CHINA'S ENGLISH
A HISTORY OF ENGLISH
IN CHINESE EDUCATION

For Annie, Maddy and Alex

CHINA'S ENGLISH
A HISTORY OF ENGLISH
IN CHINESE EDUCATION

Bob Adamson

香港大學出版社
HONG KONG UNIVERSITY PRESS

Hong Kong University Press
14/F Hing Wai Centre
7 Tin Wan Praya Road
Aberdeen
Hong Kong

© Hong Kong University Press 2004

ISBN 962 209 663 8

British Library Cataloguing-in-Publication Data
A catalogue record for this book is available from the British Library.

Secure On-line Ordering
http://www.hkupress.org

Printed and bound by Liang Yu Printing Factory Ltd., Hong Kong, China.

Contents

Series editor's preface

The English language has a long and fascinating history in China. The first English speakers arrived in southern China in the early seventeenth century, and by the late eighteenth century varieties of pidgin English were being spoken in Guangzhou (Canton) and Macau. From the outset, the reception of the English language was influenced by a range of cultural and political concerns which reflected the anxieties of Qing dynasty China to the 'strangers at the gate', whose mercantile and imperialist ambitions were perceived as a major threat to the Qing government and imperial Chinese society. Before the two Opium Wars (1839–42, 1856–60), the access to English within formal educational institutions was severely limited, and existed only in a small number of missionary schools. After 1860, access to English in the educational domain increased greatly, not only within Western Christian institutions whose numbers multiplied in the latter decades of the nineteenth century, but also in the first Chinese schools of foreign languages, including the Tongwen Guan (Interpreter's College) in Beijing (1861), Guang Fangyan Guan (School for Dispersing Languages) in Shanghai (1863) and the Jiangnan Arsenal (1867), also in Shanghai. In the late nineteenth and early twentieth century, knowledge of English was seen as essential to the modernizing efforts of 'self-strengtheners' and other reformers. Later, during the 1920s, the Nationalist government sought to regulate the teaching of English within a school system that served the aims of the government, and limited the influence of missionary institutions. Throughout many of these years, the guiding principle for state education was *zhongxue weiti, xixue weiyong* (that of 'studying China for essence, studying the West for utility').

As this book demonstrates, similar cultural and political concerns have continued to influence the attitude of the government and educational policy-makers towards the English language since the establishment of the People's Republic of China (PRC) in 1949. In this work, Dr Adamson has charted the evolution of government policy towards the English language within the state school system, and his research demonstrates the extent to which such policies have varied, and the rapidly changing status of English and English language teaching during the post-1949 era. In 1957, there were only 843 secondary school teachers of English throughout the whole country, compared with some 400,000 teachers teaching an astonishing 50 million schoolchildren by the year 2002. However, whereas previous researchers have tended to characterize the recent history of English education in China in terms of abrupt oscillations between competing language policies determined by the politics of the day, Adamson argues that a close examination of the historical record suggests a somewhat more complex picture of evolutionary development. In documenting this period of educational, political and social change, Adamson draws upon his own experience as an educator and textbook advisor in China, as well as on a wealth of ethnographic and documentary evidence. This volume is of singular importance in providing a detailed record of education policies, curriculum development and English language teaching in China from the 1949 to the present day.

Kingsley Bolton
Stockholm University
January 2004

Acknowledgements

My thanks are due to many people who helped me in the course of writing this book, and I would especially like to acknowledge the assistance given to me by Liu Daoyi, Tang Jun, Liu Jinfang, Ying Manrong, Wei Guodong and staff at the People's Education Press in Beijing, who were exceptionally generous with their time and facilitated this study in many ways, including allowing me to incorporate extracts from their English language textbooks. Bonnie Zhang Wenxia helped with translation work and a range of tedious chores with skill, efficiency and good humour; while (in alphabetical order) Kingsley Bolton, David Bunton, Jo Carr, Angus Cheng Yeung Chuen, Greg Fairbrother, Neville Grant, Peter Gu Yongqi, Gu Yueguo, Ko Po Yuk, Winnie Auyeung Lai, John Lee Chi Kin, Lee Wing On, Julian Leung Yat Ming, Jo Lewkowicz, Philip Stimpson, Anthony Sweeting, Elizabeth Walker, Ye Yuankai and Angel Yu Lai King all rendered valuable assistance. Two anonymous reviewers also provided detailed and constructive comments on a draft of this book. In particular, I owe tremendous debts of gratitude to Paul Morris, for his sharp insights and constant encouragement; and to Annie Tong and Jack and Kathleen Adamson for their unflagging support.

I am grateful to the various publishers for permission to reproduce material from my papers that had been published in their journals. Chapter 2 draws upon 'Barbarian as Foreign Language: English in China's Schools', *World Englishes* 21(2) (July 2002) published by Blackwell Publishing; parts of Chapter 7 appeared in 'English with Chinese Characteristics: China's New Curriculum', *Asia Pacific Journal of Education* 21(2) (September 2001) published by the National Institute of Education, Nanyang Technological University and Oxford University Press; and several chapters draw on data that appeared in 'Constructing an Official English for China, 1949–2000' (co-written with Ora Kwo), *Asia Pacific Journal of Communication* 12(1) (July 2002), published by John Benjamins Publishing Co.

Note on transliteration

The official system of romanization for Chinese characters in the People's Republic of China is *hanyu pinyin*, which produces transliterations such as *Beijing* for the capital city, *Yan'an* for the communist base established at the end of the Long March and *Mao Zedong* for the name of the nation's leader after the revolution of 1949. This system was not uniformly adopted in English language textbooks until Series Eight, published in 1993. In earlier textbooks, other systems of romanization were used, giving forms such as *Peking, Yenan* and *Mao Tse-tung*. In this book, *hanyu pinyin* is used, except for authors who used another styling, for institutions that have maintained long-established English versions of their name (such as Peking University), for references to names in a textbook and in direct quotations.

Map of China

1 *Introduction*

Point of departure

In 1983, I took up a teaching post in Taiyuan, Shanxi Province in the People's Republic of China (PRC). Soon after my arrival, I was being shown around the city by one of my students, Mr Liu, and we chatted about his school days. They had been disrupted by the Cultural Revolution, a period of massive social and political upheaval, and at that time, Mr Liu told me, he had joined the local Red Guards, the juvenile revolutionaries, and participated in various activities. He took me to see his former secondary school, where he indicated a third-storey window in the teachers' dormitories. That, he said, was the window from which the Red Guards had pushed their English Language teacher to his death. 'Why?' I asked. Mr Liu shrugged, 'Because he taught English.' This was my first intimation of the historically controversial, even deadly, status of English in China.

This revelation was subsequently reinforced by colleagues in Taiyuan and educators from around the country, many of whom had suffered during the Cultural Revolution. One recalled how he was accused of being an imperialist spy, simply because of his competence in English. Another recalled hearing her neighbour being beaten to death by the Red Guards for refusing to burn his treasured stamp collection that included British and Australian stamps.

Several months after my tour with Mr Liu, I was crossing the college grounds after class when I met a little boy, aged about six, who lived in a neighbouring courtyard. He greeted me with a cheerful 'Hello!' and proceeded to chat for a while in Chinese. I was surprised when he suddenly asked, 'Are foreigners good people?' Not having the linguistic resources to cope with this question in detail, I replied, 'Most are good — and we're good friends, aren't we?' He paused for thought and then said, 'Yes ... but why did you start the Opium War?' This was another forceful reminder that China has had a troubled relationship with English speakers: at different times in history, the language has been associated with military aggressors with technologically superior weapons, barbarians who ransacked imperial palaces, imperialists who seized chunks of Chinese sovereign territory and virulent anti-Communists who denounced the 'Yellow Peril'.

The perceived threat posed by the English language[1] to political, economic and social systems in China is one reason why, ever since the teaching of English began there, it has vacillated between high and low status, as indeed have all foreign languages since the Tang dynasty (Ross, 1993). In imperial times, the emperor ruled as a sovereign godhead in a hierarchical social system that combined politics and religion; erosion of power threatened the very fabric of the state. It was a system built around the notions of harmony and benevolent government, which included the observance of religious rites (Chen Li Fu, 1986). English represented very different values: it was the language of missionaries who preached Christian religions, some antagonistically denouncing Chinese beliefs and practices; of philosophers who propounded alternative social systems; of governments who pursued aggressive foreign policies; of peoples who, the Chinese believed, lacked the sophistication and refinement that a long history of unified nationhood and, in earlier times, of technological superiority bestowed upon the Chinese people. Indeed, it has been argued (e.g., Liao, 1990) that the fall of the last emperor was hastened by the controversies over how to deal with the powerful and aggressive foreign forces that were seeking to open up China for trade. And without the binding force of the imperial system, four decades of turbulence followed before the Chinese Communist Party (CCP) established the PRC in 1949.

Paradoxically, since the Chinese military was embarrassed by Western weaponry, scholars and officials in the mid-nineteenth century (and periodically thereafter) called for the learning of English to be promoted in China (Teng and Fairbank, 1979). Their aim was national self-strengthening: English would provide access to Western technology and scientific expertise (Teng and Fairbank, 1979), and it was argued that, with care, cultural erosion might be avoided. There was an added political tension after 1949, until China embraced economic reforms in the late 1970s. The English language, although desirable for national economic development in China, was perceived to embody values that were undesirable and antithetical to the nature of Chinese culture and the ideology of the CCP (Dzau, 1990). One manifestation of this was the Campaign against Spiritual Pollution (*qingchu jinshen wuran*) in the mid-1980s that targeted vices such as pornography, gambling, prostitution and even disco dancing, which were portrayed as slipping into China through the open door of international trade. As a teacher in Taiyuan at the time, I was requested by the college authorities to desist from using Western songs as teaching material and my students were warned to minimize their interactions with me to matters of grammar and pedagogy.

Nevertheless, the growth of English in China has been phenomenal. Official records for 1957 show that there were just 843 secondary school teachers of English in the whole country (Ministry of Education, 1984). Yet, despite the traumatic experiences of the Cultural Revolution and other political movements with anti-Western elements, Chinese people have embraced the study of English in recent decades with fervour. Some 50 million schoolchildren are currently learning English, taught by approximately 400,000 teachers. The figures are increasing as more and more primary schools around the nation offer the subject, and as more and more teachers take up the challenge of teaching through English across the curriculum, as part of the 'bilingual education' policy that promotes the teaching of science and maths in secondary schools through the medium of English. English competence is a key component in the tertiary level entrance examinations, a factor that enhances the status of the subject on the school curriculum. Private tutelage and tuition schools offering English courses for schoolchildren and the general public abound, popping up like bamboo shoots after spring rain, to use a Chinese metaphor. English is desirable because it is the language of trade partners, investors, advisers, tourists and technical experts, and these economic imperatives have been enhanced by China's entry into the World Trade Organization (WTO) and the awarding of the Olympic Games to Beijing in 2008.

My personal experiences as a teacher and textbook writer in China have afforded privileged access to a range of experiences. After training teachers of English in Taiyuan, I became involved in textbook development, teacher education programmes and research projects nationwide. In 1994, I visited the library in the People's Education Press (PEP), the curriculum development and publications unit in the Ministry of Education in Beijing, which has a rare, if not unique, collection of syllabuses and textbooks dating from 1949. The materials for the English Language curriculum on a secluded shelf seemed to encapsulate in a fascinating way the vagaries of China's development since 1949. Gradually, this book evolved from finding these materials. I wanted to investigate their story: the processes by which these syllabuses and textbooks had come to exist and, in most cases, then fall into disuse, and to analyse the ideas, values, and pedagogies that they incorporated. PEP officials offered generous encouragement and support for the study, and this access allowed me to build up my own collection of curriculum materials and to talk to key people who were directly involved in their production.

Analytical approach

This book explores the complex interplay of political, economic, social and educational factors that have shaped the history of English in China, with particular emphasis on the period after the founding of the PRC in 1949. The main focus is on the formal education system, most notably the English Language curriculum in junior secondary schools, on the grounds that the study of curriculum policy, including the processes of curriculum development and the products — syllabuses and textbooks — at the national level by the Ministry of Education, allows insights into the construction of an 'official' English, as well as what was considered as acceptable content in English. The book examines how, at times of heightened political tension, the state has sought to restrict the social and political impact of the language by controlling the English Language curriculum in formal education. On the other hand, the state has promoted English Language when economic development through international engagement has been a national priority. However, the findings of this book suggest that it would not be accurate to describe the shifting status of the language in the curriculum in terms of a pendulum swinging from one extreme to the other — as has been suggested by some researchers regarding general education policy in China, such as Chen Hsien's (1981) portrayal of swings between 'academic' (i.e., related to citizenship training and human resource development for economic modernization) and 'revolutionary' (i.e., ideologically-oriented) education; or a 'moderate' to 'radical' pendulum (Ruyen, 1970, cited in Löfstedt, 1980). Politicization of state policy does not mean a total neglect of economic concerns, and economic modernization does not mean that other agenda are absent. Instead, there is a contestation of economic, political, and social goals, resulting in tensions and negotiated outcomes. The nature of this contestation and subsequent outcomes has varied over time, but the general thrust towards an acceptance of English and of the need for cultural awareness has continued progressively throughout the period since 1949, with the exception of the Cultural Revolution. The fortunes of foreign language curricula, argues Ross (1992: 240), are a 'barometer of modernization', in that they register changes in pressure exerted by the prevailing socio-political climate. English, being particularly controversial, makes it a sensitive barometer.

This book uses the junior secondary school English Language curriculum as the means to examine how curriculum developers and textbook writers have confronted the shifting ambiguities and dilemmas concerning English. The reasons for selecting the junior secondary school curriculum arise partly from convenience (my involvement in curriculum development was at this level), partly from importance (curriculum developers in the PEP told me that most innovations in the English curriculum in China have been initiated at this level, and it is the stage of schooling, Year 7 to Year 9, at which most students have studied English) and partly from the need to limit the scope of the study to book length. The book asks fundamental questions concerning the English promoted by the state in China. What role has been ascribed to English, and how has it changed over time? What are the characteristics of this English, and how have they changed over time? What are the explanations for such changes? What has been viewed as appropriate content for English textbooks? The analysis adopted for this study looks at the process of curriculum development as well as the product: the nature of the curriculum as constructed by the PEP. The relationship between the two levels is shown in Figure 1.1. Studying the process — identifying the stakeholders and their contributions; sorting out the priorities; and observing how tensions were handled — illuminates the contemporary social climate and values and how they impinged upon the construction of a state English. Studying the product reveals the nature of this English. Analysing the changes over time brings out strongly the particular features of China's English.

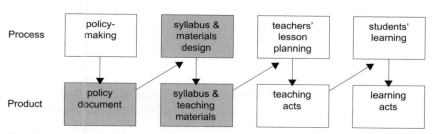

Note: Shaded area represents the main focus of this book.

Figure 1.1   Steps in curriculum decision-making (adapted from Johnson, 1989)

The study is located in the areas of the PEP's involvement in curriculum development. Despite its title as a press, the role of PEP has been to interpret state policy and operationalize it in the form of a syllabus and textbooks for individual subjects. The PEP forms a bridge between the macro-level of state policy and the micro-level of curriculum implementation in schools. Recent studies of curriculum development in China have described the complex interplay between macro- and micro-levels, thereby challenging the common portrayal of a homogeneous process, dominated by the central authorities and essentially centre-periphery in nature (e.g., Leung, 1989; Paine, 1992; Lai, 1994). Leung (1991) describes the process as 'democratic centralism'. Paine (1992) contends that the actual formulation of contemporary national educational policies has a strongly pluralistic quality through a process of *mosuo* (literally 'groping' or muddling through), whereby policies are formulated in the light of successful experiments at the grassroots and 'an evolutionary compromise' is achieved between central bureaucratic objectives and the practical lessons of local experience. While this book identifies the nature of shifts in the socio-political climate and their effect on issues of curriculum design and pedagogy in English Language teaching at the macro-level, the primary focus is on how the PEP charts a course between competing and often conflicting forces that arise at both the macro- and micro-level. Little research work has been done in the field of English Language curriculum development in the PRC, either by Chinese or international scholars. Within the PRC, a large number of journals are devoted to aspects of English Language teaching, but they tend to be descriptive and prescriptive, being principally designed to promulgate the particular pedagogy associated with a new innovation. How the PEP handles the politically sensitive issues and questions of socio-economic policy linked to English Language curriculum development has rarely been investigated: the papers on this topic surveyed for this book were all written by members of the PEP, and tended to avoid critical analysis.

The second aspect of reform, the nature of the curriculum as constructed by the curriculum developers, will be approached principally through analyses of the English Language textbooks produced by the PEP, which, in China, are the main manifestation of the intended curriculum. The PEP's task of interpreting the policy statements of the politicians and translating them into curriculum documents (such as syllabuses or textbooks) that will be used in schools is both a sensitive one, given the often volatile nature of policy statements and the historically ambivalent official attitudes towards the English language, and a difficult one, for the skills, resources and support for English Language teaching in schools place constraints on policy formulation and on the implementation of policy. Added to this is the influence of experts in the field, including specialists in applied linguistics in tertiary institutions and foreign consultants; and, as emerged from this study as it developed, of teachers, whose acceptance of new materials and pedagogies was vital to the success of any curriculum reform. The political and educational forces are often in conflict, and the PEP had to navigate a mediating course, not just through the conflicting currents of the political ('red') and economic ('expert') policy streams, but also through various competing pedagogies, to produce a syllabus and teaching materials suitable for English Language instruction and learning in Chinese schools.

The especially contentious 'desirable evil' that the English language has represented to China makes it an excellent case study of how the state handles tensions in the school curriculum, as it throws into particularly sharp relief the processes that exist for this purpose. The issue of cultural transfer (and the potential for cultural erosion that is involved in the promotion of the study of English) is a central theme to the book — how the Chinese government, through the Ministry of Education, has handled the 'foreignness' of English since 1949. This book argues that a guiding principle of selective assimilation has been applied to different degrees at different times by Chinese authorities to questions of international transfer in many fields for the past 100 years or more, and has been applied to the English Language curriculum in the various socio-political and economic climates of the different phases of history since 1949.

How has the role and status ascribed to English in the education system in China changed over time? To answer this question, evidence for the official role of English is drawn from policy documents, such as those relating to curriculum; policy actions, such as the setting up of new institutions; and policy debates. The question of status is more problematic. In this book, attention is given to both the official and popular status of English, to the relevant weighting given to English Language study in the curriculum of state educational institutions, and to the use of English in society. The attribute of 'low' status is applied in this analysis to the status of English when state policy reflected the view that the cultural or political threat of the language was greater than the technological benefits that its study might bring. Higher status is thus attributable when the balance of state policy was more inclined towards a positive view of English. Reference will also be made to popular attitudes towards the English language when these seem to be at variance with official attitudes.

Although the book is largely about language issues, it also touches on political, social and educational matters that are only tangentially related to the English Language curriculum in China. For instance, the analysis of the decision-making processes employed in the various curriculum innovations indicates how China has handled the relations between the centre and the periphery in education and other spheres of political activity. This centre-periphery tension has, historically, been an important factor in the history of Chinese politics, given the size of the country and the diversity of regional interests and ethnic backgrounds.

Major sources of data were key informants — Tang Jun, Liu Daoyi, Liu Jinfang and Neville Grant. Tang Jun had been involved in English Language curriculum development with the PEP from the early 1960s and, after the Cultural Revolution, had served as project leader for the curriculum reforms in 1978 and 1982. Liu Daoyi, who had been involved in the PEP work in the 1960s as a consultant, joined the PEP staff in 1977, and took over as project leader for the development of the 1993 curriculum. Liu Jinfang, who joined in 1977, was another long-serving member of staff at the PEP. Another key informant was from outside the PEP — Neville Grant, a textbook author working for Longman International, who had been the principal writer of the textbook series for the 1993 curriculum. I have also drawn on my own experiences as a member of the team of textbook writers working under Liu Daoyi and Grant.[2]

The data from key informants were complemented by an analysis of textbooks (in particular), syllabuses, and related curriculum documents, which were obtained from the PEP and other sources, such as the archives of colleagues in China and my own archives. Apple and Christian-Smith (1991) highlight the important role of textbook in the education process, suggesting that, in general, the curriculum as experienced by most learners is defined more closely by textbooks rather than syllabuses and other documents. Venezky (1992) argues that textbooks are both cultural and curricular artefacts, possessing an intertextuality that links them to their antecedents and a validation bestowed by various mechanisms, such as production quality (binding, design, typography, etc.), or by association with the authorship and affiliation of authors, or by implications of improvement and currency by labels such as 'revised edition'. As a cultural artefact, the nature of textbooks is circumscribed to some extent by social, economic and technical conditions, such as contemporary printing techniques:

> ... texts are not simply "delivery systems" of "facts". They are at once the results of political, economic, and cultural activities, battles, and compromises. They are conceived, designed, and authored by real people with real interests. They are published within the political and economic constraints of markets, resources and power. And what texts mean and how they are used are fought over by communities with distinctly different commitments and by teachers and students as well. (Apple and Christian-Smith, 1991: 1–2)

As a curricular artefact, textbooks reflect the intended curriculum, as well as the promoted pedagogical approaches, either explicit (e.g., presentations of concepts to be grasped) or implicit (the nature and arrangement of exercises, for example), and a hidden curriculum (such as the values and meanings of the dominant culture) (Cherryholmes, 1988; Venezky, 1992). It is this view of textbooks as reflections of pedagogical constructs and socio-political values that forms the basis of the analysis of PRC textbook resources adopted in this study. The analysis recognizes that English Language curriculum products are shaped by considerations relating to three components at the level of design (adapted from White, 1988), which are:

- pedagogy: explicit and/or implicit beliefs and practices for teaching and learning;
- linguistic components: grammar, vocabulary, and language skills (e.g., reading, writing, listening and speaking);
- content: situational contexts and topics, including political and moral messages.

Taken individually, but especially when interconnected as a coherent whole, each component contributes to an understanding of the nature and role of English in China (Figure 1.2).

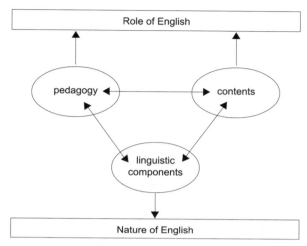

Figure 1.2   Curriculum analysis and China's English

Pedagogy

The pedagogical approach underpinning a curriculum and its related textbook resources is informative as it shows the orientation of the curriculum towards particular goals. In the case of English Language, the goals might be fostering the students' competence in oral and written English in order to produce people capable of communicating with English-speaking foreigners, or transmitting grammatical knowledge about language to develop the students' reading skills in order for them to gain access to scientific or technical information. Table 1.1 (see p. 10) shows the features of some of the more common pedagogical approaches to English Language teaching that have been identified in China and elsewhere. Each is responding to different social needs. The lack of clear pedagogical principles might indicate that priorities lay elsewhere — political indoctrination, for example. While explicit statements about pedagogy might be found in the syllabus or teacher's reference book, analysis of components such as the nature and role of grammar, and the degree of realism in the discourse can provide implicit evidence as to the pedagogy.

The use of more realistic or less realistic discourse in textbooks can be associated with different forms of English Language pedagogy. The term *discourse* has various connotations, but for the purposes of this book, it is used in the sense of a 'naturally occurring stretch of language, spoken or written' (Carter, 1993: 22), with some qualifications as noted below. *Realistic*, as used in this study, refers to the naturalness of the language in the discourse, irrespective of its actual origin. Thus a passage written by the textbook author in the form of someone else's diary would be analysed in this study as 'strongly

Table 1.1 Prevalent English language pedagogical approaches (adapted from Tang Lixing, 1983; Larsen-Freeman, 1986; Richards and Rodgers, 1986; Clark, 1987, Zhou and Weng, 1995)

Name	Focus	Pedagogy	Curriculum	Orientation/Values System
Grammar-Translation Method (from 18th century)	language forms; reading and writing	transmission of knowledge; teacher-centred; memorization of grammatical paradigms; translation	linear grading; from what is thought to be simple to complex	academic rationalism; access to literature and other written forms of language
Structural Approach (from 19th century)	grammar in context; mainly reading and writing; access to literature	transmission of knowledge; teacher as presenter and monitor; grammar focus, then creative production; use of mother tongue	linear grading; starting with what is thought to be most useful/generalizable	academic rationalism; access to the language systems
Direct Method (from turn of 20th century)	communication in context; listening, speaking, reading and writing	teacher- and student-centred; inductive learning of grammar; no use of mother tongue	cyclical, experiential learning; grading by students' needs and ability	social and economic efficiency; communicative competence to use language in society
Audiolingual Method (from late 1950s)	sentence patterns; listening and speaking, then reading & writing	language learnt through behaviourist techniques; teacher orchestrates students; habit-formation; no use of mother tongue	linear grading; starting with what is thought to be most useful/generalizable	social and economic efficiency; communicative competence to use language in society
Functional/ Notional Approach (from late 1970s)	communication in context; integration of listening, speaking, reading and writing	language learnt through modelling; teacher as manager and helper; grammar focus, then creative production; use of mother tongue	linear grading; starting with what is thought to be most useful/generalizable	social and economic efficiency; communicative competence to use language in society
Task-Based Learning (from 1990s)	holistic and purposeful communication; integration of listening, speaking, reading and writing	learning generic skills through language; student autonomy; teacher as manager and helper; providing input as needed; use of mother tongue	task as organizing focus, based on students' needs, interests and abilities; grammar and vocabulary support task completion	various: social and economic efficiency, social reconstructionism and/or individualism
Eclectic Approach	communication; listening, speaking, reading and writing skills	learning about language and generic skills through language; teacher as selector of strategies; habit-formation and cognitive learning; use of mother tongue	grading by students' needs and ability	various: academic rationalism, social and economic efficiency, social reconstructionism and/ or individualism

realistic' if the discourse displays the features of a real diary (in terms of format, topics, etc.), even though the diary was actually pseudo-realistic — i.e. written specifically for the textbook. The research focuses on the discourse contained in the textbooks, including the printed discourse that is intended to represent spoken language. Strongly realistic discourse is linked to pedagogies such as the Direct Method that stress communicative language use. Although there may be a concern to develop students' accuracy at an early stage, such a pedagogy will quickly move to a stronger degree of realism. Other approaches, such as the Structural Approach, spend longer developing students' accuracy in language use, and so strongly realistic discourse tends not to be important until later in a course. The correspondences between various pedagogies and the degree of realistic discourse shown in Table 1.2 do not imply that the degree of discourse realism exists in a precise one-to-one relationship with individual views of language learning and pedagogy. However, it is believed that realism serves as a contributory indicator, when combined with other evidence, in building up a composite picture of the views of language learning and pedagogy underpinning the textbooks.

Table 1.2   English language pedagogy and discourse

Pedagogy	Discourse
Grammar-Translation Method	realism increases as focus moves from sentence to whole-passage level
Direct Method	strong realism from early stages
Audiolingual Method	weak/medium realism, as repetition of structures can be unnatural language use
Structural Approach	weak/medium realism when focus is on discrete grammar items
Functional/ Notional Approach	strong realism from early stage when focus is on contextualized language use
Task-based learning	strong realism from early stage when focus is on contextualized language use
Eclectic Approach	weak/medium realism when focus is on discrete grammar items; strong when focus is on contextualized language use

The analysis of realism in discourse hinges upon contextualization. Carter (1993) differentiates between external and internal context. External context refers to the non-linguistic environment in which the discourse is located, while internal context refers to the linguistic environment and the inter-relationship between linguistic components. This study mainly looks at the external context, and the extent that the non-linguistic environment is explicit. Four guiding questions (and Q4 primarily) were used:

Q1. Are the participants in the discourse and their relationship made clear?
Q2. Is the setting (place and time) of the communicative event made evident?
Q3. Is the purpose of the communicative event made clear?
Q4. Is the language of the discourse appropriate to the external context as defined in the answers to the first three questions?

The realism of the written and spoken discourse in the textbooks is analysed on a three-point scale: strong, medium and weak. 'Strong' discourse has a high degree of realism, while 'weak' discourse shows little realism. Figure 1.3 shows the relationship between strong, medium and weak discourse. Strongly realistic discourse is, or is similar to, language of the real world, and comprises sentences or utterances put together in order to achieve communication; weakly realistic discourse is primarily concerned with presenting discrete linguistic components, such as a grammatical structure, for the students to master. The 'medium' category is for discourse that is quite communication-oriented, but the language is still tightly controlled (for example, a number of structures reoccur, but not to the extent as to render the discourse as 'weak'). As with the analysis of political and moral messages outlined below, the judgements made regarding discourse are subjective, being based on my experience in textbook writing and language teaching. To enhance the reliability of the findings, three English Language specialists carried out an independent analysis of a random sample of passages. Each specialist was given twenty-five extracts in total taken from various textbook series. They were asked to analyse the degree of realism of the discourse on the three-point scale ('weak', 'medium' and 'strong') to validate my construct analysis. In the event, the process resulted in some adjustments to some of my judgements.

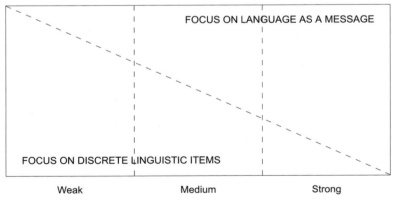

Figure 1.3   Weak, medium and strong discourse as a continuum (adapted from Littlewood, 1993)

Linguistic components

Linguistic components include grammatical items, vocabulary and functional/ notional items. The selection and organization of these components are indicative of the views of language learning and pedagogy that influence a particular series (McDonough and Shaw, 1993). For example, the sequencing of grammatical items indicates whether such items have been controlled, or whether they have been introduced randomly. A controlled sequence suggests that the textbook writers believe that language learning requires some form of progression in terms of grammatical input, be it linear, cyclical or otherwise. A random, uncontrolled sequence may suggest a naturalistic immersion approach to language learning (such as might be associated with the Direct Method) or maybe a lack of attention on the part of the textbook writers to such pedagogical aspects. The association between English Language pedagogies and the organization of linguistic components is shown in Table 1.3.

Table 1.3   English language pedagogy and linguistic components

Pedagogy	Linguistic Components
Grammar-Translation Method	grammar and vocabulary initially controlled, then dependent on passage complexity
Direct Method	grammar, vocabulary and functions/notions dependent on context
Audiolingual Method	grammar and vocabulary controlled; functions/notions dependent on context
Structural Approach	grammar and vocabulary controlled; functions/notions dependent on context
Functional/ Notional Approach	functions/notions, grammar and vocabulary controlled based on context
Task-based Learning	functions/notions, grammar and vocabulary controlled based on context
Eclectic Approach	functions/notions, grammar and vocabulary controlled based on context

The selection of vocabulary items can similarly reflect the attention paid to controlled input, which, in turn, is indicative of attention to pedagogical concerns. A simple indication of this is the number of new vocabulary items included in each lesson: a large number indicates a lack of control, either deliberate or unwitting, and a greater concern for transmitting political or moral messages than for primarily catering to the capabilities of students to master the vocabulary. Alternatively, the number of new vocabulary items may be indicative of the intended pedagogy. For instance, pedagogies such as the Functional/Notional Approach which feature more strongly realistic discourse are less likely to have a high degree of controlled vocabulary, as this would restrict the potential for realism. Functional/notional items are elements of discourse that serve a communicative purpose. They range from simple utterances, such as apologizing or telling the time, to longer stretches of language, such as arranging a meeting or arguing. A wide range of functional/notional items in a textbook series would suggest a strong orientation towards communication as the main goal of language learning and the Functional/Notional Approach, or other similar methods, as the intended pedagogy (White, 1988).

Content

For the analysis of messages in the textbooks, the study draws on the categorization (*political, moral* and *nil*) of messages used by Ridley, Godwin and Doolin (1971) in their analysis of the moral orientation of the set of Chinese Language readers for primary school students published in the 1960s prior to the Cultural Revolution. Their study found three distinct categories of passages:
1. informational passages: often politicized, about hygiene, physiology, basic science and agriculture;
2. specifically indoctrinal passages: moulding attitudes towards the nation, the CCP, foreign countries, republican China, and often containing issues relating to social and international conflict; and
3. behavioural modelling passages: anecdotes and biographies of heroes and their deeds for emulation.

Ridley, Godwin and Doolin concluded that the content of these textbooks was:

> ... clearly relevant to a predominantly agricultural society that is consciously attempting not only to transform itself into a modern, industrial society, but also one that is attempting, through education of its masses, to eradicate an old social order and to establish a new society based on radically different principles. (p. 20)

This involves attention to both economics-oriented and politics-oriented education. In the early to mid-1960s, this meant that:

> [t]he Chinese education system is charged with producing citizens to be used in the modernization of the state with both specific levels of expertise and a deep, extremely personal commitment to Mao Tse-tung. (pp. 5–6)

Kwong (1985) and Price (1979) reached similar conclusions on the moral and political contents of later textbooks. Kwong examined textbooks for Chinese Language throughout the Cultural Revolution and its immediate aftermath, and traced the changes in the socio-political climate that are reflected in the passages in various series of textbooks. She identified the abundance of political content (including eulogies of Chairman Mao and anti-capitalist diatribes) during times of mass mobilization; the moral messages advocating patriotism and diligence in study; and the later attention (when political activism had reduced) to academic skills and a more realistic portrayal of children's lifestyle. Her study concludes that analysis of language textbooks in a highly politicized society like China can reveal who formed the dominant leadership, as well as 'the assumptions and basis of China's political infrastructure, the continuities and changes in her political culture, her leaders' plans and priorities' (pp. 206–7). Price (1979) reviewed the contents of textbooks in Chinese Language and English in terms of scope of materials and intended pedagogy. For Chinese Language, Price notes that the textbooks from the late 1950s have a carefully structured linguistic syllabus, together with strong moral-political content:

> The content of the textbook is serious and moral, with almost no reference, in those studied, to play of any kind. Pleasure is to be found in hard work and in helping other people. Happy children must sit up in class and co-operate with the teacher in their studies; wash their clothes and help in the house; or join in the work of harvesting the crops. Next to earnest work, the message of thinking of the public good is put over … . Directly political material mainly takes the form of stories about heroic deeds performed during the anti-Japanese or civil wars, or a small number of stories in which life before and after 1949 are contrasted. The main message is the importance of the Communist Party, without which the improvements would have been impossible. (Price, 1979: 122)

Other contents include moralistic stories and fables; scientific passages; some anti-imperialistic diatribes, and biographies of great figures, such as Lenin or James Watt. Price's (1979) study of experimental English textbooks used in Tianjin in 1965 concentrated more on the pedagogical aspects, which, he found, were influenced by moves towards oral language production (Audiolingualism) to replace the former emphasis on grammatical rules. His later (1992) analysis focuses on the moral-political messages about patriotism, socialism and discipline in textbooks for moral education at the beginning of the 1990s. He comments that the principal aim is to justify past and present policies, rather than preparing the students for the future.

The *political*, *moral* and *nil* categories have been refined in this study because, in the course of the analysis, it became clear that not all the messages in the passages fitted comfortably in the three original categories, and these categories did not adequately discriminate between moral and political messages. For example, some passages about a 'healthy' lifestyle (such as descriptions of young people rising early, working diligently and helping others) were placed in the context of supporting a particular political movement; others did not have a political connection. The new categorization (Table 1.4) allows a distinction to be made between the two kinds of message. Three major categories (*political, moral* and *nil*) and three minor categories to distinguish between different genres of political message (*attitudes, information* and *role model*) are used — although some passages carry more than one message, and from more than one category. For the purposes of this study, a *moral* message is defined as one which promotes a mode of social behaviour, but which does not have an overt political connotation, while a *political* message is connected to ideological values. *Nil* means that there is no obvious political or moral message being conveyed. To study the messages in the textbooks, the analysis identifies *discourse units*, which are defined as any extended stretch of language oriented towards holistic communication, such as a story, a dialogue (including a communicative drill), or an anecdote. On occasions, a sequence of closely connected discourse units, such as a number of dialogues on a similar theme presented together in a lesson, were treated as a single unit for purposes of analysis.

Table 1.4   Categories for analysing political and moral messages in textbooks

Category	Description
Nil	the passage presents information or language practice (such as a dialogue) with no obvious moral or political message
Moral (M)	the message is concerned with promoting modes of social behaviour (such as a healthy lifestyle, good hygiene or courtesy), or attitudes (e.g., through fables), but there are no obvious political connotations
Political	the message is concerned with transmitting 'red' values or socialist ideology by trying to shape the reader's attitude, by providing politicized information or by projecting exemplary behaviour that has its roots in desirable 'red' values
Political attitudes (Pa)	the message aims to instil socialist ideological viewpoints, patriotism, loyalty to the CCP, its institutions and leaders, or to create negative images of other countries or societies (including pre-1949 China)
Political information (Pi)	the message provides information about aspects of society, such as agriculture, industry, science and technology, and suggests that there is a political motivation or link to the successes and achievements identified in these areas
Political model (Pm)	the passage provides examples of behaviour by ordinary people for emulation as displaying appropriate political attitudes; or of behaviour by leaders, for creating a positive image of their thoughts and deeds, and/or for emulation

The messages were categorized and counted. A predominance of political messages in a textbook series, for example, would indicate that the curriculum was influenced by the politicized climate of the time. As noted above, such an analysis is subjective, so a validation exercise was conducted to enhance the data reliability. Two specialists, one in the field of discourse analysis and the other in textbook analysis, categorized the messages in twenty-five passages. Their decisions with regard to the three main categories (i.e., 'nil', 'moral' and 'political') fully matched my own. There were some minor, insignificant discrepancies over the subcategorization ('political attitude', 'political information' and 'political model'), but after discussion, a consensus over the interpretation of the messages was reached, and no changes to my classifications were deemed necessary.

The choice of vocabulary in a series can also reflect particular moral or political messages. To investigate this aspect, the study adopts a word-list drawn up by an American educator, Edward L. Thorndike, reprinted in Thorndike and Lorge (1944: 267–74). This word-list identified 1,000 most commonly used words in textbooks, school readers, the Bible and English classics intended for children. Although other word-lists exist (e.g., Van Ek, 1980), Thorndike's list is considered the most appropriate, as it was used, *faute de mieux*, for reference by the PEP from the 1950s until the 1980s for selecting the vocabulary to be included in various series (Liu, 1995), and at different levels (Dzau, 1990). The PEP did not use the list indiscriminately: other words not on the list were included because of their specific cultural, political or economic importance. Accordingly, this study identifies those vocabulary items in textbooks that were not taken from Thorndike's list. Those extra vocabulary items may reflect dominant influences on curriculum developers in the PEP at the time. For example, the identification of a large number of vocabulary items with political meanings suggests that the textbook series reflect a time of politicization and might reveal the main political themes promoted at the time. In analysing this aspect, the non-Thorndike vocabulary items are quantified and a general estimate of the percentage with political connotations is provided. An exact figure cannot be provided, as connotations are context-dependent: for instance, *worker* could be construed in certain contexts as highly politically charged, but in others much less so.

Time frame

The main time frame of the study is the period after the founding of the PRC, but to understand the problematic nature of English as a school subject and the rationale for this subject, Chapter 2 of this book starts in the Qing dynasty, as the origins of the diverse roles of English in China lie in the Opium War of 1839–42. The war comprised an aggressive clash of cultures.

At that time, Britain, seeking to open up China for trade by creating a market for opium, met resistance from the Chinese government, who viewed foreigners as barbarians (Liao, 1990). The ensuing military struggle revealed the technological superiority of the British and resulted in the signing of the Treaty of Nanjing in 1842, which granted territorial and trading rights to the British. This defeat, and the ensuing seizure of Chinese territory by Britain and other Western powers in the following decades, were major humiliations. The process of selective assimilation was propounded by scholars in the 'Self-Strengthening Movement' during the second half of the nineteenth century, with a view to preserving China's cultural heritage while placing the country on an equal technological and economic footing with others. The principle was labelled 'Study China for essence, study the West for practical usage' (*zhongxue weiti, xixue weiyong*). Scholars recognized that this principle necessitated the study of foreign languages to gain access to Western ideas (Teng and Fairbank, 1979). The Qing dynasty, mortally wounded by internal weakness and external pressures, succumbed. During this time, state policy gradually opened the sluice gate from very restricted engagement with the language, which avoided any form of contact other than for trade and diplomatic negotiation, to one of controlled appropriation, whereby China sought to learn English in order to access technological knowledge for self-protection.

The Republican era was marked by efforts to establish a new state in a less hostile international environment with regard to English-speaking countries. The debate centred less on how to defeat the forces of external aggression and of reform, and more on how to preserve the cultural heritage, the Chinese essence, in the vacuum created by the overthrow of the last emperor. The study of English was controversial because it acted as a conduit for the introduction of new philosophies, religions and social theories. In the event, it was the synthesis of foreign ideas (Marxist-Leninist Theory) with Chinese philosophy (Mao Zedong Thought) that prevailed after the trauma of the Anti-Japanese War (1937–45) and the civil war between the CCP and the Nationalist Party — *Guomindang*, or *Kuomintang* (KMT).

Policies of the CCP, which took power after the civil war ended in 1949, may be seen as an extension of the Self-Strengthening Movement. Two of its declared aims were the ending of oppression in China by foreign countries, and the establishment of a completely independent Chinese nation (Brandt, Schwartz and Fairbank, 1952). Since 1949, these goals have been vigorously pursued, with the elimination of foreign colonies and settlements, and the introduction of various political and economic programmes to bolster patriotic sentiments and the nation's wealth. However, the economically 'underdeveloped' nature of China has meant that the English language still represents a conduit for acquiring the necessary technological expertise and for fostering international trade. The founding father of the PRC, Mao

Zedong, advocated *yang wei zhong yong* ('let foreign things serve China') as a key strategy in the nation's development, which is in line with the maxim of the Self-Strengtheners quoted above. On the other hand, some elements of the CCP have embraced at times the anti-foreignist and anti-English language stance that is uneasy about the presence of English Language in the school curriculum: to them, English bears unsavoury connotations of capitalism and imperialism, and embodies other undesirable moral values. The conflicts between the pragmatism of the Self-Strengthening Movement and the conservatism of the isolationists have affected the role and status of English Language in the school curriculum.

Five distinct phases — 1949–60, 1961–66, 1966–76, 1977–93 and 1993 onwards — form the basis for the chapters in this book (Chapters 3 to 7) that analyse the English curriculum in the post-1949 period. Each of these phases was associated with a major initiative at the macro-level, such as a drive towards modernization, a radical revolutionary movement or the promulgation of an education policy. These phases were also marked by the publication of new syllabuses and/or textbook resources that differ, in terms of their content and the processes of curriculum development that went into their production, from those of the preceding phase. The final chapter, Chapter 8, summarizes the trends arising from the study and discusses some of their implications.

The book naturally has limitations on its scope. I have already mentioned that the focus is on the junior secondary school curriculum, although passing references are made to the primary school curriculum, as well as the senior secondary school and various tertiary curricula. Likewise, it is mainly concerned with the work of the PEP, as the central agency responsible for curriculum design and, until 1993, solely responsible for producing textbooks and other resources. Since 1993, and during the Cultural Revolution, other agencies have produced materials on a regional basis. This study incorporates an analysis of some aspects of the English Language curriculum that operated during the Cultural Revolution, because there was no PEP-developed curriculum available at that time. Although there was difficulty in obtaining textbooks produced during the Cultural Revolution, friends in China were able to supply some incomplete sets that, while not permitting a full analysis, are sufficient to allow for some conclusions to be drawn. However, for the post-1993 period, I have chosen not to study the teaching materials produced by agencies other than the PEP, because of the dominance and influence of the PEP series throughout the country. While a limitation, this decision does allow for greater historical coherence in the study. Furthermore, this study is concerned with just two, albeit important, aspects of the English Language curriculum in China — the processes of development, and the product of these processes in the form of the syllabus and accompanying published resources. The questions of school-based implementation of the curriculum and strategies of teaching and learning actually employed in the classroom are not discussed in detail; nor are issues concerning assessment. These important questions would be a massive undertaking in the vastly diversified context of China, particularly if they incorporated an historical dimension.

2 Barbarian as a foreign language

The controversy surrounding English and the teaching of the language in China dates back to the late Qing dynasty, when the British, American and other trading empires sought access to Chinese markets and Christian missionaries access to Chinese souls. China's strategy to mitigate undesirable cultural transfer through selective assimilation has been in place since the mid-nineteenth century. It is akin to a sluice gate. At times, the gate has only allowed very limited contact with English, at others the inflow has been freer. In the former cases, English has not been ascribed a significant role in state policy; in the latter cases, the language has been promoted, most notably in education — in the curriculum of schools, colleges and universities.

The reason for these shifts lay in a change in the relations between China and the rest of the world, which have affected the role and status of English (Table 2.1, see p. 22). Before the mid-nineteenth century, these relations had been low key, with the main focus on trade and most crises being territorial. China had traded with the Roman Empire. She had been occupied by the Mongols in the thirteenth century and intermittently threatened by Russian expansion, but threats to Chinese cultural and territorial integrity had generally been negated — the Mongols, for instance, appeared to adapt Chinese ways rather than impose their own cultural norms (Mackerras, 1991). Foreign language learning had existed in imperial China since at least 1289, during the Yuan dynasty, when languages were learnt by aristocrats to enhance commercial and tributary relations with countries in Southeast Asia (Gu, 1996). Some Western missionaries, most notably Jesuit priests such as Matteo Ricci, Adam Schall and Ferdinand Verbiest, established themselves as scholars in the Imperial service in the sixteenth and seventeenth centuries, but their technique for gaining acceptance was generally non-threatening: they learnt spoken and written Chinese, adopted Chinese manners and contributed Western learning (most notably in science and mathematics) at the behest of the emperor.

Table 2.1   The historical role and status of the English language in China

Period		Role and Status	English Language Education
Later Qing Dynasty	1759–1860	English only permitted to be spoken (in pidgin form) by the despised *compradores;* perceived as a barbaric tongue; low official status	Private study by *compradores*
	1861–1911	Technology transfer: English as a vehicle for gaining access to Western science and technology; helpful to the development of China's international diplomacy; conduit to remunerative jobs in treaty ports; later a fad in Shanghai; medium official status	On the curriculum of institutions set up to facilitate transfer of scientific knowledge; later (after 1903) on the curricula of secondary and tertiary institutions
The Republican Era (1911–1949)	1911–1923	The Intellectual Revolution: English as a vehicle for exploring Western philosophy and other ideas; opportunities for study abroad; high official status	On the curricula of secondary and tertiary institutions
	1924–1949	English as a vehicle for diplomatic, military and intellectual interaction with the West; resistance from nationalistic scholars and politicians fearing unwanted cultural transfer; medium/high official status	On the curricula of secondary and tertiary institutions

As part of its expansion of maritime trade in Asia, Portugal seized a small port, Macau, on the south coast of China in 1535 and established it as a *de facto* colony in 1557. Contact between China and foreign nations increased steadily from the beginning of the seventeenth century, but no dealings with the outside world were quite so traumatic for China as those that occurred after 1800. The long-standing Chinese view of foreign relations was of a tributary system whereby an emissary from another country must 'kow-tow' to the emperor, whom the Chinese regarded as the link between celestial and terrestrial domains. The weakness of successive Qing emperors and the power of European nations whose technological strength had been bolstered by the Industrial Revolution forced the Chinese to re-evaluate this view: in a few decades, the imperial system that had existed for two thousand years collapsed in the face of the forces of change and modernization.

Facing pressure from countries seeking new markets, the Chinese government, concerned about preserving cultural integrity while engaging in international trade, nominated Guangzhou (Canton) as the principal port for foreign trade as it was close to the South China Sea and military fortifications.

From 1759, a court decree made it the sole port for this purpose. Foreigners residing in the cantonments in Guangzhou were restricted to a small area of Shamian Island. They could not communicate with Chinese unless supervised by *compradores* (local business agents who were registered with the authorities); they were forbidden to buy Chinese books or learn Chinese (Hsü, 1990). Thus contact between foreigners and Chinese was carried out in the language of the foreigners (usually a pidgin variety of English), with the *compradores* acting as translators. The *compradores,* also known as 'linguists', were therefore probably the first Chinese to learn English on their native soil. Although the *compradores* were often skilful entrepreneurs with influential contacts and an affluent lifestyle, they were not widely admired by their compatriots because of their contact with foreigners. Their low status is indicated by the contempt expressed in an essay, 'On the Adoption of Western Knowledge', by a reformist scholar from Suzhou, Feng Guai-fen (1809–1874), written around 1860:

> Nowadays those familiar with barbarian affairs are called "linguists". These men are generally frivolous rascals and loafers in the cities and are despised in their villages and communities. They serve as interpreters only because they have no other means of making a livelihood. Their nature is boorish, their knowledge shallow, and furthermore, their moral principles are mean. They know nothing except sensual pleasures and material profit. Moreover, their ability consists of nothing more than a slight knowledge of the barbarian language and occasional recognition of barbarian characters, which is limited to names of commodities, numerical figures, some slang expressions and a little simple grammar. How can we expect them to pay attention to scholarly studies? (Translated by Teng and Fairbank, 1979: 51)

One of the earliest extant English Language textbooks was produced for the benefit of 'linguists'. Dating back to the 1830s, the *Hong Mao Tong Yong Fan Hua* (literally 'Common Foreign Expressions of the Red-Haired People') presents approximate transliterations in Chinese characters which, when pronounced in the Cantonese dialect, resemble English and other European terms for numbers, weights, measures, jobs, commodities, relationships, geographical locations, colours, common adjectives, furniture, utensils and colloquial expressions for trade and conversation. For instance, on the first page, the Chinese characters for numbers from one to twenty-one are set out (from top to bottom, and from right to left), and under each character is the transliteration (Figure 2.1, see p. 24).

The Opium War of 1839–1842, when Britain, seeking to open up China for trade, met resistance from the Chinese government, revealed the technological superiority of the British and resulted in the signing of the Treaty of Nanjing in 1842, which granted territorial and trading rights to the British. This defeat and the ensuing seizure of Chinese territory by Britain and other nations in the following decades revealed China's inability to protect its

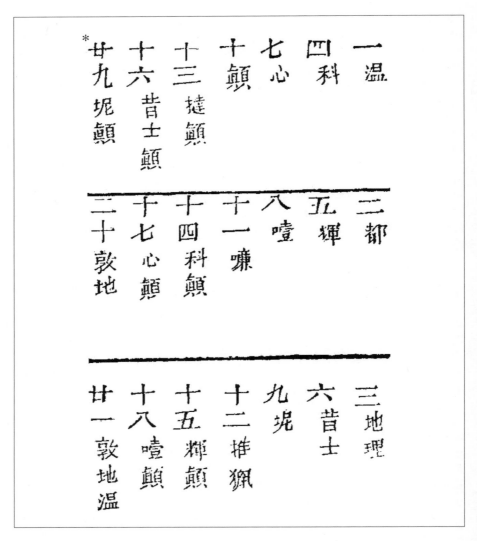

Figure 2.1   Extract from the textbook for *compradores;* the full text is provided in Bolton (2003). In romanized form, the text reads as follows:

19*	16	13	10	7	4	1
nai-din	sik-si-din	tat-din	din	sum	for	won
20	17	14	11	8	5	2
dun-day	sum-din	for-din	lim	ai	fi	dow
21	18	15	12	9	6	3
dun-day won	ai-din	fai-din	tui-fung	nai	sik-si	day-lay

* The Chinese characters actually show 29, which is presumably a misprint.

territorial integrity, with all the implications that this had for the nation's cultural and political well-being. China was threatened or perceived herself to be threatened by Western nations in three areas: military technology and hardware, industrial machinery and products, and culture and philosophy.

The Chinese response to these threats took the form of two conflicting strands:

> One was the intellectuals and the government forces, the other was the masses which were not directly under the tight control of the government. The former were represented by prominent scholars and officials. They sought to understand the West and searched for an organized and institutionalized approach to deter "imperialism". Modernization by means of Westernization has been the key approach to building up the strength of China to resist foreign aggression. The failure of this approach gave rise to the second force: the antiforeign sentiments of the unorganized masses — the peasants, workers, students and merchants. (Liao, 1990: 3)

Thus some Chinese officials came to accept, albeit reluctantly, the need to study Western ideas and languages to strengthen the nation so that future humiliations might be avoided (Bastid, 1987). A strategy of synthesis was propounded by scholars in the Self-Strengthening Movement during the second half of the nineteenth century, which sought to preserve China's cultural heritage while placing the country on an equal technological and economic footing with others. Scholars recognized that the study of foreign languages was necessary to gain access to Western ideas (Teng and Fairbank, 1979). Feng Guai-fen's suggestion, which was highly controversial, was to set up official colleges to study foreign languages with a view to strengthening China through technology transfer:

> If today we wish to select and use Western knowledge, we should establish official translation offices at Canton and Shanghai. Brilliant students up to fifteen years of age should be selected from those areas to live and study in these schools on double rations. Westerners should be invited to teach them the spoken and written languages of the various nations, and famous Chinese teachers should also be engaged to teach them classics, history, and other subjects. At the same time they should learn mathematics ... If we now wish to adopt Western knowledge, naturally we cannot but learn mathematics. (Translated by Teng and Fairbank, 1979: 51)

Feng's ideas, as well as those of like-minded scholars, gained imperial consent. In 1861, the Chinese government established the Tongwen Guan (literally 'School of Combined Learning'), an institute of translation in Beijing. A similar establishment, the Guang Fangyan in Shanghai, opened in 1863. The Tongwen Guan was subordinate to the Zongli Yamen, an office responsible for foreign affairs that was also created in the decree of 1861. One duty of the interpreters trained in the Tongwen Guan was to pass on to the Zongli Yamen intelligence garnered from foreign newspapers produced in the treaty ports. Thus the study of English had a dual role: to gain access to Western technology through the translation of scientific and technical books into Chinese, and to enable the Chinese government to engage in diplomacy with the Western powers. Ironically, the Tongwen Guan initially suffered from the stigma that its proponent, Feng Guai-fen, had noted with regard to the *compradores*. At first, as Borthwick notes, it was:

> filled with the dregs of an old official school for Manchu bannermen [military officers]. The students and their families were ostracised by friends and relatives for surrendering to the West. Some even had difficulty in finding wives. (Borthwick, 1982: 63)

One reason for the low popular standing of the institution was the belief that a sound knowledge of Chinese would endow students with a status and position in society, whereas a knowledge of English promised an uncertain future (Biggerstaff, 1961). However, by the late 1870s, graduates from the Tongwen Guan began to gain appointments within the civil service or even diplomatic postings overseas and the status of the school, and therefore of studying English, rose accordingly (Spence, 1980).

The forced opening of China meant that English was also taught in schools set up by missionary organizations. From 1842, missionary schools were established in Macau, Guangzhou, Tianjin, Shanghai, Ningpo and other treaty ports, and, following the Opium Wars, in the hinterland (Bolton, 2002). Teaching English was seen as a medium to change China peacefully and to proselytize. An editorial in the missionary journal, *The Chinese Repository*, on the importance of the English language in British imperial history, comments:

> We entertain no mean opinion of the strength of the Chinese; yet we do not by any means regard them as invincible either by arms or argument. They could never stand against the discipline of European forces — and we hope they will never be put in such a woful [sic] position; but if they can be brought into the open field of argument, we are, if possible, still more sure they must yield. It is impossible that forms, and usages, and claims founded in error and falsehood, can stand against the *force of truth*. By a free intercourse of thought, commercial and political, social and religious relations can, and sooner or later, certainly will be improved. (*The Chinese Repository*, 1834: 5; emphasis in original)

However, it was the economic rather than spiritual benefits of learning English that attracted most students: the study of the language offered access to lucrative posts with foreign companies, in the customs service, or the telegraph service. The work of English-speaking *compradores*, which had previously been associated with outcasts, became a means for budding entrepreneurs to make quick capital and useful connections (Hsü, 1990).

The positive view of the English language that predominated among residents of the treaty ports was not shared by all Chinese, many of whom reacted against any form of interaction with foreigners, particularly after the Opium Wars. This opposition was occasionally expressed in violent terms. The nobility, especially, whose status and power were derived from traditional social and political structures, periodically showed overt hostility towards the English language by directing mass anti-foreignist movements that sought to eradicate its traces from China (Liao, 1990). Much of the violence was directed against the missionaries, whose religious messages allied to English teaching were perceived as a threat to the mixture of Daoism, Buddhism, Shintoism and Confucianism, the state philosophy that embraced religious, governmental, social and familial affairs in China. Anti-foreign riots took place at various times in Hunan, Hubei, Jiangxi, Tianjin and Nanjing, *inter alia*, and culminated in the Boxer Uprising of 1900–01, which saw the death of 231 foreigners and many more Chinese Christians. While many participants in these riots were peasants, they were encouraged and organized not only by the local aristocracy, but also by high-ranking officials and even the Empress Dowager, Cixi, who wielded significant power in the Imperial Court (Hsü, 1990).

These anti-foreign sentiments formed a strong counterpoint to the trend towards strengthening China militarily, economically and diplomatically through an education programme based on technical transfer from overseas, as advocated by scholars such as Zhang Zhidong. Zhang's view that foreign science and technology needed to be grafted on to the moral traditions of China was encapsulated in the slogan *zhongxue weiti, xixue weiyong* ('study China for essence, study the West for practical usage'). Immediately prior to the Boxer Uprising (and one of its probable causes) was the reform movement of 1898, known as the Hundred Days' Reform because from 11 June to 30 September, over forty reform decrees were issued. To assuage anti-foreignist sentiments, scholars attempted to encapsulate in the reforms the principle of assimilating Western ideas and preserving the fundamental state philosophy (Ayers, 1971). Foreign language study, for instance, would be slotted into this ethical framework for purely functional, rather than cultural, goals; according to Wen Ti, a scholar at the time of the Hundred Days' Reform:

> If we wish to receive the benefit of Western methods, we must first acquire a knowledge of Confucius, Mencius, Ch'eng and Chu, and keep it as the foundation to make people thoroughly familiar with filial piety, younger-brotherhood, loyalty, sincerity, ceremony, righteousness, integrity, a sense of shame, obligations and the teachings of the sages and moral courage, in order to understand and demonstrate the foundation, before we can learn the foreign spoken and written languages for some practical use. (Translated by Teng and Fairbank, 1979: 183–4)

The decree of 10 July 1898 established higher educational institutes based on the model of the Tongwen Guan, and a range of other reforms intended to facilitate the transfer of technology. However, officials undermined many of the reforms. For instance, the Board of Rites, which supervised entrance to the imperial civil service strongly resisted the imposition of changes to traditional examinations. Other reform edicts were ignored by central and provincial officials (Hsü, 1990). The aftermath of the Boxer Uprising, when an army despatched by the various nations with territorial interests in China crushed the rebellion and exacted harsh indemnities from the Chinese government, witnessed some half-hearted attempts at reform by a dispirited Imperial Court, mortally wounded by internal strife and external force. In 1902, China finally rejected the traditional system of schooling, which was linked to the imperial civil service. In its place, one based on the Japanese system of education was adopted as a suitable model for grafting Western ideas on to an Oriental culture (Hayhoe, 1984); the Chinese had also been forced into grudging admiration of Japan following their humiliating defeat in the Sino-Japanese War of 1894–1895. English (as an alternative to Japanese) was among the subjects included in the mainstream curricula of secondary schools according to the 'Regulations of Primary and Middle Schools' edict issued by Emperor Guangxu in August 1902, although English was recommended to be taught only to senior secondary school students. Further regulations were issued in 1904, spelling out the underlying objective of assimilating Western ideas:

> The principal idea in establishing any school is a basis in loyalty and filial piety. In other words, traditional Chinese learning must be the basis of education to form students' character. After that, the importance of Western learning is emphasized to enrich knowledge and to give technical skills to students. (translated in Abe, 1987: 65)

The new model aimed to counter the exclusivity of Confucian and neo-Confucian education by making schooling universal for all children of seven years of age or older. Units of educational administration were set up throughout China to implement the new measures, but a lack of money and facilities, as well as a shortage of teachers sufficiently qualified to meet the demands of the new curriculum, hampered such an ambitious project. Japan provided some resources and helped in teacher education. However, the imitation of the Japanese model was short-lived, as fear of Japanese hegemony spread and the traditional elements lacked relevance to the needs of China's development programme, which, in any case, was thrown into temporary chaos by the revolution of 1911.

The eventual abolition of the traditional examinations and the adoption of a modern education system was a victory for the Self-Strengtheners. The last emperor of China, Pu-Yi Aisin Guoro (who adopted the English name, Henry), epitomized the official recognition of the value of English by hiring a tutor, Reginald Fleming Johnston, who used 'Alice in Wonderland' as a textbook (Pu-Yi, 1964: 54).

English during the Republic

The overthrow of the Qing dynasty and the establishment of the republican era in 1911 may be regarded as a Pyrrhic victory for the modernizers. The English language had played a significant role in the modernizers' cause, but without an emperor, the philosophical, religious and social constructs of the nation were undermined. The Republic, founded on 1 January 1912, was marked by political uncertainty. The brief provisional presidency of Dr Sun Yat-sen was followed by the appointment of Yuan Shikai as President of the Republic of China, but Yuan's inclinations appeared monarchical rather than republican. After his death, China experienced a further breakdown in law and order: warlords established control of regions of the country and it was only in 1928, with the setting up of a Nationalist Party government in Nanjing, that a semblance of unity was restored. Even then, the relative stability was short-lived, with the outbreak of the Anti-Japanese War in 1937, followed by the Civil War that culminated in 1949 with the founding of the People's Republic of China.

In the early days of the Republic, studying abroad, most notably in the United States of America, grew in popularity (Keenan, 1977). In 1922, China decided to follow the model of the US education system. The USA had ploughed back the reparations received following the Boxer Uprising at the turn of the century into the establishment of educational institutions in China, many of which had American missionaries and other teachers on the staff. Military co-operation had also reached a considerable level.

A major advocate of learning from the industrialized world was Dr Sun Yat-sen. At times, he lived abroad in order to study foreign languages (particularly English), literature, politics, mathematics and medicine. His goals, encapsulated in the Three People's Principles, were the development of Chinese nationalism, freedom from domination by the Manchu Qing dynasty as well as from foreign powers, democracy, and socialism. He sought to create a modernized China that existed on an equal footing with the industrialized nations, but which synthesized Chinese tradition with new imported ideas. The young intelligentsia that supported Sun Yat-sen included several scholars who had studied overseas. The ideas of Thomas Huxley, John Dewey, Bertrand Russell, Paul Monroe, Adam Smith and Charles Darwin, among others, fuelled what Hsü calls the 'New Cultural Movement' (Hsü, 1990). The notion of Progressivism, when espoused (and reinterpreted) by influential reformers such as Tao Xingzhi, briefly filled the vacuum created by the ousting of Confucianism as the basis for the political rationale of education.

This reform movement, epitomized by the May Fourth Movement of 1919, aroused great debate in China, with language as a central issue. Most notably, the direction of Chinese Language education was the most hotly debated question: whether the vernacular and oral-focused *baihua* version should be emphasized in the curriculum or the classical, literary-focused *wenyan* version. Debates surrounding English, too, were prominent during the 'Intellectual Revolution' between 1917 and 1923, as attitudes towards the language were still ambivalent. English (or another foreign language) was one of the three core subjects in the secondary school curriculum, but the wider role for English, as a medium for accessing philosophical, economic, social and political ideas, was resisted by traditionalists. Writing in 1933, a scholar, Fan Shou-kang, sought to curb what he perceived to be the pernicious influence of English upon Chinese culture by boosting patriotic education and restricting the study of English to enable pupils to:

> ... use the most common foreign language in speech and writing in order to ... meet the most common and simple needs in business and in society, establish the foundation for further study in that language, and promote their interest in the study of the daily life conditions of foreign countries. (cited in Tsang, 1967: 72–3)

Some scholars called for the removal of English and other foreign languages from the school curriculum. In an article entitled 'Nationalistic Education and the Movement for the Abolition of English in the Elementary School', Li Ju-mien wrote in 1925:

> Not until recently has there been the realisation of the necessity for nationalistic education. Elementary education has the primary function of cultivating patriotic and efficient citizenship. All kinds of training and all branches of the curriculum should be centred on this mission. Subjects unimportant or irrelevant to this purpose of education should be taken out of the curriculum. English is a foreign language. It has no relation to the training of citizenship and should be abolished. (cited in Tsang, 1967: 72)

In time, the American model of education was, in turn, discarded, on the grounds that it swung too far from Chinese tradition and, more persuasively, the nationalist movement felt it politic for China to shed the least hint of foreign intervention in domestic affairs. The Nationalist Party sought to establish an indigenous philosophy and system of education. It faced conflicting forces: the traditional notion of self-cultivation against the progressive idea of social utility; elitist against broad-based education, and, particularly, the aspirations of the Nationalist Party itself against the needs of the country in general. Indeed, the Nationalist Party introduced mandatory propaganda courses into schools. However, investment in education was severely limited by economic difficulties and the inability of the Nationalist Party to administer a nation which, politically, was rapidly devolving into a patchwork of warlord states. A few warlords, like Yan Xishan in Shanxi, demonstrated an appreciation of the importance of education and invested in its development (Gillin, 1967). In the background to the reforms and instability, Confucian schools (*si shu*) remained in operation, particularly in rural areas, and the teaching of traditional values were preserved in such places.

On the other hand, interest in learning English was enhanced by other factors. One was the growth of international mass media and mass entertainment. Chinese people, particularly in the major cities, experienced a wider exposure to English than previously through the increased availability of foreign newspapers, journals and films, with the result that the popularity of English learning was heightened. Shanghai especially had a Westernized élite, typified by the Soong sisters, Ailing, Meiling — who married Chiang Kai-shek, the leader of the Nationalist Party — and Chingling, who married Sun Yat-sen. They were educated in a girls' academy run by Western missionaries: such schools were favoured by rich Chinese families wishing to enhance their commercial dealings with industrialized nations and to prepare their children for overseas study (Cleverley, 1991). For some, knowledge of English offered social advancement as a mark of education, to the outrage of some members of the aristocracy (Borthwick, 1982). Lower down the social scale, a smattering of English still represented a passport to employment in the treaty ports, albeit in humble positions (Borthwick, 1982).

International events also brought China closer to English-speaking nations. Chinese pressure led to the number of treaty ports being reduced, and the Nine-Power Treaty (6 February 1922) assured China, at least on paper, of political independence and territorial integrity. When Japanese aggression against China flared up seriously in 1937, China turned to the USA for support, which came, particularly after Pearl Harbor, in the form of advisers such as Joseph Stilwell and *matériel* flown in 'over the hump' (the Himalayas) from India. One source of support in the Anti-Japanese War was China's private recruitment of Claire Lee Chennault from the US Army Air Corps to oversee the Chinese Air Force. His commitment to the Chinese cause was enhanced by a meeting with Soong Meiling, in which he was apparently impressed by the way she spoke English in a rich Southern drawl (Spence, 1980).

In the Chinese Civil War, which followed the Anti-Japanese War, both sides, the CCP and the Nationalist Party, wanted support from the USA in particular — the CCP for international legitimacy and the Nationalist Party for military assistance. US diplomatic activity was generally even-handed when the two political groups first emerged as potential governors of postwar China, and both Zhou Enlai of the CCP and Chiang Kai-shek of the Nationalist Party were able to communicate with US officials in English (Spence, 1980; Wilson, 1984). After the meeting between US President Roosevelt and the USSR leader, Stalin, at Yalta in 1945, the US policy to back the Nationalist Party emerged. This engendered the ambivalent attitude of the CCP towards the USA and her allies that was to set the tone for the early decades of the PRC: the CCP understood the importance of international recognition and appreciated the individual friendship and assistance of sympathetic doctors and journalists such as Norman Bethune, Edgar Snow, Agnes Smedley and Anna Louise Strong, but it abhorred the anti-Communist stance of the US government and retaliated in 1949 by announcing that it would seek solidarity with the forces of socialism to combat imperialism.

Summary

English was perceived in imperial China as a threat to the nation's cultural integrity, but also, paradoxically, as a means to help shore up that integrity. The cultural threat embodied by English led to violent resistance at times, especially when scholars and aristocrats, whose interests were most at risk, believed that the Imperial Court was incapable of resisting the impact of the language and the values it embodied. The status of English was as ambivalent as its role. The negative connotations of English meant that the language had low official status initially, when communication was conducted by virtual outcasts from Chinese society, but as the national crisis developed, English was accorded higher official status with the government's establishment of foreign language institutions. Popular approval of English also rose because of the social mobility that knowledge of English made possible.

In the Republican period, the role of English was enhanced in China's modernization programme. The official status of the language also grew, with its institutionalization in the curriculum. Opportunities to learn the language increased, although the agrarian masses that made up the vast majority of the population had little time or opportunity for schooling. The incidence of violent anti-foreignism decreased (and where it did occur, was mainly directed against Japanese militarism). One reason for the greater acceptance of English could be that the debate had lost its political edge: China was facing less of a territorial crisis than in the latter years of the Qing dynasty. Although she had not yet shaken off the foreign imperialistic yoke, China strengthened her international position, tending towards alignment with Western rather than Eastern powers such as Japan. At the same time, China was adopting Western ideas to fill some of the void left by the demise of the imperial system, although not at the expense of a total rejection of her cultural heritage. These shifts towards a more equitable relationship with industrialized countries are reflected in the development of an indigenous education system built on a US model and operating in parallel and in competition to that of the expanding missionary movement.

Nonetheless, there were dissenters who saw the influx of foreign ideas as a threat. The tension between the modernizers and the traditionalists centred on the question of nationalism. The former sought a re-evaluation of China's heritage with reference to social, political, economic and philosophical ideas from abroad; for this to take place, the study of English was necessary. The traditionalists saw the English language as the thin edge of a wedge that would destroy China's rich culture. The tension was not resolved during the Republican era. Indeed, it was to become an issue of great controversy after the CCP assumed power in 1949, particularly in the light of the international politics surrounding the Chinese Civil War, which created or heightened antipathy towards the USA and her allies.

3 The Soviet influence, 1949–60

The establishment of the PRC on 1 October 1949 marked the end of more than twelve years' fighting, firstly arising from the Japanese invasion in 1937, and then the civil war between the CCP and Nationalist Party. Internal strife and weakness were major challenges to the CCP, whose main priority in the 1950s was nation-building. State policy addressed two major historical tensions (Hsü, 1990). The first arose from the immediate past: the need to consolidate the CCP's power in the face of the lingering influences of the Nationalist Party and traditional feudal ideas, by using mass campaigns to unite the populace in support of CCP policies. The second was connected to the long-standing strategy of national self-strengthening: the need to build a strong China politically, economically and militarily, in order to enable her to play what was viewed as an equitable role in international affairs.

The early years after the revolution were characterized by united front activities in urban areas to engage the loyalties of former Nationalist Party sympathizers, particularly the entrepreneurs in the prosperous seaboard areas who could provide the means to develop the nation's economy. At the same time, land reform in the rural areas was carried out to eradicate the influence of wealthy landowners (whom the CCP considered to exploit the peasants); to reward the poorer peasants for their support in the civil war; and to prepare for the introduction of new agricultural programmes. These programmes sought to establish a collectivized system of agricultural production that was designed to even out former inequalities and increase efficiency. Help was solicited from the Union of Soviet Socialist Republics (USSR), which had undergone a similar process after the revolution in 1917. Policy advisers and technical experts from the USSR arrived in China to assist in the developmental process. The CCP also initiated a series of reforms to create new political structures.

In the early 1950s, English was rarely found in the school curriculum. Education policy efforts were oriented towards mother-tongue literacy as a part of the provision of mass education, and Russian was the main foreign language in schools because of the strong link with the USSR. Political events rendered

English unpopular. A number of English-speaking countries failed to recognize the PRC, and the USA, which remained a strong supporter of the Nationalist Party that had decamped to Taiwan in 1949, imposed an economic blockade. A tide of anti-US sentiment swept the country with the effect that it 'became somehow unpatriotic to study the language of our enemies' (Tang Lixing, 1983: 41). Recalling this period, Tsang Chiu Sam writes:

> The social movements and thought reform movements have scared the people to such an extent that, as far as possible, they keep away from any association with imperialism. It was reported that the sons and daughters of the professors of English in the universities were unwilling to take up the study of English. It was explained that they did not want to face the same misfortune of their fathers in the social movements and thought reforms when they had to pay the penalty for having been English scholars. At one time, in elementary English in the lower schools, "Jack" and "John" were superseded by such Chinese names as "Li Fong" or "So Ming", and "sir" was replaced by "comrade". Progress in foreign language learning is handicapped by this emotional strain. (1967: 203–4)

On the other hand, the government did not completely lose sight of the practical value of the English language as a means of access to science and technology. The draft curriculum for foreign language faculties in tertiary institutes issued in 1950 stated that the main purpose of studying foreign languages was for the purposes of translation (Ministry of Education, 1950a). Interpreters of Russian were required for the Soviet specialists working in China, and translators of Russian and English were needed as most technical and scientific manuals imported by China were in these languages.

The official recommendation was that Russian should be the foreign language studied in schools, although schools teaching English would be allowed to continue (Ministry of Education, 1950b). However, there were no school textbooks for English produced in China at that time, and the importation of books from the USA, UK and other English-speaking nations was banned. Schools had to rely on revisions of old Nationalist Party textbooks for English (which were tolerated by the authorities because of the lack of alternatives) or write their own materials (Tang Jun, 1986). These conditions favoured the teaching of Russian, for which expertise and teaching materials were more readily available. Many former English Language teachers switched to teaching Russian — to the extent, when official records began in 1957, there were only 73 junior secondary school English Language teachers in the whole country (Tang Lixing, 1983; Ministry of Education, 1984). On 28 April 1954, the ministry announced that all foreign language teaching other than Russian would cease in secondary schools in order to reduce the demands of the curriculum on students. Priority was given to learning Chinese and other subjects (Löfstedt, 1980; Tang Lixing, 1983; Tang Jun, 1986).

Industrial expansion in the mid-1950s served to rekindle official interest in English as a valuable language of science and technology. At the same time, China's foreign policy was developing, largely through the diplomacy of Premier Zhou Enlai, towards a degree of *détente* with countries in Asia that were not aligned with either the communist or capitalist blocs. An example of this diplomacy was the agreement of the Five Principles of Peaceful Coexistence at Bandung in 1955, involving non-aligned countries. The increased international activity, together with a general review of educational standards in the country resulted in a range of educational reforms (Wilson, 1984; Pepper, 1996). In 1956, the Ministry of Education announced that, from the following year, junior secondary schools would teach either English or Russian, and that the target ratio of schools offering Russian to those offering English would be 1:1 (Qun and Li, 1991), although this provision would be initially limited to those schools in the big cities, such as Beijing, Shanghai and Tianjin, that possessed sufficient resources to teach English (Tang Lixing, 1983). In the event, the number of full-time junior secondary school English Language teachers multiplied more than 25 times to 1,859 between 1957 and 1959 (Ministry of Education, 1984).

The decade ended with political movements that had a drastic effect on people's lives: the Anti-Rightist Campaign in 1957 against dissent or criticism directed towards the government; the institution of People's Communes, in which many aspects of work and family life were collectivized, and the frenzied Great Leap Forward. The last of these, which started in 1958, was designed to mobilize all sectors of society to make contributions to industrial development — even to the extent of establishing small, makeshift steel furnaces in work units and communes. While output did increase, quality was sacrificed and the emphasis on industry over agriculture meant that the Great Leap Forward resulted in mass famine, especially in the rural areas, and an estimated 50 million deaths. All these movements placed pressure on the high degree of national solidarity and consensus that the CCP had achieved after taking power: factionalism appeared in the CCP; the persecutions for political errors were bewildering; the People's Communes were unproductive and wasteful; the Great Leap Forward was a disaster, and discontent was growing among the people (Löfstedt, 1980; Hsü, 1990; Liao, 1990; Wang, 1995).

Between 1957 and 1960, there were three sets of innovations in the junior secondary school English Language curriculum in China; and their features are summarized in Table 3.1 (see p. 38). The common features of this phase lie in the process of development. All innovations were produced at the time of Sino-Soviet collaboration, which clearly impinged upon the English Language curriculum, especially in terms of political content and intended pedagogy. The PEP in the Ministry of Education relied on staff in tertiary institutions to write the syllabuses and textbook resources, and there was little planning or consultation with grassroots members of the teaching profession.

Table 3.1   Features of the English Language curriculum, 1949–60

	1957: Series One	1960: Series Two	1960: Series Three
Genesis	reassessment of role of English in economic development	call to strengthen political content	plan to create unified primary and secondary curriculum, during politicization
Role and status of English	technology transfer; cultural information; low/medium official status	promote loyalty to CCP and patriotism; low official status	promote loyalty to CCP and patriotism; low official status
Role of agencies PEP: Consultants: Teachers:	commissioning and publishing writing syllabus and textbooks none	commissioning and publishing writing textbooks none	commissioning and publishing writing syllabus and textbooks some piloting and feedback
Process	adaptation of tertiary materials; reference to Soviet models	adaptation of Series One; reference to Chinese Language textbooks for political messages	reference to Chinese Language textbooks and political tracts for political messages
Syllabus	not published; guidelines stress accurate pronunciation and basic grammar	unchanged	not published (experimental curriculum)
Resources	two textbooks	three textbooks	18 textbooks (8 for junior secondary)
Organization	integrated topic-based; linear sequence	integrated topic-based; linear sequence; disjointed between Book 1 and Books 2 and 3	no clear underpinning organization; passage-based; widely varying number of vocabulary items
Discourse	from weakly to strongly realistic	from weakly to strongly realistic	mainly strongly realistic
Linguistic components	focus on pronunciation, grammar, vocabulary; some control	focus on reading and vocabulary; little control	focus on reading and vocabulary; little control
Intended pedagogy	Structural and Grammar-Translation: teacher-centred; focus on accuracy and written language; memorization; Kairov's five steps	Structural and Grammar-Translation: teacher-centred; focus on written language, pronunciation and grammatical structures; memorization	Grammar-Translation: teacher-centred; focus on written language; memorization
Political and moral messages	mainly 'healthy' lifestyle; patriotism and participation in CCP youth activities	mainly political values; some social values and 'healthy' lifestyle	almost exclusively political messages

The curriculum of 1957

The first curriculum stemmed from the increase in China's international diplomatic activity, which was followed by a review of the education system. The focus was on how education could help socialist economic construction and cultural development (Tang Jun, 1986). When the Ministry of Education announced on 10 July 1956 that English, as well as Russian, was to be a junior secondary school subject from September 1957, the need for appropriate resources became pressing. The PEP, being responsible for curriculum development in secondary schools, was asked to produce a syllabus and a set of textbooks for English.

Previously there had been no recommended textbooks for English in China: schools had to rely on pre-Revolution materials or produced their own, and there was no unified syllabus, apart from rather sketchy guidelines in the 'English Curricula Criteria for Junior Secondary Schools' (1948). These guidelines (cited in Zhou, 1995: 880–1) promoted a positive approach to Western countries, listing, as two objectives, 'Understanding the British and American national mindset and customs', and 'Arousing interest in learning Western things'. The intended pedagogy focused on building a 'foundation' in the four skills of listening, speaking, reading and writing, with the latter stages of the course centring on reading. Also, the guidelines stipulated that 'all oral and written exercises should be strictly limited to repetition. Free creative use or practice should be avoided so that students can learn purer English.' However, the senior secondary school guidelines encouraged free use of English by students, once they had a solid foundation. Students were encouraged to study from films and gramophone records featuring native speakers.

The task of developing the new curriculum was pioneering work, as there was no strong tradition of indigenous textbook production for the teaching of English in junior secondary schools in China. Previously, schools had used textbooks produced overseas or written by foreigners working in the country. Although the target readership was relatively small — the Ministry of Education envisaged English being offered only by those schools in large cities that had the necessary resources, including competent staff — the ability range of teachers was broad. The teachers in schools offering English would have been trained before the revolution of 1949, and their own competence in English would depend, to a large extent, upon the kind of education they themselves had received. According to Tang Lixing (1983), those who had graduated from missionary schools or schools with a good academic reputation would probably have good all-round ability in English, whereas graduates from non-religious and less prestigious schools would scarcely be able to read or write in English. Another complicating factor facing the PEP was the relatively short time available for producing the materials. Commissioned in July 1956, the textbooks were required for use in classrooms from September 1957. The process of subsequent curriculum development process was quite centralized, but pragmatic. The crucial defining factor of the curriculum was the available resources, not the centrally-determined educational policy, which only set the parameters. Three major influences are discernible: the socio-political climate, that set a role for English Language curriculum in national development during a time of some tension with English-speaking countries; an international influence from the USSR on the contents and pedagogy; and an historical intertextuality, whereby the writers referred to their own past experience and materials, as well as those from overseas.

The PEP had been established in December 1950 to research, compile and publish teaching materials in the new PRC (PEP, 1990). When they received instructions to produce an English curriculum, PEP officials felt they lacked the expertise in English to write the syllabus and textbooks in-house. Therefore they decided to seek help from tertiary institutes, but the majority of universities and colleges specialized in Russian Language teaching. The exception was the Beijing Foreign Languages Institute. As this institute had been set up to train cadres and interpreters for the Ministry of Foreign Affairs, it possessed a strong English department. Its staff were also experienced curriculum developers and textbook writers at tertiary level, and, more importantly, had considerable experience in designing and teaching courses for beginners, as many students at the institute had not previously studied English. For these reasons, the PEP engaged a team of lecturers from the Beijing Foreign Languages Institute, under the leadership of Ying Manrong and Fan Ying, to produce an English syllabus for junior secondary schools and to write accompanying textbooks (which we will refer to as Series One).[1]

In writing the syllabus and textbooks, Ying Manrong, Fan Ying and their colleagues first drew up a plan of the materials to be covered in three years of junior secondary schooling, given that only three lessons a week would be devoted to English. According to Ying Manrong, they used two sources for reference: the courses for beginners that they had written at the Beijing Foreign Languages Institute, and secondary school English textbooks from the USSR.[2] The latter choice was restricted by the political climate, which ruled out the possibility of borrowing from Western countries. The obvious source was the USSR, where the teaching of English created similar dilemmas for educationalists, in that the two countries shared an antipathy towards Western nations, and both the USSR and China used school textbooks as a means for promoting a similar prevailing political ideology. Furthermore, Soviet textbooks were readily available, unlike Western textbooks, which had been banned from China. There were pedagogical reasons that also made the Soviet textbooks attractive. These books generally stressed grammatical rules and followed the pedagogical principles of 'three-centred' teaching — classroom-centred, teacher-centred and textbook-centred — propounded by the Soviet educator and one-time Minister of Education, I. A. Kairov (Tang Lixing, 1983). These approaches resembled traditional, indigenous methods for learning Chinese (Dzau, 1990).

After the team had drafted the syllabus, one group under Ying Manrong then took responsibility for writing the first textbook in Series One, while Fan Ying and two colleagues wrote Book 2. Because of time constraints and to ease the division of labour, only two textbooks were written, but they contained sufficient material for the three-year junior secondary programme. The PEP published the two textbooks in Series One, 'English Book 1' and 'English Book 2', in September 1957 and August 1958 respectively.

Although the syllabus was written concurrently with Book 1 of Series One, it was never published. Instead, it remained an internal working document that guided the material development teams. Focusing mainly on pedagogical goals, it set out a number of aims for teaching English, notably to 'motivate students to learn English in the future, and to provide students with the necessary knowledge, skills and techniques that are needed when they use English'.[3] The syllabus stresses that particular attention should be paid to accurate pronunciation and to basic grammar, and lists approximately 1,000 vocabulary items and formulaic expressions, as well as identifying the tenses and other grammatical structures to be taught. Ying Manrong acknowledges that the orientation of the syllabus was influenced by her work at the Beijing Foreign Languages Institute, where good pronunciation and grammatical accuracy were held to be important attributes of capable interpreters.[4] The use of a specified vocabulary list was intended to control the level of difficulty of the textbooks. This measure had been used prior to the founding of the PRC: the 1948 curriculum guidelines stipulate that two-thirds of the 2,000 words to be covered in secondary school should be drawn from the list of 5,000 words drawn up by Thorndike and Lorge (1944). The notion of using vocabulary to control language difficulty was also used in Chinese Language teaching, where a restriction was placed on the number of characters to be taught per school year.

As Series One were the only textbooks permitted to be used in junior secondary schools, the relationship between the syllabus and the textbook content was inextricably and symbiotically linked. This did not arise from the skilful writing of a new set of textbooks to precisely meet the requirements of a newly-created syllabus. Essentially, Series One was the syllabus. This unified entity was developed by adapting an existing course (in which materials and syllabus were likewise a unified entity) for a different set of learners.

Technically, the two books were relatively simple productions, measuring 13 cm x 19 cm, with plain white covers and the title printed in green (Figure A.1, p. 211). The paper was of poor quality. Some pages were illustrated with black and white line drawings. Book 1, with 186 pages, contains 46 'lessons' (or units, as a lesson does not correspond to a class period), while Book 2 has fewer (36 lessons) to allow time for revision, and is consequently shorter, with 168 pages.

Pedagogy

According to Ying Manrong, the course was organized to follow an integrated topic-based approach.[5] The main feature of this approach is the interaction between the discourse and the linguistic components (such as the grammar, vocabulary and pronunciation): each lesson has a theme, which is explored principally in the reading passage, and the theme dictates the vocabulary, grammar and other linguistic components (such as pronunciation) to be covered in the relevant sections of the lesson. At the same time, the level of difficulty of the linguistic components in the reading passage was intended to be carefully controlled so as to facilitate students' comprehension and learning. In Series One, the integrated topic-based approach is evident in that the main organizational feature is a piece of discourse (i.e., an extended stretch of language). The lessons generally start with the discourse, which, in the early stages of the course, cover topics related to daily life, and then broaden to include societal issues and literature. The vocabulary, grammar and other items that are presented are all derived from the discourse. At the same time, the linguistic components are controlled in order to follow linear syllabuses that are set out on the contents pages.

The general organization reflects close attention to pedagogical considerations, as evidenced by the linguistic control and the linear sequencing, which are features of the Structural Approach. However, the centrality of discourse indicates a view that language has a communicative function, and that language teaching should not be restricted to the learning of grammatical rules. The focus on written passages is indicative of the Grammar-Translation Method.

The lessons in Series One all contain examples of discourse in English. In this study, 'strong' discourse is language, either oral or written, that is oriented more towards the purposes of communication than just towards the practice of discrete linguistic components. An analysis of the discourse, using the strong–weak discourse continuum, will provide insights into the kind of communication that is being promoted, as well as into the views of language pedagogy that underpin the contents.

The discourse in Series One is mainly found in the reading passages, although some exercises for students to complete in Book 2 involve the production of communicative text. Most of the discourse in the first part of Book 1 is weak, being relatively unrealistic. For instance, the main purpose of Lesson 4, 'I see Ann', the first to include complete sentences, is to present the syntagmatic paradigm *I see + OBJECT(S)*. The passage comprises sentences, such as:

> I see Ann.
> I see Pete.
> I see Ann and Pete.
>
> I see Ann.
> I see a cat.
> I see Ann and a cat. (Series One, Book 1: 14)[6]

In a few passages, the discourse is expressed in stilted, relatively unrealistic language ('medium' realism). An example is Book 2 Lesson 5, 'What Are You Doing?', which clearly serves to show the use of the present continuous tense, but, at the same time, has a message about exemplary behaviour:

> What are you doing, boys?
> We are working in the fields.
> We are picking cabbages.
> We are helping the farmers.
>
> What are you and your friends doing here, Wang Ping?
> I am working on the bus.
> Chang Li is helping an old woman to find a seat.
> Yang Pao is helping the conductor to collect the tickets.
>
> What are those boys and girls doing there?
> They are digging holes in the ground.
> They are planting trees.
> They are making our country green and beautiful. (Series One, Book 2: 14)

Another technique used to balance realistic discourse with a focus on individual language structures is the use of question and answer dialogues following a description. Thus, in Book 1 Lesson 30, a description of a classroom is followed by questions and answers that provide practice in the use of *there is/are* and *it is* in both statement and interrogative forms:

> Our Classroom
>
> We have a large classroom. It has two doors and three windows. It is bright and clean.
>
> There is a picture of Chairman Mao on one of the walls. On another wall there is a map. It is a map of China.
>
> There are three blackboards in our classroom. There is a table for the teacher. There are forty-five desks and chairs. They are for the pupils.

— Is there a map in your classroom?
— Yes, there is.
— What map is it?
— It is a map of China.
— Where is it?
— It is on one of the walls.
— What is there on another wall?
— There is a picture of Chairman Mao.
— How many blackboards are there in your classroom?
— There are three.
— Are there desks for the pupils?
— Yes, there are. There are forty-five pupils in our class. There are forty-five desks and chairs in our classroom. (Series One, Book 1: 98–9)

This passage is 'medium' strength, in that it combines relatively strong discourse (such as in the description of the classroom in the passage), with relatively weak discourse (such as the unrealistic nature of the dialogue, and the repetitive use of structures, such as *There is/are* throughout).

There is a shift from weak to strong discourse in the series, with the first part of Book 1 carefully controlling linguistic components in the discourse, and the rest of the series gradually loosening the control. The linguistic control in the last passage in the series (Book 2 Unit 36) is less evident than in 'Our Classroom', for instance, although some degree of control is found in the passages:

Summer

Summer is the hottest season of the year, and now summer is here. The nights are short; the days are long. There are flowers and green leaves everywhere.

Very soon examinations will be over and summer holidays will begin. My friends and I are going to a pioneer camp. We shall get plenty of exercise and fresh air. We shall gather firewood and cook our own meals. We shall collect insects and study them. When it rains, we shall listen to stories about heroes and model workers. We shall discuss how pioneers can help to build Socialism. When it is fine, we shall visit factories and work on farms. The workers will show us how they work at the machines. The farmers will tell us how they work in the fields. We shall work with them and learn a lot about the working people. We shall understand them better and love them more. (Series One, Book 2: 115–6)

This supports the indications noted earlier that the pedagogical underpinning of these two textbooks is a view that language learning is best brought about initially through the presentation and practice of discrete linguistic components, such as vocabulary and grammatical structures, and later through the presentation of more complex and realistic written passages. A specific pedagogical approach is described in a reading passage in Book 2 Lesson 15:

Our English Lessons

We have a new text every week. Our teacher reads the text and we read after her. Then she explains the text. We listen carefully because there are many new words in it. If we do not understand, we put up our hands, and she explains again. Our teacher asks us questions. When we answer her questions, we must try to speak clearly. We do a lot of exercises in class. We make sentences. We have spelling and dictation. Sometimes we write on the blackboard. Sometimes we write in our notebooks. We learn to write clearly and neatly.

I like our English lessons. I think we are making good progress. (Series One, Book 2: 46)

This pedagogical approach bears the hallmarks of the Grammar-Translation Method, which is characterized as: emphasizing reading and writing skills; making constant references to, and explanations in, the learners' mother tongue; focusing on grammatical forms; requiring memorization of grammatical paradigms; and highly teacher-centred (Tang Lixing, 1983; Larsen-Freeman, 1986). Another passage, in Book 1 Lesson 25, reinforces several of these features, most notably the focus on forms of the language rather than on communication. The teacher conducts the pupils in activities which involve reading aloud, reciting and writing, but the language produced is not spontaneous or generated freely by the pupils:

At an English Lesson

Teacher: Good morning, boys (girls).
Pupils: Good morning, comrade teacher.
Teacher: Sit down, please. (The pupils sit down.)
Teacher: Open your books. Li Ming and Liu Teh-lan! Stand up and read lesson 25! (Li and Liu stand up and read.)
Teacher: Very good. Sit down, please. (Li and Liu sit down.)
Teacher: Close your books, boys (girls). Count from one to twenty. (The pupils count from one to twenty.)
Teacher: Good. Now, Wang Min and Chang Li! Come to the blackboard. Please write the numbers eleven to twenty. (Wang and Chang go to the blackboard and write.)
Teacher: That's good. Go back to your seats. Now boys (girls), put your books in your desks and take out your notebooks. (The pupils put their books in their desks and take out their notebooks.)
Teacher: Write in your notebooks: "This is an English lesson. At this lesson we read and write in English." (Series One, Book 1: 84–5)

The work of Kairov, the Soviet educator, was influential on English Language pedagogy in China in the 1950s (Penner, 1991). Ying Manrong[7] does not explicitly attribute the intended pedagogy of Series One to Kairov's influence, saying only that the writing teams made reference to Soviet textbooks, but these Soviet books were based on Kairov's methods (Tang Lixing, 1983). Kairov's pedagogy had five steps (Yu, 1984; Penner, 1991), namely:

1. reviewing old material
2. siting new material
3. explaining the new material
4. consolidating newly learned material
5. giving assignments

There are echoes of these steps in the two passages from Series One quoted above: the teacher explaining the new material in a reading passage, and a class reviewing newly learned material by reading the passage aloud and recalling the numbers. The arrangement of the components of a lesson also indicates an adherence to the five steps. Typically, the grammar items to be taught are sited in a short passage or dialogue first. The next section of the lesson presents the new vocabulary in a box, followed by the grammatical structure in tabulated form, to facilitate explanation of the material. This structure is then practised for consolidation through various exercises, such as transformation drills (rewriting a sentence, changing an element such as the tense), translation (from/into both Chinese and English), blank-filling (with or without a cue word in Chinese) or substitution exercises (e.g., replacing italicized phrases with a pronoun). The approach to grammar exemplified by such exercises (and which runs throughout the series) — a graded, linear syllabus starting with the present simple tense, presented in reading passages, explained in Chinese and practised through translation or transformation exercises — is consistent with the Structural Approach blending with the Grammar-Translation Method.

At first sight, there is an apparent contradiction between the pedagogical approaches overtly advocated in these lessons and the approaches inherently suggested by the nature of some of the passages. For instance, although the emphasis as stated in Book 1 Lesson 25 is on reading and writing in English, there are a number of passages in both books that take the form of a dialogue. This would suggest an emphasis on spoken English. However, closer examination of the exercises in the textbooks reveals that there are no exercises that allow free or guided oral production by the pupils: the spoken work is limited to recitation of the passages. In other words, spoken production only involves reading aloud.

Linguistic components

There is also a reflection of the influence of the USSR in the linear progression and controlled presentation of linguistic components. The early stages of Series One pay attention to accuracy, especially in pronunciation and grammar. Much of Book 1, as noted above, contains weak discourse, denoting a focus on grammatical forms rather than on communicative messages. From Book 1 Lesson 4 onwards, sentence structures are introduced, such as *I see a pen. I see a nib. I see a pen and a nib.* Work on the present simple tense is then developed in the rest of the book. A typical lesson in the textbook has the following format (Book 1 Lesson 38):

1. 'Can You Swim?': a dialogue between friends with repetition of the modal *can + swim* in positive and negative statements and questions.
2. Grammar: *can + swim* in positive and negative statements and questions.
3. Exercises: phonetic practice of vowel sounds; transformation of statements into questions and negative responses; questions based on *Can you … ?* for the students to answer (e.g. *Can you count the stars in the sky?*); and a further transformation exercise converting sentences into question forms using highlighted words.

The grammar sections of the first thirteen lessons of Book 2 are mainly concerned with regular and irregular verb forms. In the latter part of the book, verb forms and different tenses are covered — the future simple, present continuous, past simple and present perfect tenses — as are ordinal numbers, adverbs, possessive and relative pronouns, reported speech, and so on. The grammar syllabus of Book 2 builds on the foundation of Book 1 without overlap, thus creating a linear grammar syllabus. Liu Daoyi[8] notes that this arrangement reflects Professor Zhang Daozhong's ideas expressed in 'A Practical English Grammar', which were based on Soviet practices prevalent in China during the 1950s.

Vocabulary items are controlled to no more than 17 new words or phrases in a single lesson in Book 1 (at an average of approximately 9 new items per lesson), and 21 in Book 2 (average = approximately 12 new items per lesson), although some lessons have an extra load in the shape of past tense verb forms. This average is similar to later series that emphasize pedagogical more than political goals. The vocabulary is presented in boxes after the passage, and occasionally through pictures. In the boxes, a translation into Chinese is given, as well as phonetic transcriptions for words that are problematic for pronunciation.

The principal features of the linguistic components are the focus on pronunciation, vocabulary and grammar, which indicates careful attention being paid to accuracy of language production; and the focus on linguistic components — vocabulary, grammatical items, etc. — in written discourse (as opposed to spoken discourse).

The importance attached to reading skills is evidenced by the fact that both textbooks are centred on reading passages, with comprehension and grammar exercises, although there are instances of dialogues and phrases for oral use, particularly in Book 1.

Content

The genres of discourse in Series One cover three basic categories: those related to the students' daily experiences; those with a moral message, and those that have an explicit political message. The passages include descriptions of the daily activities of characters at home, at school or at play (such as 'Li Ming's Day' in Book 1 Lesson 34), fables (such as 'The Lame Man and the Blind Man' in Book 2 Lesson 26), informational passages (such as 'The Moon' in Book 1 Lesson 42), and positive or negative descriptions of life in other countries (such as 'Two American Boys' in Book 1 Lesson 39 and 'A Negro Boy in the Soviet Union' in Book 1 Lesson 40). The orientations in the discourse reveal a belief that the English Language curriculum can be a vehicle for broader educational (informational, moral and political) goals, and that language competence is not the sole aim. Thus, English is not seen as a threat to the socio-political fabric of the nation, but rather as a means for transmitting desirable messages. Having said that, Series One is not highly political. An analysis of 88 examples of communicative discourse in Series One found 94 messages, of which 56 are of a moral or political nature. The other 38 present information that has no obvious moral or political connotation (Table 3.2). Compared with later series, the percentage of moral and political messages (60% of all messages) is relatively low, and most occur when examples of strong discourse predominate, from the latter stages of Book 1 onwards.

Table 3.2   Political and moral messages in Series One

Discourse total	Messages total	Nil	Moral	Political	*Political (attitude)*	*Political (information)*	*Political (role model)*
88	94	38 (40.43%)	30 (31.91%)	26 (27.66%)	*16*	*2*	*8*

Of the series analysed in this study, the moral messages in Series One are the highest in percentage terms, at 31.91% (30 messages) of all 94 messages. The overall projection of ideal moral behaviour contained in the messages is leading a 'healthy' lifestyle by rising early, studying hard and happily, going to bed early, keeping fit, helping others, and enjoying a harmonious relationship at home and with friends.

Political messages, which form 27.66% (i.e., 26 messages), are a relatively low percentage, compared with later series. They are primarily concerned with fostering positive attitudes towards the CCP and its institutions, such as the Young Pioneers and the Communist Youth League; and towards the nation. The passage in Book 2 Lesson 8, 'On National Day', for instance, describes pupils waving to Chairman Mao in Tiananmen Square; the passage in Book 2 Lesson 31 includes a geographical description and a political message:

China

China is the largest country in Asia. It has many rivers, mountains and cities. The Yellow River is in the North. The Pearl River is in the South. The Yangtze is between the two. The Yellow River is longer than the Pearl River, but the Yangtze is the longest of the three. It is the longest river in China.

Peking is the capital of China. It is a big city. It is in the North. Peking has many beautiful buildings. It is one of the most beautiful cities in the world. Our great leader Chairman Mao lives and works there.

The Chinese people work hard and love peace. They are building Socialism. Now there are more schools, more factories and more hospitals in China than before. How happy the Chinese people are! (Series One, Book 2: 97–8)

The Young Pioneers are portrayed as enjoying healthy outdoor pursuits during summer camps, or helping farmers by catching rats, killing sparrows or cleaning the farmers' houses. These activities are linked to political aims (such as imbuing enthusiasm for socialism and socialist policies), as shown in the passage from Book 2 Lesson 36 quoted earlier. Another example is Book 2 Lesson 16:

A Visit to a Farm

It is a bright autumn day. A group of pioneers are visiting the Red Star People's Commune. They tell the chairman of the commune that they like the farm very much.

"May I come to work with you when I finish school? I shall try hard to be a good farmer."

"I want to work on the farm too," says a girl. "You have many pigs and cows. I think I can learn to take good care of them."

"And I shall learn to be a tractor-driver. There will be many tractors on the farm."

"What will you be, little girl?" the chairman of the commune asks the youngest girl of the group.

"I shall be a teacher. In the morning I shall teach the children here, and in the afternoon I shall work in the fields with all of you."

"Thank you, boys and girls," says the chairman of the commune. "We shall be glad to have you with us." (Series One, Book 2: 49–50)

The Youth League, an organization for older children, is portrayed as requiring virtuous behaviour, although it is not specified in the passages what the virtues are. Book 2 Lesson 32 tells of a fourteen-year-old boy returning home, presumably from boarding school or from living with relatives, to spend a week with his sister and brother. It concludes:

> We had a very good time together. We often played ping-pong. I can play ping-pong quite well, but my sister plays better than I. She is the best player in her class.
>
> I stayed with my brother and sister for a week. When I left home, my sister said to me, "You are making good progress in many ways. But if you want to join the Youth League next year, you must try harder to overcome your shortcomings." (Series One, Book 2: 101–2)

One influence from the Soviet Union is the use of propaganda, mostly bleak portrayals of aspects of life in capitalist countries. One theme is the hardships of the black community in the USA: 'Two American Boys' (Book 1 Lesson 39) contrasts the privileged life of a white boy with that of a black boy:

> Jimmy and Billy are two American boys. Jimmy is a Negro boy, and Billy is a white boy.
>
> Jimmy and Billy's fathers are workers. They are poor.
>
> Jimmy and Billy are friends, but they do not go to school together. They do not go to the cinema or the park together.
>
> Jimmy and Billy like to go to school together. They like to go to the cinema and to the park together. They like to play together. But they cannot, because Jimmy is a Negro.
>
> — Who are Jimmy and Billy?
> — They are two American boys. Jimmy is a Negro boy, and Billy is a white boy.
> — Are they friends?
> — Yes, they are. They are good friends.
> — Do they go to school together?
> — No, they do not. They like to go to school together, but they cannot.
> — Do they go to the cinema together?
> — No, they do not. They like to go to the cinema and to the park together, but they cannot.
> — Do they often play games together?
> — No, they do not. They like to play games together, but they cannot, because Jimmy is a Negro boy. (Series One, Book 1: 124–5)

The theme of the following lesson, Book 1 Lesson 40, presents a much rosier portrait of life for a black boy:

A Negro Boy in the USSR

> Sam is a Negro boy. He is an American, but he does not live in America. He lives with his father in the Soviet Union. His father works there.
>
> Sam does not feel lonely. He has many Soviet friends. Sam and his friends go to school together. They often go to the cinema and to the park together.

Sometimes Sam goes to his friends' homes, and sometimes his friends come to his home. In winter they often go to skate together. In summer they go to camp together.

— Does Sam live in America?
— No, he does not. He does not live in America.
— Where does he live?
— He lives in the Soviet Union.
— Does he feel lonely there?
— No, he does not. He does not feel lonely, because he has many Soviet friends.
— Does Sam go to school together with his friends?
— Yes, he does. And in summer he goes to camp with them too.
— Is Sam happy?
— Yes, he is. He is very happy in the Soviet Union. (Series One, Book 1: 126–8)

This indicates that these passages are borrowed directly from textbooks published in the USSR. Other passages in a similar vein include 'Black Jimmy' (Book 1 Lesson 46) and 'Jimmy Picks Cotton in the Field' (Book 2 Lesson 17). 'Lizzy', the description of the life of a twelve-year-old girl working in a cotton factory in northern England, is written in the past tense and therefore does not suggest that the context is contemporary, but the final paragraph draws a modern conclusion:

> Today many children in capitalist countries are like Lizzy. They are poor and miserable. (Series One, Book 2: 112)

The view that children in capitalist countries were poverty-stricken was commonly held in China at this time: recalling her childhood in the 1950s, Jung Chang writes, 'When I was in the boarding nursery and did not want to finish my food, the teacher would say, "Think of all the starving children in the capitalist world!" ' (Chang, 1991: 326).

To a lesser extent, the political messages incorporate role models. These are mainly descriptions of young people joining politically-related activities, such as helping farmers, but there is one heroic story in Book 2 Lesson 33 that was to reappear in future series of textbooks:

Lesson Twenty-four   第二十四課

Grandfather

It is evening. Mother, Li Ming, Li Lan and Li Feng are at home. They are sitting round the table.

Li Ming: Mother, tell us about Grandfather. Tell us about his life.

Mother: All right. Your grandfather was a poor worker. He worked from morning till night. He had little time for rest. Very often he had no money to buy food. He was always tired, and we were often hungry.

Before liberation, a worker's life was very hard. His home was poor. His food was poor. His clothes were poor. When he was ill, he had no help. His children, too, worked all day. They could not go to school. The schools were for children from rich families.

Now in China the workers live in good houses. They have time for rest. Their children can go to school. The workers in New China are living a very happy life.

· 75 ·

Figure 3.1   Reading passage from Series One Book 2 (p. 75)

The passage promotes the message that the revolution has benefited those who suffered under the previous régime. The linguistic components are controlled, although there are authentic touches to the dialogue, such as the mother's response 'All right'.

Lo Sheng-chiao

There is a monument in Korea. It tells the world who Lo Sheng-chiao was. It tells us how Lo Sheng-chiao gave his life for a Korean boy.

Lo Sheng-chiao was a brave soldier of the Chinese People's Volunteers. He loved the Korean people and helped them in many ways.

One morning Lo Sheng-chiao was working near a river. Four Korean boys were skating on the ice. They did not know that the ice was thin. Suddenly one of them fell through the ice into the water. The boys cried for help. When Lo Sheng-chiao heard them, he ran to the river and jumped into the water. With great difficulty he helped the boy up through the hole. He saved the boy, but he himself died in the river.

Lo Sheng-chiao is dead, but his name will always live in the hearts of the Korean and the Chinese people. (Series One, Book 2: 104–5)

The selection of vocabulary in the series reflects the mild political orientation. Slightly more than one quarter of the vocabulary items (253 out of 852, or 29.69%) are not found in Thorndike's word-list, the prescribed source for the core vocabulary. This is not a high percentage when compared with other series, and most of the non-Thorndike items are non-political, being related to the students' daily life and interests (such as clothing, furniture, school, sports and leisure activities, animals in a zoo), and to the needs of second language learners (such as numbers, days of the week and months of the year), and China-specific terms (such as place-names). Only about forty are related to political themes (such as *comrade, pioneer, commune, Youth League, Communist, liberation, Socialism* and *Chinese People's Volunteers*).

The curriculum of 1960

The curriculum of 1957 was short-lived. It was replaced in 1960 by a new curriculum, which included a new set of textbooks published by the PEP. The change was generated by a shift in the political climate, as China underwent a period of politicization, with campaigns such as the Great Leap Forward. Anti-Soviet rhetoric also built up at the end of the 1950s, as tensions over Khrushchev's policies — including a reassessment of Stalin — emerged. Members of the CCP such as Kang Sheng, a close ally of Mao Zedong, expressed concerns, shared by Mao, that the political messages transmitted through education were insufficient (Löfstedt, 1980; Pepper, 1996). In 1958, various reforms in education sought to address this issue, including the establishment of part-study, part-labour schools and the revision of all school textbooks (Pepper, 1996).

In a statement in July 1958, Kang Sheng declared that textbooks should be revised to incorporate a more labour-oriented theme, and that students and technicians should assist professional educators in revising the textbooks.

This resulted in eighteen provinces writing their own English Language textbooks (Tang Jun, 1986). The criticisms by national leaders that current textbooks failed to devote sufficient attention to political education and were contaminated by the borrowings from the USSR also applied to Series One. Despite (or because of) the political content, the series 'was criticised and condemned as being divorced from politics, from production and from reality', according to Tang Jun.[9]

In April 1960, the Ministry of Education ordered a revision of all the PEP textbooks published since 1954. In revising the English Language textbooks, the PEP decided that the new series (Series Two) should have three textbooks instead of two, in order to correspond with the three-year junior secondary school programme. As with Series One, the PEP turned to an outside agency for assistance. Staff from Shanghai Foreign Languages Institute were commissioned by the PEP to write Junior English Book 1, to be used the following September. The Ministry of Education, which was overseeing the work of the PEP, then decided to rush through the production of the complete series, at very short notice. As Tang Jun recalls:

> In the summer of 1960 the Ministry of Education suddenly assigned the Beijing Foreign Languages Institute the task to write Junior English Book 2 and Book 3 which were to be used in September when schools began. Perhaps they thought that the Institute had a great number of experienced English teachers and could take on the work. To write two books within two months was really hard work. All the teachers of the English Department of the Institute were mobilised. With the effort of the teachers the two books were written and published in the autumn.[10]

Tang Jun worked on this series, as she was then a lecturer at the Beijing Foreign Languages Institute. The writers used two principal sources: Series One (many passages and exercises are reproduced in Series Two) and Chinese Language textbooks, mainly for political passages. Some of these antecedents are shown in Table 3.3 (see p. 55). All the passages from Series One were adapted in Series Two, with changes to phrasings and content. Despite the now tainted association, some passages of Soviet origin were retained and (curiously) some new ones praising the USSR introduced, although those explicitly located in the USSR were not used. The antecedents in Chinese Language textbooks are primary school textbooks, as these have traditionally contained the stories and messages that were considered most suitable for English Language curriculum developers to transfer to their textbooks, according to Liu Jinfang.[11]

Given the very short notice for producing a new set of textbooks, no syllabus was issued to go with Series Two. Tang Jun recollects that the linguistic components and organization of Series One were used for Series Two.[12] Thus the Soviet influence noted in this regard with Series One was retained.

Table 3.3   Antecedents of some passages in Series Two

Passage in Series Two	Title	Antecedent
Book 1 Lesson 21	The New Term	Series One Book 1 Lesson 26
Book 1 Lesson 36	A Negro Boy	Series One Book 1 Lesson 46
Book 2 Lesson 2	Our Classroom	Series One Book 1 Lesson 30
Book 2 Lesson 15	Black Jimmy	Series One Book 1 Lesson 46
Book 2 Lesson 18	In Spring	Series One Book 2 Lesson 29
Book 2 Lesson 19	Counting	Series One Book 2 Lesson 22
Book 3 Lesson 5	On Duty	Series One Book 2 Lesson 21
Book 3 Lesson 7	Lizzy	Series One Book 2 Lesson 35
Book 3 Lesson 13	Lo Sheng-chiao	Series One Book 2 Lesson 33
Book 3 Lesson 17	Yu Kung Removed the Mountains	'Chinese Language for Primary School' Book 3 Lesson 19 (1948)
Book 3 Lesson 19	Chairman Mao and the Wounded Soldier (I)	'Chinese Language for Primary School' Book 3 Lesson 15 (1948)
Book 3 Lesson 20	Chairman Mao and the Wounded Soldier (II)	'Chinese Language for Primary School' Book 3 Lesson 15 (1948)

Series Two was published in time for use in junior secondary schools in September 1960. The books are the same dimensions, 13 cm x 19 cm, as Series One, but the covers are more sophisticated, with a white and green background, the title in red, and the English alphabet printed in white on the green background, with vowels in red (Figure A.2, p. 211). The series contains black and white illustrations. The three books comprise a total of 82 lessons, but there is difference in the number of pages. 'Junior English Book 1', written by members of staff at Shanghai Foreign Languages Institute, is about twice the length, with 212 pages as opposed to 111 and 96 respectively of the second and third books, which were written by staff at Beijing Foreign Languages Institute. Book 1 has 37 lessons and three appendices, while Book 2 has 25 lessons, and Book 3 just 20 lessons plus one appendix. The total of 82 lessons is the same as in Series One, which comprised two books for three years' study. The division of content into three books in Series Two was intended be consistent with the number of years of junior secondary schooling, but the allocation of lessons to each book is lopsided, suggesting that the lack of time prevented a more coherent arrangement.

Further differences between Book 1 and Books 2 and 3 are evident, most notably in the internal organization of lessons, which is compared in Table 3.4 (see p. 56). The lessons in Books 2 and 3 follow the pattern of reading passage

Table 3.4   Organizational structure of lessons in Series Two

Book 1	Books 2 and 3
1. Vocabulary list 2. Reading Passage 3. Focus on one item 4. Exercises 5. Homework exercises	1. Reading Passage 2. Vocabulary list 3. Notes to the Text 4. Grammar/Phonetics focus 5. Exercises 6. Revision

— vocabulary lists — grammatical notes to the text — [phonetics/grammar] — exercises. In Book 1, presentations of grammatical points are found in the 'Exercises' section, but in Books 2 and 3, they are accorded an individual section ('Grammar') of their own. Another difference is the positioning of vocabulary lists: in Book One, the new vocabulary comes before the reading passage, whereas in Books 2 and 3 the new vocabulary is placed after the passage. The comparison in Table 3.4 shows that the organization is consistent in Books 2 and 3, which means that the variances from Book 1 arose from a different approach by the two writing teams, rather than from a deliberately planned progression in instructional techniques.

Pedagogy

In terms of pedagogy, however, these differences in organization are not significant — they are just variations on a similar approach. Like Series One, Series Two adopts a thematic approach, in that the central focus is the reading passages, to which the presentation of new vocabulary, grammar and phonetics is related. At the same time, these linguistic components are controlled in the passage, so that the amount of new language is not too demanding for the pupils. In this respect, the organization resembles Series One, reflecting a concern for principles of language teaching and learning, and a view of language learning as being best achieved through mastery of grammatical paradigms and the study of written passages.

The discourse in Series Two shifts from weak to strong, suggesting a pedagogy that starts as grammar-oriented and then moves to the study of grammar and vocabulary in the context of a more realistic reading passage. This is consistent with a blend of the Structural Approach and the Grammar-Translation Method. Book 1 starts with a number of weakly realistic passages that are designed to present specific linguistic components, such as common vocabulary items, e.g., Book 1 Lesson 3:

This is a pencil.
That is a pen.
This is a book.
That is a map. (Series Two, Book 1: 8)

These sentences are presented without pictures or indication as to the location of these objects. They are uncontextualized, although the sentences which follow do have a picture of a finger pointing at a near and a far object to distinguish between 'This' and 'That'. Likewise, some discourse presents grammatical structures, such as positive and negative statements in Book 1 Lesson 5, which includes five short dialogues, such as:

— Is this a book?
— Yes, that is a book.
— Is that a map.
— Yes, that is a map. (Series Two, Book 1: 13)

Again, no context or illustration is provided to show the meaning of this dialogue. As the linguistic resources incorporated into the passages increase, the degree of realism likewise increases. In the following example from Book 1 Lesson 19, the passage, which incorporates numbered paragraphs for ease of reference, describes the children's routine on a Sunday, using a limited range of linguistic items (present simple tense, short sentences, common action verbs and adverbs, etc.):

(1)   On Sunday we do not go to school. We get up early in the morning. Before breakfast we do morning exercises. We clean our rooms. After breakfast we go out to play.

(2)   Sometimes my schoolmates and I go to the park in the afternoon. The park is very large. We like it very much. Sometimes we have our Pioneer meeting in the park. We sing and dance. We play games. Sometimes we work in the fields. Sometimes we go to the factory. We work there.

(3)   After supper we review our lessons. Then we brush our teeth and go to bed. (Series Two, Book 1: 82)

The intended pedagogical approach is described explicitly in a passage in Book 2 Lesson 13 (see p. 59):

Exercises   課堂練習

1. 拼讀下列單詞的音標：

[frɔm]   [houm]   [faiv]

[kʌm]   [plei]   ['fæmili]

[wɔːm]   ['fɑːðə]   [mʌnθ]

2. 聽寫。

3. 填空白:

(1) China is _____ countries in the _____.

(2) Under the leadership of _____ we are building socialism.

(3) New factories, schools and hospitals are_____
everywhere in China.

(4) All over the country _____ take place day
after day.

(5) Workers and peasants are _____ in socialist
construction.

(6) _____ from many countries _____ our
people's communes.

(7) We are good _____ and _____ of our
country.

4. 漢譯英:

(1) 中國人民是勤勞、勇敢、愛好和平的。

(2) 中國有悠久的歷史。

(3) 我們積極地參加社會主義建設。

• 155 •

Figure 3.2   Grammar exercises from Series Two Book 1 Lesson 32 (p. 155)

The first exercise is to transform the words in phonetic script to regular orthography. The second exercise is a dictation given by the teacher. The third exercise asks the students to fill in the blanks with suitable words and phrases, while the fourth exercise is a translation from Chinese to English. The sentences are:

(1)   The Chinese people are hard-working, brave and peace-loving.
(2)   China has a long history.
(3)   We are enthusiastically participating in socialist construction.

In Class

It is nine o'clock in the morning. The pupils of Class Four, Grade Two are having an English lesson. The teacher gives them a quiz. First they recite the text and translate some sentences, then they have dictation. After the quiz the teacher explains the new words in the next lesson. The pupils learn to spell them. Then they begin to read the text. The pupils read after the teacher. They read carefully and clearly. They read the difficult sentences again and again. After that they learn how to use some of the new words and phrases. the teacher writes the word "Party" and the phrase "to be proud of" on the blackboard. He asks the pupils to make sentences with them. The pupils soon get the sentences ready. One of them reads his sentences aloud.

"We must be good sons and daughters of our Party."
"We are proud of our great motherland."

They are very good sentences. The teacher is very glad. (Series Two, Book 2: 56–7)

The features of this lesson again match those of the Grammar-Translation Method, with its emphasis on reading and writing, discrete grammatical forms (in this case, sentence construction) and memorization (of spellings in this lesson). The lesson is teacher-centred, as are lessons depicted in other reading passages. Such an approach is consistent with the organization of materials in the series, with the reading passages being supported by grammar practice that involves the pupils in mechanical translation and structural manipulation exercises, including phonetic transcriptions, dictation, grammar practice and recitation of the reading passage. As noted above, the linguistic components are organized in a linear syllabus, which accords with the Structural Approach. There is thus no change in the intended pedagogy — a blend of the Structural Approach and the Grammar-Translation Method which merges Soviet principles and traditional Chinese English Language teaching practices.

Linguistic components

The new series has a broadly similar arrangement of linguistic components to Series One, but there are internal discrepancies in the three books. For instance, in the grammar syllabus, the sequence of tenses starts with the present simple tense, followed by the present continuous in Book 1. In Books 2 and 3, the present simple is re-introduced, then the future simple, present continuous, past simple and present perfect tenses. Books 2 and 3 therefore follow the same tense sequence as Series One, but there is an obvious lack of articulation with Book 1. Book 2 includes existential structures, irregular verbs and *wh-* questions, thus covering exactly the same ground as the middle stages of Book 1. This arrangement, with a linear syllabus covering Books 2 and 3, and revision incorporated in clearly marked sections, suggests an accidental repetition of grammatical items from Book 1 in Book 2, rather than deliberate recycling of revision points.

In terms of vocabulary, Book 1 lists 417 new words and phrases (an average of nearly 12 vocabulary items per lesson), Book 2, 487 items (average = nearly 20 per lesson), and Book 3, 463 items (average = nearly 23 per lesson), a higher set of averages than in Series One. The vocabulary lists in the textbooks have a total of 1,367 items, at an average of nearly 17 new words or phrases per lesson, which arises from the loosening of control of this linguistic aspect in favour of more realistic reading passages, many of them with a political message. The noticeable relaxation of control on the vocabulary is accounted for by the more politicized content of the passages, which requires greater realism and more specialized terms.

Content

Series Two carries a large amount of political and moral messages in its discourse. In 90 examples of discourse, only 12 were found to have no explicit moral or political message. In the remaining discourse examples, 102 messages were identified, of which 90 had a political or moral connotation. The percentage of political messages (67.65%) is a large increase from Series One (27.66%), while there is a decline in proportion of moral messages (20.59%, from 31.91%). Details are shown in Table 3.5. The increase in political messages reflects the instruction by the Ministry of Education to increase the messages of this kind. Of the 79 political messages in Series Two, more than one-third are related to the promotion of national policies, patriotism and loyalty to CCP leaders. However, there is a large increase from Series One in the passages about role models, to also over one-third. Many of these were translations from Chinese Language textbooks, as indicated earlier. Role models are a feature of traditional Chinese education: in *The Analects*, Confucius often exhorts his followers to imitate great leaders.

Table 3.5   Political and moral messages in Series Two

Discourse total	Messages total	Nil	Moral	Political	Political (attitude)	Political (information)	Political (role model)
90	102	12 (11.76%)	21 (20.59%)	69 (67.65%)	28	12	29

There are three kinds of role models: ordinary people who perform heroic deeds; CCP leaders who show exemplary behaviour; and children who take part in politically-related activities. The heroes include Lo Sheng-chiao, who died saving a drowning Korean boy, and Liu Wen-hsueh (Book 3 Lesson 16):

Let's All Learn from Liu Wen-hsueh

Liu Wen-hsueh was a Pioneer of fourteen. One evening when he was going home from school he found a landlord in the fields, stealing the crops of the people's commune. "Thief! Thief!" he began to shout loudly. The landlord was afraid. He tried every way to keep the boy from shouting. First he offered Liu Wen-hsueh a one-yuan note and then threatened to kill him. But all this failed. There was only one thing in the Pioneer's mind: "I must protect the property of the people's commune." That was why he fought the landlord so bravely until he got killed.

Liu Wen-hsueh hated the enemy of the people. He loved the commune and the commune members. He loved his classmates and everyone in his class loved him. He worked hard and was always ready to help others.

Liu Wen-hsueh was a fine pupil of Chairman Mao. Let's all learn from him! (Series Two, Book 3: 72–3)

Mao (depicted personally treating a wounded soldier in Book 3 Lessons 19 and 20) and Lenin ('Doing Physical Labour with Lenin', Book 3 Lesson 18) are shown setting a good example. Ordinary children also provide a role model with their work on a commune — as in Book 2 Lesson 4:

I am a commune member. But I am a student at the Agricultural Middle School too. I study in the morning and work in the afternoon. I live a happy life.

My father is a peasant. He is a team leader. He takes an active part in farm work.

My brother is a tractor driver. He is a model worker. He likes to study too. He goes to the spare-time school at night.

My sister works at the farm tool factory. She works very hard. She is a fine worker.

We all love our commune. (Series Two, Book 2: 15)

A recurring theme, which appears in the above passage, is the connection between work and school. The pupils in the passages work in a factory or on the school farm, or help various workers, including a pig farmer (Book 2 Lesson 14) and a cook (Book 2 Lesson 23). Book 2 Lesson 17 highlights a number of 'worthy' jobs for pupils to aspire to:

There are forty-three pupils in our class. Everybody has his own wish.

Some of us want to be engineers, textile-workers, doctors, nurses or teachers. But most of us want to be peasants or steel workers.

Hsiao Chang says that she will go to the countryside. "I shall look after the pigs and cows," she says.

Our monitor says, "I shall be a tractor driver. I shall go to the Northwest and work in the countryside all my life."

Li Ming, the strongest boy in the class, says, "I want to be a steel worker. I shall produce iron and steel for our motherland."

But what shall I be?

I shall be a PLA [People's Liberation Army] fighter and defend our motherland. I shall do anything that the Party wants me to do. (Series Two, Book 2: 74–6)

Other passages praise the work of the CCP, including the changes in Tibet under Chinese rule since 1951. 'A Tibetan Girl' (Book 3 Lesson 15) describes a happy group of children singing and dancing outside the Potala Palace. One of the group is a girl named Chuma:

Like thousands of Tibetan people, Chuma's parents were slaves of a big serf-owner. They toiled all day long, but still suffered from cold and hunger. The cruel serf-owner often beat them black and blue. Chuma can never forget those bitter days.

But times are different now. The slaves have become their own masters. Chuma's parents have got their own land and cattle. "We owe all our happiness to Chairman Mao and the Communist Party," they often said to Chuma. "You must always bear this in mind."

Chuma is a good child of her parents and a fine pupil of Chairman Mao. She works very hard. She knows she must study hard in order to do more for her motherland. (Series Two, Book 3: 67)

As with Series One, there are Soviet-inspired passages portraying life in other countries in a poor light, including 'Lizzy' (Book 3 Lesson 7), the young factory worker in England, and the various passages describing the hardships, such as racial discrimination, endured by black people in the USA: examples include 'The Cotton Fields' (Book 3 Lesson 3) and 'Black Jimmy' (Book 2 Lesson 15), which reproduces almost verbatim the contents of 'A Negro Boy' in Book 1 Lesson 36. This repetition is further evidence of the lack of co-ordination between the writing teams based in Shanghai and Beijing.

The moral messages are also similar to those in Series One. Schoolchildren portrayed in the series display a 'healthy' lifestyle that involves attention to personal hygiene, early rising, physical fitness, selflessness, and diligence in study. Schooling in particular is projected in very positive terms. Book 1 Lesson 24 describes a typical school day as follows:

We come to school early in the morning. At half past seven we go to the playground and do our morning exercises. We are strong and active.

At eight o'clock the bell rings. The class begins. We all keep quiet and listen to our teacher.

We have four lessons in the morning. We usually have Chinese, English mathematics and other subjects.

After lunch we have a rest. We play on the playground or read newspapers in the reading room. In the afternoon we usually have two lessons. Sometimes we have sports. All of us like sports. We like ping-pong, basket-ball or other games.

Sometimes we have Pioneer meetings or science activities. Sometimes we work in the factory or in the fields.

After school we go home. Our school life is very happy. We love our school very much. (Series Two, Book 1: 112)

Analysis of the vocabulary shows that, of the 1,367 new words in Series Two, 479 (35.04%) are non-Thorndike (131 out of 417 in Book 1; 163 out of 477 in Book 2, and 185 out of 463 in Book 3). Approximately two-thirds of the new words are related to political themes (socialist terminology, names of leaders, names of political campaigns, etc.), while the rest are connected to school life and common functions and notions (such as telling the time). However, the figures have to be treated with some caution, because several of the items appear as 'New Words' on more than one list; for instance, in the lessons containing almost identical reading passages (Book 1 Lesson 36 and Book 2 Lesson 15), the vocabulary lists are likewise almost identical. Nevertheless, the vocabulary indicates a much stronger political content in Series Two compared with Series One, which is evident from the analysis of the messages in the discourse.

There are a number of strong similarities and also striking differences between the curriculum of 1960 and that of 1957. The genesis for each was rooted in macro-level national policy, although the nature of the policy had a different orientation: the 1957 curriculum arose from the policy of national construction through technology transfer from overseas; the 1960 curriculum had a more political aim, seeking to instil loyalty to the CCP and patriotic sentiments. The process of designing the curriculum of 1960 was similar in some ways to the process adopted for the 1957 curriculum. The PEP commissioned outside agencies (staff from tertiary institutions) to write a series of textbooks according to broad guidelines relating to the overriding aims of the curriculum. Teachers at the grassroots had no role in the process in either instance of curriculum change. The expediency of 1957 was exacerbated in 1960, when the PEP commissioned writers from two different institutions, one in Shanghai and the other in Beijing, whereas writers from a single institution in Beijing had been chosen in 1957. The process of writing the resources also

Lesson Twenty-One

The Young Pioneers

The Young Pioneers is our own organization. It educates us and helps us to become fine builders of communism.

Every week we have Pioneer activities. We visit exhibitions. We have outings or go to films. Sometimes we work in factories or on farms.

We all love to go to the Pioneers' Palace. There we learn to operate machines and make radio sets. There we sing and dance. Sometimes we invite writers and advanced workers to speak to us.

We Pioneers are also called "Red Ties", because we wear them. We are proud of them. The red tie represents a section of the red flag. It makes us think of the revolution. We are all ready to devote ourselves to the cause of socialism and communism.

• 90 •

Figure 3.3   Reading passage from Series Two Book 2 (p. 90)

The Young Pioneers are members of a communist youth organization. They regularly feature in reading passages as moral and political exemplars.

had similarities and differences. In 1957, the writers referred to existing sets of materials, namely their own courses and textbooks from the Soviet Union. In 1960, the writers referred to existing materials, the textbooks in Series One and (a new source) Chinese Language textbooks.

Series Two naturally resembles Series One, as it was derived to some extent from it. This is reflected in the topic-based, linear organization and Structural Approach/Grammar-Translation pedagogy of both series. Several of the original reading passages were retained in Series Two, although, in terms of political and moral messages, the political element is stronger in Series Two. Likewise, the grammar and vocabulary covered in Series Two are similar to Series One, but there is less control over the vocabulary, with more items relating to political themes, and grammar receives less treatment. Another difference between Series One and Series Two is the coherence of the textbooks as a series. Whereas Series One (comprising two books written at a single location) was well co-ordinated in progression, there are serious flaws in Series Two (comprising three books written in two separate locations), with much of the material presented in Book 1 being repeated, at times verbatim, in Book 2. Thus the politically-motivated changes to the curriculum turned out to be to the detriment of the pedagogical quality of the resources, as Tang Jun notes:

> In the revised textbooks [i.e., Series Two], the vocabulary items concentrated on political life but reduced the emphasis on everyday life. Political ideas were improperly stressed: this led to a neglect of language training. Furthermore, there was a lack of linkage between the textbooks, which had a negative impact on teaching.[13]

It was this pedagogical weakness that eventually led to the replacement of Series Two, as will be seen in Chapter 4.

The experimental curriculum of 1960

Parallel to the development of Series Two, moves were underway to promote foreign language teaching in primary schools, whose numbers had expanded from 346,769 in 1949 to 726,484 by 1960 (Ministry of Education, 1984). On 27 October 1959, the Ministry of Education held a meeting in Beijing with language specialists to discuss resources for foreign language teaching. The idea of starting foreign language classes at primary level was mooted and accepted. The Ministry of Education commissioned a new series (Series Three), designed to cover primary, junior secondary and senior secondary school curricula over a period of nine years. It was decided to use these books on an experimental basis for two years in selected schools in Beijing and

Shanghai before they would be introduced nation-wide. The books were published between March and May 1960. This meant, as the introduction in each book indicates, that the textbooks were written 'in a relatively short time'.

The period was one of increasing politicization, and textbooks were under scrutiny for their political content. The pattern of curriculum development remained consistent with earlier series. The PEP commissioned an outside agency, the Foreign Languages Department of Beijing Normal University, to write the materials. Writing English Language textbooks for primary and secondary schools represented a new undertaking for this department, and the socio-political climate made the task complicated. According to the introductory notes in each book, there were two aims, namely, 'to strengthen the students' proletarian communist ideology and their competence in studying foreign languages'. The notes went on to say that the textbooks were still at the draft stage and suggestions for improving the materials from teachers would be welcome. This indicates that the writers were aware of the political dimensions of their work. The request for feedback could either denote concern about pedagogical imperfections in the series, or serve as a protection against any criticism, political or educational. (Such disclaimers were also a feature of textbooks produced during the Cultural Revolution, which was another period of politicization.)

Series Three was not a success. It was used briefly in experimental primary and secondary schools for two years before being abandoned, partly because of changes in the political climate, and partly because the contents of the series were poorly constructed. Teachers complained that the textbooks were impossible to teach, but, in any case, the period of politicization had come to an end and the Sino-Soviet split had occurred, rendering many of the passages in Series Three obsolete. Because of the focus of this book on the junior secondary curriculum, only the textbooks for junior secondary schools are analysed below.

It has not been possible to trace any of the team involved in writing the textbooks, but internal evidence suggests that they used Series One, Chinese Language textbooks and English-language translations of political tracts as sources for some reading passages. For instance, the similarity of phrasing in 'Lo Sheng-chiao' (Book 7 Lesson 3) to the passage with the same title in Series One Book 3 Lesson 33 suggests direct borrowing. On the other hand, 'The Cuckoo is Late' in Book 8 Lesson 2 has a similar story to its namesake in Series Two Book 3 Lesson 12, but there are marked differences in the phrasing, suggesting that, as with Series Two, this passage was translated from a Chinese Language textbook. At the end of the passages in Book 13 Lesson 3 ('The Chinese Nation') and Lesson 9 ('How Yu Kung Removed the Mountains'), there is an acknowledgement that the passage is excerpted from an English version of *Selected Works of Mao Tse-tung* published in London in 1956.

Other examples of antecedents are shown in Table 3.6. The use of translations of political tracts was an innovation for the junior secondary curriculum.

Table 3.6   Antecedents of some passages in Series Three

Passage in Series Three	Title	Antecedent
Book 7 Lesson 13	A Visit to a Farm	Series One Book 2 Lesson 16
Book 8 Lesson 3	A Man and a Snake	'Chinese Language for Primary School' Book 1 Lesson 13 (1951)
Book 10 Lesson 8	Commander Chu Teh's Shoulder Pole	'Chinese Language for Primary School' Book 2 Lesson 24 (1951)
Book 13 Lesson 6	The Nightingale (I)	'Chinese Language for Primary School' Book 2 Lesson 23 (1946)
Book 13 Lesson 7	The Nightingale (II)	'Chinese Language for Primary School' Book 2 Lesson 23 (1946)

As with previous series, no official syllabus was published for Series Three. This was partly due to the experimental status of the curriculum, and partly, as the analysis below shows, pedagogy, linguistic components and discrete language skills were not the primary concern of the curriculum developers during this period of politicization.

The new series, entitled 'English', comprised eighteen volumes, each of which was intended for use in one semester. They were divided into three sections: the first six books were designed for Primary 3 to Primary 5 pupils, the next eight books for junior secondary school pupils, and the last four books for senior secondary school pupils. The primary school textbooks have colourful covers showing children engaged in study, physical labour or Young Pioneer activities, while the secondary school books are green-grey with a line drawing of a leaping horse in front of an industrial skyline, with a clock face superimposed (Figure A.3, p. 212). The colour of this design varies according to the school level: Books 7 and 8, for instance, are brown, while Books 9 and 10 are green. The books measure 13 cm x 19 cm (5.12 inches x 7.25 inches), and the number of pages in the junior secondary series are: 46 (Book 7), 48 (Book 8), 63 (Book 9), 76 (Book 10), 56 (Book 11), 58 (Book 12), 64 (book 13) and 74 (book 14). The experimental nature of the textbooks is reflected in inconsistencies of format (e.g., the contents page is sometimes before the Foreword, sometimes immediately after, or sometimes at the back of the book) and typographical errors (e.g., the title 'Lessen 1' in Book 7 Lesson 1).

Pedagogy

The books each have fourteen to sixteen lessons. The organization of the lesson follows the same basic format. First, there is a reading passage, usually illustrated by a simple black and white line drawing, although Book 8 Lesson

5 contains a colour reproduction of a photograph depicting Tiananmen Square on National Day. The passage is followed by a list of new vocabulary items in the passage, together with phonetic symbols and Chinese equivalents. The third and final section of each lesson comprises exercises, although when a passage is divided into two parts across two consecutive lessons, this section is placed only at the end of the second lesson — no exercises are given for the first lesson. Compared with earlier series, the organization of Series Three is inflexible and insubstantial. The passage remains the central focus of each lesson, but, apart from vocabulary lists, there are no clearly delineated pedagogical components such as grammar presentations and spelling rules. This either reflects the relative inexperience of the materials writers, or a very strong politicization of the series to the detriment of pedagogical quality.

The passages in the junior secondary section are oriented towards strongly realistic discourse: there are no examples of 'weak' discourse serving merely to present discrete vocabulary or grammatical items. The vast majority of passages are politicized and examples of non-political passages are rare. Only the description of a library in Book 9 Lesson 4, and the scientific passages, 'How Plants Make Food and Use It' (Book 10 Lesson 13) and 'The Atom and Its Nucleus' (Book 14 Lesson 11), do not have overt political or moral messages. The reason for this limitation in genres is explained in the introductory notes in the textbooks:

> Previous textbooks were centred on the children's family and daily life. This series uses simple sentences and political passages to instil a communist mentality, according to the children's learning ability. One long-term aim is to develop children best fitted for New China.[14]

The use of so much realistic discourse could indicate a pedagogical inclination towards the Direct Method, which is associated with the use of realistic discourse from an early stage. Alternatively, and more persuasively when evidence from other analyses is taken into account, it could demonstrate a conception of the whole course in which the primary section provides a controlled linguistic foundation, while the junior and senior secondary sections pay much less attention to pedagogical matters in favour of politicized discourse, wherein the linguistic components are less controlled than in non-politicized discourse.

The introduction to the books in Series Three offers some insights into the intended pedagogy. The series, it says, is designed to develop the students' competence in the four language skills (reading, writing, listening and speaking) as well as a basic ability in pronunciation and grammar. The contents of the textbooks are to be used for intensive study, and the teacher should feel free to choose suitable materials for extensive study, for writing in different genres (letters, diaries, compositions) and revision work. 'Intensive' study (*jin du*) means that the passages should not just be read for meaning, but also parsed and recited. This approach, which accords with the Grammar-Translation Method, is reinforced in the design of the lessons in the textbooks. The new words are presented with Chinese translations and the exercises are predominantly concerned with translation and reciting parts of the passages. They are few instances of reading comprehension exercises. The claim in the introduction that the series is designed to develop the four language skills is only justified if a narrow interpretation of speaking and listening is applied, i.e., reciting a written passage and listening to a recital. As noted above, one of the reasons for the demise of Series Three was that teachers complained that there was a lack of attention to pedagogy. Tang Jun and other PEP staff were told by the teachers that the series needed a coherent linguistic progression underpinning the course — in other words, the Structural Approach.[15]

Linguistic components

The large numbers of strongly realistic passages, together with the lack of pedagogical components noted above, suggest that there is no predetermined graded linguistic syllabus underpinning the series. The emphasis is placed on the political and moral messages rather on than a structured presentation of the linguistic medium that conveys them. However, in analysing the linguistic components of Series Three, it should be remembered that the series for junior secondary pupils does not stand alone: it follows six books for primary pupils and precedes, in turn, four books for senior secondary pupils. In terms of linguistic components, the junior secondary material is apparently designed to build upon the language that was taught in the primary textbooks, where the level of complexity of the vocabulary, grammar and discourse increases as the course progresses. In the primary textbooks, the vocabulary is initially concerned with personal information, daily activities and classroom English. The range then expands to include lexis relating to political and nationalist themes. The grammar starts with simple sentences in the present simple tense. Other tenses are introduced occasionally, but the textbook offers no explanation or practice other than a copying exercise. By the end of the primary section, the textbooks have included the present simple, present continuous, future simple, present perfect and past simple tenses, as well as verbs in the passive voice. The discourse starts with short sentences, moving on to two-line dialogues, short passages and poems, and by the end of Book 6 has passages of three or more paragraphs and more than 120 words.

In the junior secondary section (Books 7–14), the linguistic components are determined by the nature of the passages. New vocabulary arising from the passage is listed in each lesson, but varies significantly in quantity: for example, 6 new words are presented in Book 12 Lesson 10, whereas 38 new words appear in the passage in Book 12 Lesson 14 and 52 in Book 13 Lesson 2. There is no overt presentation of grammar, but the complexity of the sentences is raised quite rapidly. The passages range from eight-line poems to passages and dialogues that increase in length from just over 100 words in Book 7 to over 500 words in Book 14. Towards the end of the series, many of the passages are taken directly from real-life sources apparently without modification. Book 14 Lesson 10 comprises the following:

Pulling Through

When we were trying out the shells, one of them exploded unexpectedly. I was seriously wounded and sent to hospital at once.

Now I was in bed, my left hand and leg held rigid by splints, and my head, and the whole of my body from the stomach downwards, swathed in bandages. I felt as if I were clamped to the bed. I couldn't even wriggle. It dawned on me that I was in a pretty bad way, but I wasn't going to die — not a bit of it. It wasn't the first time I should have been a dead one by rights and I'd got over it. Anyhow, even if I did die or come out a crock, it was no use crying over spilt milk. For the great cause of the liberation of the working class, we must not be afraid of making sacrifices. The words of Nikolai Ostrovsky, put into the mouth of Pavel Korchagin, the hero of his novel *How the Steel Was Tempered*, came to me:

"Man's dearest possession is life, and it is given to him to live but once. He must live so as to feel no torturing regrets for years without purpose, never know the burning shame of a mean and petty past; so live that, dying, he can say: all my life, all my strength were given to the finest cause in all the world — the fight for the liberation of mankind."

It was true. Life *is* short, but our cause endures for ever. As an individual I might suffer, but as long as I'd done my bit to help bring victory for all I should have a share in their happiness. As long as I was alive, I should go on working for the Party and for the people.

I remembered how back in the spring of 1943 the Party had called on us to model ourselves on Pavel Korchagin and so give ourselves a deeper political understanding. I'd borrowed the book from a friend who had the only copy in Huainan. It had already passed through many hands and its pages were worn and dog-eared. For several nights Pavel Korchagin and I kept vigil together over a tiny lamp. Compared with him I thought I was pretty small beer, but I vowed I'd do my best to live as if I were a fit friend and comrade of my hero.

1. New Words: 27 words and phrases
2. Exercises:
    I. *Recite the words of Nikolai Ostrovsky on life.*
    II. *Translate the following into Chinese:*
        1. *As an individual I might suffer, but as long as I'd done my bit to help bring victory for all I should have a share in their happiness.*

2.   *As long as I was alive, I should go on working for the Party and for the people.* (Series Three, Book 14: 44–7)

The liberal use of new vocabulary, averaging just over twenty new words per unit across the series, is much greater than in Series One or Two, and is indicative of the preference for strong, realistic discourse. It also reflects the lack of attention in the junior secondary section of Series Three to the established norms of linguistic control which are found in pre- and post-1949 series, and is directly influenced by the intention to increase the emphasis on political content.

Content

Overall, Series Three contains a very large number of political messages. Altogether 119 examples of discourse were identified in the series, containing 125 messages. Of these, 121 (96.80%) were classified as political, one as moral (0.80%) and three (2.40%) as neither political nor moral. This percentage of political messages was the highest in all the series studied, and was only rivalled by a textbook published in Shaanxi Province during the Cultural Revolution (see Chapter 5).

As Table 3.7 indicates, the politicized passages mainly concerned with attitudes and role models. The former category includes passages recording pre-revolutionary events, such as incidents from the Long March or life in the Communist base at Yan'an (e.g., Book 8 Lesson 9; Book 9 Lesson 13).

Table 3.7   Political and moral messages in Series Three

Discourse total	Messages total	Nil	Moral	Political	*Political (attitude)*	*Political (information)*	*Political (role model)*
119	125	3 (2.40%)	1 (0.80%)	121 (96.80%)	*43*	*29*	*49*

Other messages celebrate the achievements of the nation under the leadership of the CCP since 1949, such as Book 10 Lesson 3, 'Grandpa and I':

When my grandpa was of my age,
He worked for the landlord;
But I study for our country with joy.
The food for him was soy-bean cake;
But mine is buns and rice.
My grandpa went about in rags;
But I can wear shirt, uniform and jacket.

The house for him was old and shaky;
But mine is splendid and clean.
Why are we so different?
The time is different.
When he was of my age,
The imperialists and reactionaries
Made our country as dark as hell.
But the Chinese Communist Party saved us.
Long live the Chinese Communist Party!
Long live Chairman Mao! (Series Three, Book 10: 6)

Other recurring themes include stories of heroes, such as Lo Sheng-chiao (Book 7 Lesson 3), Liu Hu-lan (Book 9 Lessons 11 and 12) and Hsiang Hsiu-li (Book 11 Lesson 8), who all performed acts of selfless bravery; the activities of CCP youth organizations, such as the Young Pioneers (e.g., Book 7 Lesson 4); descriptions of educational visits by pupils to farms and other places (e.g., Book 7 Lesson 13); fables in which animals and rivers express admiration at changes that have occurred since 1949 (e.g., Book 7 Lessons 11 and 12), and negative portrayals of Western capitalist countries (e.g., Book 10 Lesson 10). Book 14 Lessons 4 and 5 contain writings by Mao and his speech at the meeting to celebrate the 10th anniversary of the founding of the PRC. It also contains translations of stories by Soviet writers (Gorky, in Lesson 2 and Fadeyev in Lessons 12 and 13).

Even the less politicized passages carry positive portrayals of national leaders, state policies and those implementing them. 'Sunnie' (Book 7 Lesson 1) extols the virtues of rising before dawn and retiring after sunset:

O Sunnie, don't you see
You aren't so good as we?
We rise early and work,
While you still lie in bed.
When you are up, o Sun,
Much of our work is done!
We stay up and work,
But you have gone to bed. (Series Three, Book 7: 1)

'A Sweet Potato Rolls Down into the River' (Book 7 Lesson 6) is an amusing poem featuring 'uncle farmers' who are 'happy' in their work:

Eastwards flows the river,
So clear is its water.
On the bank lies a little slope.
Gay and happy are our uncle farmers,
Digging sweet potatoes on the slope.
A loud noise rises from the river,

Lesson 15

U. S. Imperialists, Get Out of Taiwan!

Taiwan, the Penghu Islands and other coastal islands have been Chinese territory since ancient times. But since the liberation of the Chinese mainland, the U. S. imperialists with the reactionary Chiang Kai-shek gang as their lackey have occupied these islands. They have been carrying out destructive activities on the mainland, especially on the coastal regions.

The liberation of Taiwan and the other islands is China's internal problem. This is crystal clear to the world. To protest against U. S. aggression, to maintain our sovereignty and territorial integrity, and to defend peace in the Far East and the world, the Chinese people throughout the country are carrying on a resolute struggle. We shall never stop until Taiwan is liberated. The powerful socialist camp and the peace-loving countries and peoples of the world all have condemned

`44`

the U. S. imperialists for their aggression and expressed their support for the just struggle of the Chinese people. The Soviet Government has repeatedly warned the U. S. Government: to attack China means to attack the Soviet Union.

The Chinese people love peace dearly. We are now carrying out a peaceful construction which astounds the world with the immensity of its scale and the speed of its progress. But we are not afraid of war. We can never be cowed into submission by the war threats of the imperialists. Nothing can shake our will to liberate Taiwan and other islands. Ours is a just struggle, and we are confident of our strength. With the support of all the peace-loving countries and peoples of the world, we will certainly make the Taiwan Straits a grave for the aggressors and win final victory for our cause.

New Words

Taiwan n. 台湾
strait [streit] n. 海峡
Penghu n. 澎湖

island [ailənd] n. 島嶼
territory ['teritəri] n. 領
    土

`44`

Figure 3.4   Reading passage from Series Three Book 10

The issue of Taiwan has been a major preoccupation for the PRC since the island provided refuge for the Nationalist Party after its overthrow.

Ten feet high splashes its water.
"Aiya!" I shouted aloud,
"Who has fallen into the river?"
All laugh and laugh and laugh.
"It's not anybody at all, you see,"
Answered a little girl,
"It's a big sweet potato
that rolls down into the river." (Series Three, Book 7: 12–3)

'A Wolf in Sheep's Clothing' (Book 9 Lesson 16) could be construed as having a covert political message, with its conclusion that 'the most dangerous enemies are those who pretend to be friends'. 'Loushan Pass' (Book 11 Lesson 6) is a poem by Mao Zedong, while 'Parachute Jumping' (Book 11 Lesson 14) and 'A Trip to the Moon' (Book 11 Lesson 15) focus on military activities 'for national defence' and space travel (with special reference to the Soviet space programme) respectively. Book 14 Lesson 14 is a story of cooperation between China and the Soviet Union, which also allows a negative portrayal of the Nationalist Party (referred to as the 'Kuomintang' in the passage):

Hands of Friendship

Hsu Hsueh-hui is the daughter of a handicraft worker of Tengchung county of Yunnan Province in southwest China. Since 1956, she has been serving as an accountant in a branch banking office on a state farm near the border.

At dead of night on March 2, 1959, six bandits, remnants of the Kuomintang troops, armed with knives, crossed the border and broke into the branch office with intent to rob. The seventeen-year-old Hsu Hsueh-hui clung to the safe with all her might in a desperate attempt to prevent it from being taken away. In the courageous fight, both her hands were slashed off by the robbers.

The Communist Party and the people showed her every care and she was restored to health. In 1959, she was elected delegate to the National Conference of Labour Heroes held in Peking. Her heroism has been a source of inspiration to the Chinese people as well as friends in the Soviet Union and other socialist countries, who showered her with letters expressing their kind concern for her.

Among them was A.A. Romanov, Director of the Artificial Limbs Factory at Chita, who invited Hsu Hsueh-hui to visit Chita to be fitted with a new pair of "hands". She accepted the invitation and arrived there on January 15, 1960. Thanks to Director Romanov and the workers, the young Chinese heroine was fitted with special artificial hands to use in eating and other specialized "hands" to enable her to work. She regained her ability to use her "hands" and to do quite complicated work.

Filled with joy and hope she said, "I will certainly learn how to use my new hands well so that I can contribute something towards Sino-Soviet friendship and the socialist construction of my country." She has now returned to China with her new hands and she is deeply grateful to the people of the Soviet Union. (Series Three, Book 14: 62–3)

The continued presence of passages praising the USSR indicate that the CCP's misgivings over Soviet 'revisionism' had not yet entered the domain of political messages in school textbooks, although Series Three was the last to provide such a positive portrayal of the Sino-Soviet relationship.

The moral message in Book 7 Lesson 1 is similar to those in earlier series, stressing a healthy lifestyle (such as by rising early and working hard). However, it is completely overshadowed by the heavy politicization of Series Three, which ties in with the political orientation of the planned curriculum. The vocabulary lists are also a very strong indicator of the political orientation and the lack of linguistic control in Series Three. Out of a total of 2,394 new vocabulary items, 1,793 are non-Thorndike (i.e., 74.90%). The non-Thorndike words and phrases are predominantly related to industry, agriculture and military affairs, which reflects the themes of the passages (most notably, socialist achievements in these areas).

Series Three was viewed as flawed on two counts. Its political messages became quickly outdated with the Sino-Soviet split, which turned such passages as 'Long Live the Great Sino-Soviet Alliance — Powerful Bulwark of World Peace!' (Book 12, Lesson 2) into an embarrassment. Second, it was heavily criticized on pedagogical grounds by teachers piloting the series in Beijing, who described it as 'unteachable' to Tang Jun because of the neglect of pedagogical concerns, such as attention to the presentation of linguistic components in a controlled linear sequence or of a limited number of new vocabulary items in each lesson (although the series does appear to promote, at least rhetorically, the Grammar-Translation Method).[16] For these reasons, Series Three was abandoned without being published for general use.

Summary

The period 1949–60 marks the first phase of English Language curriculum development in China. In this phase, there were three major socio-political influences on the curriculum. Firstly, the nation was embarking upon economic construction through technical and industrial expansion with the assistance of the USSR. Secondly, China was developing its own international diplomacy, particularly with regard to the non-aligned Asian nations. Thirdly, there was a period of politicization. Under these circumstances, English was perceived to have a useful role for technology transfer, diplomacy and transmission of political messages, but was generally accorded lower official status than Russian. This was because of the ambivalent attitudes towards English. Despite its utility, it was the language of a number of Western nations that had not yet recognized the PRC and whose political orientation placed them in an opposing bloc during the cold war at this time.

The three English Language curricula had different macro-level triggers. Series One was the linkage between English and national development; Series Two, the linkage with the transmission of political messages, and Series Three, an educational policy to provide a unified curriculum across primary and secondary schooling. In reality, however, the aim of Series Three was subordinated by the politicized climate.

Overall, the subsequent pattern of curriculum development is similar to the 'garbage can' pattern identified by Elmore and Sykes (1992), in that the process of development for all three curricula was pragmatic and expedient, resulting in varying degrees of incoherence in the curriculum. The 'complex ecology' that Elmore and Sykes view as giving rise to competing interest groups and agenda-setting was exacerbated in China by the shortage of suitable resources and expertise. The PEP did not perform a centralized function in curriculum development, other than to ensure that an appropriate degree of 'redness' and/or 'expertise' was included. The PEP reacted to policies from the central government by publishing the textbook resources, but, because of a perceived lack of experience and expertise in pedagogical concerns, commissioned outside agencies (specialists at various leading higher educational institutes) to carry out the actual writing of the textbooks. This commissioning was in turn constrained by the expertise available at this level: few tertiary institutes had even vaguely relevant experience. As a result, the curriculum was initially more influenced by socio-political forces and — as far as the choice of textbook materials was concerned — by happenstance than by the grassroots pedagogical realities of junior secondary school English Language classrooms. Teachers were not involved to a large extent, although a small number of teachers in the experimental schools piloting Series Three played a major role as critics, contributing to the rejection of the series.

In terms of content, the first two series attempted to maintain a bureaucratic balance between political, social, linguistic and pedagogical concerns in keeping with the 'red and expert' philosophy, although Series Two was more political than Series One. The textbooks writers took the politically and pedagogically safe option of referring to, and even borrowing from Soviet models that interlaced reading-based teacher-centred pedagogy with passages that carried strong political messages. Meanwhile, Series Three was heavily skewed towards political goals, to the detriment of considerations of pedagogical and language learning principles that were acceptable to teachers. The series reflected the contemporary climate of 'politics to the fore' by making use of political tracts written by or about national leaders, but was abandoned not just because of political developments, but also because teachers found the textbooks to be unteachable.

The experience of the first phase of the English Language curriculum proved salutary. As a result of both pedagogical and political factors, none of these series was long-lived, as each was judged by CCP leaders and/or by teachers to lack sufficient attention to either contemporary socio-political imperatives or pedagogical considerations. The problem of politicization was hard to resolve, as the shifts in the prevailing political winds were beyond the control of curriculum developers. On the other hand, the rejection of Series Three showed to the PEP the importance of paying attention to pedagogical principles and of respecting teachers' opinions. Addressing this issue was within the capacity of the PEP, and in the next phase, teachers were consulted in the development process.

4 Towards quality in education, 1961–66

The early 1960s in China was a period of 'leadership dissension and economic recovery' (Wang 1995: 24). Political radicals, including Mao Zedong, were under pressure from other CCP leaders, such as Liu Shaoqi, Peng Dehuai, Lu Tingyi and Deng Xiaoping, after the failure of the political movements. On top of this was the acrimonious Sino-Soviet schism. The denunciation of Stalin by the Soviet leader, Khrushchev, and consequent re-orientation of policies were repudiated by the Chinese government and this led to Soviet experts being withdrawn from China at short notice, leaving many projects incomplete. Consequently, the status of English was boosted while that of Russian declined. The subject was extended to secondary schools nation-wide, leading to the retraining of many Russian teachers as English Language teachers (a reversal of the previous trend). English thus became a major foreign language in the curriculum and the official syllabus stated that the explicit political functions of learning the language were to receive less attention than in the previous period (Tang Lixing, 1983; Tang Jun, 1986). The syllabus stated that English was:

> … an important tool to developing cultural and scientific knowledge, to carry out international interaction, to foster cultural exchanges, and to increase the understanding between peoples of different countries. English is commonly used throughout the world. A good grasp of English enables us to absorb the aspects of science and technology which will help socialist construction; to introduce our experience to friendly countries and people; to strengthen our relationship with people in different countries; and to empower people in different countries to combat imperialism. (PEP, 1963: 1, in translation)

Competence in English became important for individuals to gain access to higher education, and attention was paid to improving the quality of English Language teaching, which, during this period, 'boomed', according to Tang Lixing (1983: 42).

This chapter examines the English Language curriculum in this relatively depoliticized period from 1961 to 1966 when attention was paid to strengthening the quality of education in terms of curriculum, pedagogy and teaching materials. After the break with the USSR and the disastrous Great Leap Forward, the roller-coaster experiences of the first phase of the English curriculum outlined in Chapter 3 were replaced in the early 1960s by an era of relative stability. This second phase, from 1961 until the beginning of the Cultural Revolution, is distinct from the phases that immediately preceded and followed it. The process of curriculum development underwent change, with the strengthening of the role of the PEP (as it lessened its dependence upon outside agencies), and also of the teachers, who became more involved in the process. A clear mechanism for developing and monitoring the quality of syllabuses and textbook resources was established. There were also changes to the intended pedagogy, incorporating some features originating in Western countries.

The chapter analyses two series of textbooks produced during this time: Series Four (published incrementally from 1961) and Series Five (from 1963). Another series was also planned and a draft version published for piloting in 1965, but was abandoned at a very early stage because of the Cultural Revolution. It is not analysed in this chapter because it was an adaptation of Series Four (unlike Series Three, which was also abandoned after piloting, but which was analysed in Chapter 6 because of its distinct characteristics).[1] Table 4.1 summarizes the English Language curriculum during this phase.

The ten-year schooling curriculum, 1961

Placed in a state of self-reliance after the schism with the USSR, China reorganized its approach to education. Some of these changes arose because Soviet ideas were unfashionable, but others came from the grassroots. In schools, there was, according to Tang Lixing (1983), a 'Renaissance', which was a reaction against the Soviet-influenced textbooks and pedagogy in many subjects, including English Language:

> With a focus on reforming the curriculum, compiling teaching materials, experimenting with new teaching methods and improving teaching facilities, education boomed. And TEFL, formerly an almost lifeless profession, boomed as well. (Tang Lixing, 1983: 42)

A National Cultural and Educational Conference was held in the summer of 1960 to discuss future initiatives in education, such as length of schooling, curricular content and pedagogy (Löfstedt, 1980). Two tasks for the English

Table 4.1 Features of the English Language curriculum, 1961–66

	1961: Series Four	1963: Series Five
Genesis	reaction to politicization; desire to improve pedagogical quality in education	desire to improve pedagogical quality in education
Role and status of English	national economic construction; high official status	national economic construction; high official status
Role of agencies PEP: consultants: teachers:	production of syllabus and resources; production of syllabus and resources; suggestions and feedback	production of syllabus and resources; suggestions and feedback; suggestions and feedback
Process	team established to develop syllabus and then materials; piloting in some schools	research into English Language teaching in China and abroad; team established to develop syllabus and materials; piloting in some schools; advisory consultative editorial committee reviewed materials
Syllabus	not published, but guidelines to materials writers; stresses oral and written language development	published; stresses oral and written language development, specific teaching and learning strategies; symbiotic with textbooks
Resources	three textbooks and a teacher's handbook	six textbooks, tape recordings and teacher's handbooks
Organization	integrated topic-based; linear progression	integrated topic-based; linear progression
Discourse	initially weak/medium realism, but soon strong	progression from weak to strong realism
Linguistic components	focus on phonetics, intonation, grammar and vocabulary	focus on phonetics, intonation, grammar and vocabulary
Intended pedagogy	reading aloud, memorization, Structural Approach, Grammar-Translation	reading aloud, memorization, oral practice, sentence writing, students' independent learning, Structural Approach, Grammar-Translation
Political and moral messages	emphasis on moral education; some political values	emphasis on moral education; some political values

section of the PEP emerged: the first to prepare materials for the new integrated ten-year programme covering primary and secondary schooling, and the second to revise the syllabus and textbooks used in other secondary schools (in the event, the majority) that did not adopt the new programme. These tasks resulted in the production of Series Four and Series Five respectively. As part of the educational reforms, the use of nationally unified textbook resources was reinstated by the Ministry of Education in 1961 (Pepper, 1996). The trigger for the ten-year curriculum was an amalgam of different forces. The shift in the socio-political climate prompted a macro-level movement for change in the political orientation of the English Language curriculum, but there was also a combination of meso- and micro-level forces for educational change, corresponding to Elmore and Sykes' (1992) concept of a 'complex ecology' bringing about change, which is different from the triggers for change in the first phase analysed in the previous chapter.

A committee was formed, including PEP staff and consultants, to prepare new English syllabuses and resources for the new ten-year primary and secondary curriculum. The consultants enlisted by the PEP came from the Foreign Languages Department of Beijing Normal University, who had played a major role in the conference, and, in time, from Beijing Foreign Languages Institute, where Ying Manrong and Tang Jun were able to recruit colleagues including David Crook, Isabel Crook, Margaret Turner, Wang Zuoliang, Xu Guozhang and Zhou Xiaohong (Qun and Li, 1991).[2] This organizational structure, permitting a largely in-house production of the syllabus and textbooks, was a significant change from previous practice, whereby the writing of such materials was contracted out by the PEP to scholars in tertiary institutions. The developers' goal, says Tang Jun, was to write a series that was more structured, more complete and of a higher standard than previous series.[3] When finished, the series comprised five books, three of them for junior secondary schools. Book 1 and Book 2 were trialled in draft form in key secondary schools in major cities such as Beijing and Tianjin from the autumn semester of 1961. Book 3 was produced for the following semester in 1962. After favourable feedback from teachers in the piloting project, the series was adopted for general use in schools operating the ten-year system from the autumn of 1962. This process of curriculum development has more pluralistic features than the first phase, but, paradoxically, there was also a degree of centralization. The PEP assumed the central role as curriculum developers, but acted as mediator between various outside agencies and teachers. Reference was made to earlier series, as well as to the expertise of outside specialists (including foreigners). This indicates historical and, to a lesser degree, international influences on the curriculum. The contribution of Westerners also reflects the relative depoliticization in the socio-political climate.

The committee initially decided to produce a syllabus and teaching materials for the five-year secondary stage of the new ten-year schooling system. These materials would be designed for three years' junior secondary and two years' senior secondary schooling. Following a conference held in April 1961, which discussed the development of teaching materials for arts subjects, the committee decided upon the objectives for the English Language curriculum and drew up a draft syllabus, but no formal document was published, as had also been the case with earlier series. Instead, the syllabus served as guidelines for the writers of Series Four. According to Tang Jun (1986), the guidelines stipulated that English should be learned, as with Series One, as a tool for national construction and for students' future studies and career. The students should acquire the ability to read, write and speak English, and the teaching materials should be taken from original sources or should be as colloquial (and therefore as realistic) as possible. The students were also intended to achieve a 'basic knowledge' of phonetics and grammar, as well as a vocabulary of 2,700 words. In this sense, the plan is closer to those that underpinned Series One and Series Two: the view that language is best studied through a thematic approach with graded linguistic components. In advocating the inclusion of original English language materials, the draft syllabus also reflects the aim of moving away from the highly politicized curriculum that was embodied in Series Three.

The objectives identified the use of colloquial English and the ability to read professional publications in English as two major goals. Another aim, according to Tang Jun, was 'to overcome the inappropriate stress on political content and the lack of attention to language learning' that had been a criticism of the curriculum in the previous phase, as manifested most notably in Series Three.[4]

The draft of Series Four was prepared during the summer of 1961. In addition, a set of reference books to assist teachers in teaching the series was published (Tang Jun, 1986). This innovation represents awareness, on the part of the PEP, of the needs and difficulties of teachers, and a response to provide them with support. The textbooks vary in size and cover (as the available copies of Books 1 and 2 are from the piloted series, and Book 3 is from a later edition). Book 1 (146 pages) and Book 2 (164 pages) measure 20.32 cm x 13.97 cm (8 inches x $5\frac{1}{2}$ inches), while Book 3 (213 pages) is 18.42 cm x 13 cm ($7\frac{1}{4}$ inches x 5.12 inches, Figure A.4, p. 212). Books 1 and 2 have a soft paper cover with a coloured illustration of Tiananmen Square and three-colour printing of the title and other information; Book 3 has a similar design in a single colour (red). In all three books there are some pages with black and white illustrations.

One of the guidelines called for the use of materials from original English sources, rather than translations of Chinese passages (Tang Jun, 1986). The writers referred to earlier series as a major source: for example, Book 1 Lesson 15 closely resembles Series One Book 1 Lesson 30:

Our Classroom

This is our classroom. It has two doors and four windows. It is bright and clean. There are many desks and chairs in our classroom. There is a blackboard on the wall. There is a picture of Chairman Mao over the blackboard. (Series Four Book 1: 58–9)

Our Classroom

We have a large classroom. It has two doors and three windows. It is bright and clean.
There is a picture of Chairman Mao on one of the walls. On another wall there is a map. It is a map of China.
There are three blackboards in our classroom. There is a table for the teacher. There are forty-five desks and chairs. They are for the pupils. (Series One Book 1: 98)

The wording in the versions in Series Four is sometimes exactly the same, apart for some abridgements, clarifications or more felicitous renderings than in previous versions. For instance, the story of the cock in Series Three begins with the following paragraph:

When Kao Yu-pao was a child, he worked for a landlord. The landlord was greedy and shrewd. He made the farmhands work hard and long, and gave them little to eat. Of course, they hated that landlord very much. (Series Three Book 7: 31)

The version in Series Four starts:

When Kao Yu-pao was a child, he worked for a landlord. The landlord was cruel and greedy. He made the farmhands work long hours, but gave them little to eat. Of course they hated him. (Series Four Book 2: 132)

The second version uses easier vocabulary ('cruel' for 'shrewd') and more precise renditions ('work long hours' instead of 'work long and hard'; 'but' for 'and' as a conjunction expressing apposition), but is basically the same. The use of passages from Series Three reflects the contribution of authors from Beijing Normal University who worked on both series. Liu Daoyi also recalls that passages for potential inclusion were contributed by some of the consultants, including the foreign teachers from Beijing Foreign Languages Institute.[5] A few passages, mainly with a moral message, were based on Chinese language sources, despite the recommendation in the guidelines not to do so. Table 4.2 shows some of the antecedents.

Table 4.2   Antecedents of some passages in Series Four

Passage in Series Four	Title	Antecedent
Book 1 Lesson 17	Our Class	Series Two Book 2 Lesson 5
Book 2 Lesson 14	The Little Swallow (I)	Series Three Book 7 Lesson 11
Book 2 Lesson 15	The Little Swallow (II)	Series Three Book 7 Lesson 12
Book 2 Lesson 18	The Wolf and the Lamb	'Chinese Language Primary Readers' Book 8 Lesson 34 (1958)
Book 3 Lesson 11	A Blanket	'Chinese Language Primary Readers' Book 7 Lesson 4 (1958)
Book 2 Lesson 22	The Cock Crows at Midnight	Series Three Book 7 Lesson 15

Pedagogy

The developers attempted to pay more attention to pedagogical rather than political concerns. Tang Jun recalls:

> In structuring the textbooks, the need to nurture the students step by step in their ability to read, speak and write was the guiding factor. The basic components of phonetics and grammar, and the selection of vocabulary and passages were designed to take students' ability to learn into consideration, and were organised from simple to complex.[6]

The draft syllabus suggested that the textbooks should cater to students' ability to learn by adopting a carefully controlled linear progression of discrete linguistic components, in accordance with the Structural Approach. In turn, so as to promote realistic language use rather than just knowledge about language, a thematic approach that closely integrated the level of difficulty of passages with the graded grammatical items would be adopted. The theme of the reading passage or dialogues determines the linguistic components in each lesson. However, the number of new linguistic items in the passages are restricted by the view that pupils should not be given too many at one time while another constraint is the need to cover the prescribed linguistic syllabus. As a result, many passages are pseudo-realistic: they resemble real-life passages in discourse characteristics, but the linguistic components are controlled. However, the aim of having more realistic passages is realized in Book 3 and the number of new linguistic items increases correspondingly, as the control is weakened.

There are 30 lessons in Book 1, 24 lessons in Book 2 and 18 lessons (plus supplementary readings) in Book 3. The organization of individual lessons shows some variation over the series. A typical lesson in Book 1 contains the following elements: a reading passage (including, sometimes, a script for an oral dialogue); a box showing one or two new structures; a list of new words and expressions; expressions for conversation; phonetics; grammar; and exercises practising the phonetics and grammar, as well as some open questions about the reader's own experience. A lesson in Book 3, on the other hand, typically comprises: a reading passage (occasionally it takes the form of a script for oral production); a box showing one or two new structures; a list of new words and expressions; notes to the reading passage; grammar; and exercises practising phonetics, grammar, composition and translation skills — a more holistic approach to the language than the discrete focus in Book 1.

Overall, the pedagogy of Series Four embraces three distinct approaches. There are strong elements of the Structural Approach in the presentation of linguistic components, and of the Grammar-Translation Method, most notably in the later books, but there are hints of another method — Audiolingualism — in some sections of the book. The Grammar-Translation Method is spelt out in Book 1 Lesson 21:

> It is half past nine in the morning. We are having an English lesson. First the teacher explains the new words in the new lesson. He teaches us to spell them. Then he reads the text. We read after him. We read carefully and clearly. (Series Four Book 1: 88)

Many exercises in the later part of the series reflect this pedagogy, together with the Structural Approach. They practise discrete grammatical items and translation between English and Chinese. This focus on the written word, the explanation of the vocabulary, and the practice of grammar rules all match the pedagogy of Series One to Three. Series Four therefore adds another pedagogical approach to the two identified in previous series. It starts with a main focus on teaching oral English, predominantly through the strategies of recitation and memorization. Then it moves to the Grammar-Translation Method, with the focus on written discourse from Chinese into English and vice versa. The oral dimension is not totally ignored in the later stages of the series, as some dialogues and passages are retained in the 'Exercises' sections for reading aloud. Thus in Book 2 Lesson 8, the contents of the lesson are:

1. 'After the Test': a passage in the form of a dialogue
2. New Words and Expressions
3. Notes to the Text, with translations and explanations of specific grammatical points
4. Dialogues (classroom expressions)
5. Phonetics, with a study of stress patterns
6. Exercises: learning irregular past tense forms; producing some regular and irregular past tense forms; converting statements into questions; translation of Chinese sentences into English; a single comprehension question based on the passage.

Lesson Twenty-one 第二十一課

We Like Our English Lessons

I

It is 'half past 'nine in the ↘morning. We are 'having an 'English ↘lesson. ↗First the 'teacher ex'plains the ↗words in the 'new ↘lesson. He 'teaches us to ↘spell them. 'Then he 'reads the ↘text. We 'read ↘after him. We 'read 'carefully and ↘clearly.

'English is a 'useful ↘tool. The 'lessons are 'very ↘interesting. We 'like our 'English 'lessons 'very ↘much.

II

— 'Do you 'like your 'English ↗lessons?
— ↘Yes, I ↘do.
— 'Why do you 'like your 'English ↘lessons?
— Be'cause 'English is a 'useful ↘tool. I 'want to 'master this ↗tool and 'use it for our 'socialist con↘struction.

> **Why** do you like to study English?
> **Because** it is a useful tool.

Figure 4.1   Extract from Series Four Book 1, p. 88

The description of the lesson reflects a structured, mimetic approach to learning English. It also shows the association of English with national political and economic goals. The marks on the text show stress (´) and intonation patterns (↗).

The discourse in Series Four is, in general, strongly realistic, in that the purpose of the reading passage is to convey a description, a story, a dialogue or other genre in colloquial English, rather than to present discrete linguistic components. Only three passages out of 72 are classified as 'weak'. These all occur early in Book 1 and are aimed at establishing some simple sentence structures, such as 'What is this? It is a …' (Book 1 Lesson 2). No situational context is provided for these questions and answers; the dialogue in Lesson 2 is practising the structures for naming vocabulary items. Most of the passages up to Book 1 Lesson 15 are classified as 'medium'. These are often stilted dialogues because of the heavy control on the linguistic components, but some form of context is provided (such as a picture) or is implicit in the discourse. For instance, the first part of the passage in Book 1 Lesson 8 reads:

> I am a young pioneer. I have a red tie. He is a young pioneer. He has a red tie. Has she a red tie?
>
> Yes, she has. She is a pioneer too. (Series Four Book 1: 28)

Although there is no picture in the textbook, it is clear that the passage is describing people. The language is highly controlled (short sentences using a limited range of structures) and the realism of the discourse is therefore classified as 'medium'. From Book 1 Lesson 16 to the end of the series, the passages are all classified as 'strong' discourse.

This arrangement, moving from weak to strong discourse, is similar to that of Series One, and accords with the integration of the Structural Approach and the Grammar-Translation Method. However, Book 1 and the first part of Book 2 contain a number of dialogues and significant amounts of oral practice, which fit neither of these two pedagogies. Instead, it has features, superficially at least, akin to those of Audiolingualism, which was emerging internationally as a preferred second language pedagogy at the time. For instance, students are advised on how to learn English in Book 3 Lesson 1:

Learn to Speak English

Student: Good morning, teacher.

Teacher: Good morning. How did you enjoy the holidays? Are you glad to be back at school?

Student: Yes, I am very glad to be back and to begin my lessons again. I want to improve my English this term. I should like to be able to speak correctly. What should I do?

Teacher: You must try to talk in English as much as possible. Don't simply say "yes" or "no" and then stop. You can't learn to talk by keeping your mouth shut, can you?

Student: No. But suppose I make mistakes …

Teacher: Don't worry about mistakes. First of all, learn the expressions by heart. Learn whole sentences, not single words. Another thing,

> don't be afraid to talk. Just try to say what you want to say, and don't
> be afraid that people will laugh at you. Keep on trying and you'll
> make fewer and fewer mistakes. And, there's another thing to
> remember: always say complete sentences. That's the way to learn
> to speak a language.

Student: Thank you. I'll do as you say. (Series Four Book 3: 1–2)

The features of Audiolingualism include emphasizing oral skills before written skills; encouraging pupils to use English as much as possible; and learning through habit-formation (see Table 1.1 in Chapter 1, p. 10). Curiously, the advice in the reading passage is not followed through in the exercises that the students are expected to carry out. For instance, there are no sentence pattern drills for oral practice, which would be expected as part of an Audiolingual approach (Larsen-Freeman, 1986). The pedagogy does not fit any of those identified in Table 1.1 as major international English language teaching methods. An alternative interpretation is that the pedagogy advocated implicitly in this dialogue is a part of the traditional mimetic teaching and learning practices in China (Paine, 1997), and was introduced to meet the requirement in the curriculum guidelines to develop students' oral skills. Most passages in the first half of the course are also intended for reading aloud, as intonation patterns are marked in the text.

Linguistic components

The development of the linguistic components in Series Four is consistent with the syllabus guidelines that stipulate a foundation course in English phonetics and grammar, and a restricted vocabulary of 2,700 items for the whole secondary school course. The series starts with the alphabet, in both printed and cursive form, some common vocabulary items and simple deictic structures (*this, that, here, there*, etc.). The international phonetic alphabet is covered systematically in Book 1, with an individual focus on vowel sounds and/or families of consonant sounds in each lesson from Lesson 7 to Lesson 15. The grammar follows a similar progression to that of Series One and Series Two, starting with the verbs *to be* and *to have*, and other verbs in the present simple tense in statements and interrogatives. The tenses are then introduced in the following sequence: present continuous, future simple, past simple, present perfect, past continuous, past perfect and future-in-the-past. Series Four goes further than Series One and Series Two by introducing the three latter tenses.

The vocabulary is presented in the 'New Words and Expressions' list in each lesson. The total for the three books in the junior secondary component of the course is 1,272 new vocabulary items, which is an average of approximately 18 new words and expressions per lesson, ranging from 1 new word in Book 1 Lesson 7 to 34 in Book 3 Lesson 17. The number of new words and expressions per lesson increases as the series develops. In Book 1, there are 421 new words and expressions at an average of 14 per lesson; in Book 2, there are 480 at an average of 20; and in Book 3, there are 371 at an average of just over 20. This increase reflects the strengthening of the realism of the discourse and an expectation that the students can handle more new words as their linguistic competence develops.

Content

In general, the themes in the early stages of the course are centred on the everyday experiences of schoolchildren, such as family and school life. In Books 2 and 3, the themes are broadened to include fables and other stories, literature (including simple poems) and descriptions of social conditions in China and other countries. There are fewer political messages in Series Four than in Series Two or Three, but still a higher percentage than in Series One. However, the kind of political messages are less ideologically oriented than those in Series One. A total of 81 examples of discourse were identified and analysed in Series Four, and 83 messages were found, 64 of them having a political (46 or 55.42%) or moral (18 or 21.95%) orientation. The details are shown in Table 4.3.

Table 4.3   Political and moral messages in Series Four

Discourse total	Messages total	Nil	Moral	Political	Political (attitude)	Political (information)	Political (role model)
81	83	19 (22.89%)	18 (21.69%)	46 (55.42%)	26	8	12

A few passages have a strong patriotic message (e.g., 'National Day' in Book 2 Lesson 4), while some others contrast life before and after the CCP came to power (e.g., 'The Little Swallow' in Book 2 Lessons 14 and 15). One such passage, 'Tibet Reborn' in Book 3 Lesson 9, extends this to the question of minorities:

> Our country is a big family of many nationalities. In the southwest of it live the Tibetans.
>
> In the past, most of the Tibetans were serfs. They led a miserable life. Men and women, old and young, had to work all the year round for the serf-owners, but never got enough food to eat or clothes to wear. If they tried to run away, they were cruelly punished, or even killed by their masters. Many serfs toiled all their lives, but when they became too old to work they were thrown out and left to die.

In 1951 Tibet was peacefully liberated. Social reforms were carried out step by step. But the reactionary serf-owners openly opposed the Party's policy of peaceful reform in Tibet. In 1959, they started an armed rebellion. However, it was quickly put down by the People's Liberation Army.

Now the serfs of yesterday have become the masters. Under the leadership of the Party they are carrying out important reforms. Factories have been built. New schools have been set up for the children. Grown-ups, too, are learning to read and write. Like their brother nationalities in our country, the Tibetans are working with great enthusiasm to build their new life. (Series Four Book 3: 78–9)

This passage is unusual in Series Four in addressing a specific political incident (other than general inspirational stories from the history of the PLA). However, it was a topical theme, as the Tibetan uprising occurred in 1959, just two years before the textbooks were written, and China was facing strong international criticism of its Tibetan policies. Another political theme in Series Four is People's Communes, an innovation that sought to create large agricultural units that catered for most aspects of daily life, including schools, factories and communal dining, which is described in Book 1 Lesson 19:

Our Commune Dining-Room

This is our commune dining-room. My mother and I have our meals there. There are three cooks in the dining-room. They cook for over one hundred people. They keep everything clean. They do their work well.

My mother and aunts do not have to cook at home. They can go out to work. They take an active part in socialist construction.

We like our commune dining-room very much. We are grateful to the commune and the Communist Party. (Series Four Book 1: 80)

'A City People's Commune' (Book 2 Lesson 16) returns to the theme, and the level of difficulty of the passage also demonstrates the anticipated rise in students' comprehension over one year:

The Erh-lung-lu People's Commune in Peking was set up in 1958. Since then, great changes have taken place in the people's life. They have set up a lot of factories, dining-rooms, nurseries, kindergartens and service centres.

The commune factories make various kinds of things, from pins to machine parts. They play an important part in socialist construction. At harvest time, many commune members go to the countryside and help the peasants with their work in the fields.

The commune members work very hard. They know they are working for socialism and communism. They are eager to study and many of them go to spare-time schools. Some of them are now studying Chairman Mao's works. Their political consciousness is rising rapidly.

The Erh-lung-lu City People's Commune was the first city commune in Peking. Now there are thousands all over our great country. (Series Four Book 2: 97)

Passages portraying other countries in a poor light are sparse compared to the previous phase. One, 'Eddie Lewis' in Book 2 Lesson 20, tells the tale of a black child in the USA who died after being refused admission to hospital by white doctors, while 'The Little Match Girl' in Book 3 Lessons 12 and 13, the story of a poor girl freezing to death in a rich neighbourhood at Christmas, and 'Joe Hill' in Book 3 Lesson 5, about a murdered labour activist in the USA, also are unflattering towards Western countries. Many passages present positive images of the Young Pioneers, and of farmers, factory workers and soldiers, although the overall percentage of role model passages is lower than that in the previous two series.

The major thrust of moral messages in Series Four is similar to Series One and Two: a healthy lifestyle is promoted, involving hard work and keeping fit (e.g., Book 1 Lesson 13), cleanliness (Book 1 Lesson 24) and positive attitudes towards school (Book 2 Lesson 1). This reduced emphasis on explicitly political messages is confirmed by the non-Thorndike components of the new vocabulary lists. One-third of the vocabulary items (420 out of 1,272, or 33.02%) in Series Four are non-Thorndike, but less than 30 might be classified as 'political' vocabulary (i.e., related to socialism, CCP policies, capitalism or imperialism).

The 1963 curriculum

The trigger for Series Five was complex, but the development of the curriculum was essentially influenced by macro-level factors, both external and internal to education. The schism with the USSR made Series Two obsolete, and the ten-year programme of primary and secondary schooling (for which Series Four was intended) was not adopted throughout the country: it was mainly used by schools whose students were deemed capable of covering the twelve-year syllabus in ten years. Most schools retained the twelve-year system (Pepper, 1996). To provide materials for these schools, and thereby replacing Series Two, the Ministry of Education first engaged a group of university scholars to summarize the experience of the previous sixty years of English Language teaching in China and, in order to access international trends in education, including those emanating from Western countries, the group was also asked to look at ideas from Japan, the USA and the United Kingdom. The findings of this group, presented to the Ministry of Education, included recommendations that oracy as well as literacy should be stressed, and that the syllabus and teaching materials should be carefully graded according to linguistic complexity (Tang Jun, 1986).

The process of curriculum development continued the move towards centrally-dominated pluralistic strategies that were noted in Series Four, in that the PEP and teachers were involved to a greater extent than previously. The PEP strengthened its English editorial staff to ten members in 1962 by recruiting more educationalists from leading tertiary institutions. This meant that the production of the syllabus and textbooks could be carried out in-house, without the need to commission an outside agency to do or share the work. Outside agencies were still involved, however. The team of consultants from tertiary institutions continued to comment on and polish the textbook materials as Series Five was being written. Tang Jun remembers that much of the polishing work was carried out by David Crook and Xu Guozhang from Beijing Foreign Languages Institute.[7] The materials production team were given clear-cut responsibilities, as managing editors, text editors and writers, and — in a move designed to enhance commitment to quality — all team members would be credited by name in the final version of the textbooks. In the event, the textbooks list ten writers.

The process of writing the textbooks was also reorganized. The credits in the textbooks acknowledge the help received from various individuals as well as 'teachers and educationalists [who] also made a number of invaluable comments'. Questionnaire surveys were conducted among senior teachers to gather their opinions on the content, organization and methodology of the textbooks; feedback was also collected at seminars and by means of a post-piloting survey of teachers at three schools in Beijing and Tianjin in 1962–63. Tang Jun recalls that the teachers made many suggestions, of which the most influential were: that the contents should be relevant to the students' educational needs and should be written in idiomatic English; that extra care should be taken in the early stages of the course in facilitating the teaching of pronunciation, handwriting, spelling and oral English; and, the presentation of new vocabulary should be sequenced from concrete to abstract, with words that frequently occur in daily life being placed at the beginning of the course.[8] The developers also took into account criticisms by teachers of Series Four, which was considered to place a very heavy learning burden upon students. Accordingly, adjustments were made to the number of vocabulary items to be covered, and the early stages of the course were designed to incorporate a more simple progression from the alphabet to short passages. After the textbooks had been piloted in three schools, adjustments were made in the light of feedback from teachers. One major recommendation was to replace the gothic form of handwriting presented in the draft version with italic style. There was some deliberation among the consultants and the textbook writers concerning the pedagogical approach to be adopted. Xu Guozhang preferred a much stronger literary, Grammar-Translation orientation to the move in Series Four to incorporate more colloquial oral components. However, Tang Jun and other members of the project team decided to follow this latter trend, given the support of teachers for more realistic oral English.[9]

According to notes in the syllabus, the textbook writers had three ways of producing passages. The first was to create their own: these formed the majority of passages in Books 1 and 2 in Series Five. The second way was to use (and adapt as necessary) stories, fables, articles and political tracts from English language sources, including passages in Series Four, and this made up about one-third of the passages in Books 3 and 4 and the majority of Books 5 and 6. The third way was to use translations of Chinese passages (which accounted for a small part of Books 3 to 6). This balance was designed to ensure that the language was as realistic (i.e., resembling what was perceived as real-life English) as possible. The antecedents of some of the passages in Series Five are shown in Table 4.4.

Table 4.4   Antecedents of some passages in Series Five

Passage in Series Five	Title	Antecedent
Book 3 Lesson 10	The Fox and the Crow	'Chinese Language for Primary School' Book 2 Lesson 22 (1948)
Book 3 Lesson 13	Study as Lenin Studied	Series Four Book 2 Lesson 13
Book 3 Lesson 15	The Wolf and the Lamb	Series Four Book 2 Lesson 18
Book 3 Lesson 19	The Cock Crows at Midnight	Series Four Book 2 Lesson 22
Book 4 Lesson 1	A Blanket	Series Four Book 3 Lesson 11
Book 5 Lesson 1	Chairman Mao and the Wounded Soldier	'Chinese Language Primary Readers' Book 7 Lesson 3 (1958)
Book 5 Lesson 14	Sambo (I)	'Chinese Language Primary Readers' Book 10 Lesson 31 (1957)
Book 5 Lesson 15	Sambo (II)	'Chinese Language Primary Readers' Book 10 Lesson 31 (1957)

Another innovation of the 1963 curriculum was the publication of a syllabus. This was a 28-page document in Chinese, setting out teaching aims and requirements, teaching content, the organization of the teaching content, pedagogical considerations, and the detailed requirements and content for each year group. Although the linguistic components of the syllabus were drawn up before the textbooks in Series Five were written, it is clear that parts of the syllabus were written after the contents of the textbooks had been decided, as indicated by the sections in the syllabus that describe and name the various passages that appear in the textbooks. This means that the symbiotic relationship between syllabus and textbooks that was noted in previous series existed in the case of the 1963 curriculum, with the exception that the 1963 syllabus was actually published for public reference.

The syllabus covers a comprehensive range of issues relating to the macro- and micro-level aims and objectives of the curriculum. It also sets out how the 'red and expert' balance between political and subject-specific goals might be handled, and begins to explicate a view on pedagogy and learning. The preamble to the syllabus, which appeared in May 1963, identifies international understanding, as well as information transfer as a goal:

> Foreign language learning is an important tool in developing cultural and scientific knowledge, to carry out international interaction, to foster cultural exchanges, and to increase the understanding between peoples of different countries. English is commonly used throughout the world. A good grasp of English enables us to absorb the aspects of science and technology which will help socialist construction; to introduce our experience to friendly countries and people; to strengthen our relationship with people in different countries; and to empower people in different countries to combat imperialism. (PEP, 1963: 1, in translation)

The reference to imperialism links the syllabus to a major theme of Chinese diplomacy that emerged after the Bandung agreement on the Five Principles of Peaceful Co-existence in 1955. China's policy was to seek solidarity with other Asian countries, by highlighting their shared experiences of imperialism (Wilson, 1984).

For junior secondary students, the syllabus has the following targets:

> … students are required to master 1,500 to 2,000 words and some set phrases, to acquire basic knowledge and skills in pronunciation, vocabulary and syntax; and to develop a preliminary ability to read simple texts, a certain ability to make sentences and to conduct simple everyday conversations. (PEP, 1963: 1–2, in translation)

These are broken down into annual targets, which are summarized in Table 4.5 (see p. 96).

According to the syllabus, the vocabulary should be chosen carefully:

> Those words which the students are required to master … should be drawn mainly from frequently used vocabulary in daily life, study, production, labour and social activities, as well as some words and phrases about the customs and habits of English speaking countries. An appropriate number of words from natural science, social science and key words, such as the names of places, countries and people should also be selected. (PEP, 1963: 3, in translation)

Table 4.5   Specific learning targets in the 1963 syllabus (adapted from PEP, 1963)

Junior Secondary Year 1

1. Mastering the alphabet and transcriptions; accurate pronunciation of single and double-syllable words that conform to regular pronunciation patterns; reading all lessons aloud and reciting the passages
2. Answering simple questions about passages and making simple sentences; using standard handwriting and basic punctuation
3. Speaking by imitating passages and using conventional conversation; understanding simple classroom language; completing a simple dictation of 25 words within about 10 minutes
4. Acquiring about 600 words and a few idioms

Junior Secondary Year 2

1. Reading aloud clearly and correctly; mastering stress and intonation of simple sentences; being able to recite about 80% of passages
2. Writing sentences without serious error using the present simple, present continuous, future simple and past simple tenses; copying skilfully with neat handwriting
3. Asking and answering questions relating to the passages; understanding the teacher's retelling of the passage; understanding and responding to classroom language; completing a short dictation of 40 words within about 10 minutes
4. Acquiring another 600 words or so and a few idioms

Junior Secondary Year 3

1. Translating passages correctly into Chinese; reading the passages fluently with correct pronunciation and intonation; being able to recite about 70% of passages; being able to use small dictionaries to prepare the passage in advance; being able to understand passages with a limited amount of new vocabulary and grammar
2. Writing sentences correctly or translating accurately from Chinese; retelling the passage in writing; using neat handwriting and appropriate layout
3. Answering questions relating to the passages; talking about familiar daily life topics; understanding the teacher's introduction to the passage; participating in conversations with the teacher about certain classroom activities
4. Acquiring another 600 words or so and a few phrases

This attention to vocabulary reflects the expertise of Tang Jun in the field.[10] Her technique was to draw up categories of vocabulary that she considered relevant to the pupils' needs. She then selected words from existing lists such as Thorndike's that were based on frequency counts in English-speaking countries. Then she added any words not on the lists that she felt were useful in the Chinese context.

The syllabus also sets out some principles for choosing reading passages, and they reflect the suggestions made by teachers in the consultative process:

> The language should be appropriate and include sufficient examples to enhance learning English. The content and ideas should be beneficial to the students — or at least have no harmful effects. ... There should be a wide range of topics: passages should include ones about class struggle and the

struggle over production in English-speaking countries, the life, customs, culture and historical traditions of these countries, and there should also be some passages introducing our own country. Some passages about popular science and socio-political issues can also be chosen. (PEP, 1963: 5, in translation)

The guidelines suggest that the English curriculum serves some political purposes, but there is an acknowledgement of the problems caused to teachers and curriculum developers by changes in the political climate, as occurred with Series Two and Series Three:

We should not have a one-sided view that foreign language study serves proletarian politics, or over-emphasize the ideas and contents of the reading passages. However, as textbooks are fixed but the social situation is changing, teachers should use the textbooks flexibly according to the prevailing climate, should some passages not be compatible with the times. (PEP, 1963: 11, in translation)

It offers advice on principles of learning:

The passage in each lesson and the vocabulary and grammar of the passage should be compatible with the students' receptive ability, and arranged in accordance with such principles as from superficial to deep, from easy to difficult, and from concrete to abstract ... The presentation of grammar can usually be carried out using the inductive method, ... which is adopted because it makes it easy for the students to imitate and apply grammatical phenomena. (PEP, 1963: 9–10, in translation)

The syllabus thus shows a stronger concern for pedagogy, teachers' views and student learning than was evident in earlier curricula. It is consistent with Tang Lixing's (1983) description of this period as a time of development in English Language teaching practices.

For Series Five, the PEP published six textbooks, a set of teacher's handbooks and, another innovation, cassette tapes of the reading passages. Each book was intended for use in one semester: Books 1 and 2 for Junior Secondary Year 1, and so on. Despite the sophistication of the curriculum development process, the technical aspects of the final product are inconsistent, with some books being larger than others. Books 1, 3, 5 and 6 measure 18.42 cm x 13 cm ($7\frac{1}{4}$ inches x 5.12 inches), while Books 2 and 4 are 20.32 cm x 13.97 cm (8 inches x $5\frac{1}{2}$ inches). Books 1 to 5 have a pale yellow cover with single colour printing (a different colour for each book in the series), but Book 6 has a grey cover (Figure A.5, p. 212).

Pedagogy

The organization of Series Five follows familiar patterns. The books are divided into lessons, and the series is also topic-based. Book 1 has 32 lessons, Book 2 has 30, Book 3 has 21, Book 4 has 20, Book 5, 16 and Book 6, 14. The early stages of the course have more lessons because the content of each lesson is less time-consuming. In the later stages, the reading passages are longer and appear to require more intensive study. Throughout the series, the lessons are organized around the passage, which provides the topic that is the context for the practice of individual linguistic components. There is no vocabulary list related to the passage, but in Book 3 (alone) new words are presented in bold in the main body of the passage. Generally, the lessons contain the following elements:

1. the passage
2. highlighted phrases or a rhyme
3. grammar focus
4. exercises (e.g. phonetics, reading comprehension, parsing, transformation exercises focusing on grammar points, fill-in-the-blanks)

However, by the later stages of the course, there are basically two elements: the reading passage and exercises.

The passages in Series Five start with relatively weak discourse. Individual vocabulary items or dialogues about objects are presented in uncontextualized forms. For instance, Book 1 Lesson 6 has dialogues such as:

> What is this?
> It is a desk.
> What is that?
> It is a lamp. (Series Five Book 1: 19)

The speakers and the reasons for asking the questions are not clear, although pictures of the relevant objects are given. The dialogue serves to present deictic question and answer forms, rather than to give a realistic model of conversational English.

As with Series Four, Book 3 is a turning point in the series. The amount of new grammar explicitly taught is reduced (only 5 lessons out of 21 have a grammar section). The reading passages become longer and there are fewer dialogues than in the previous two books. Instead of the lesson consisting of a number of discrete learning elements (such as a teaching and learning focus on phonetics, grammar, etc.) topically related to the passage, the reading passage itself becomes the major learning experience, supported by related exercises. Thus the study of the written word in the form of literature becomes dominant. This is consistent with a shift from the Structural Approach to the

Grammar-Translation Method — a focus on building up the students' knowledge of the language system early in the course is followed by a focus on reading passages for detailed analysis and translation. The presence of dialogues is an indication of attention to oral skills, which was an emergent trend in Series Four.

By Book 3, the discourse is uniformly strong. In accordance with the syllabus, the genres of passages include stories, such as 'Chairman Mao and the Wounded Soldier' in Book 5 Lesson 1; scientific passages, such as 'How Coal is Formed' in Book 5 Lesson 3; descriptions of socio-political situations in China and elsewhere, as in 'National Day' in Book 3 Lesson 3 and 'New Awakening of the American Negroes' in Book 5 Lesson 16; personal letters and diaries, such as 'A Letter to a Friend' in Book 3 Lesson 11; situational interactions, as in 'Shopping' in Book 4 Lesson 7; and political tracts, such as 'Imperialism and All Reactionaries are Paper Tigers' in Book 6 Lesson 1. This shift from weak to strong discourse is compatible with the aims of the guidelines to move from simple to difficult and from concrete to abstract: essentially, it is moving from the tightly structured to the loosely structured, in terms of linguistic control, and is associated with the change in pedagogy to a greater focus on reading skills.

In the pedagogical approaches, as with other aspects, there is a strong resemblance between Series Five and earlier series, with the exception of Series Three. All these series move from an initial emphasis on discrete linguistic items to one on reading skills. The intended pedagogy in Series Five, as spelt out in the syllabus, stresses practice by the students for developing all four language skills. Teachers can contribute to the process by giving clear explanations, but the following strategies are strongly recommended: getting students to read aloud and recite passages from memory; holding question and answer sessions with the students about the contents of a passage; giving a dictation; getting the students to write sentences; and getting the students to translate and compose passages. Furthermore, extracurricular activities were suggested in the syllabus to supplement regular lessons: these could include reading simplified novels; singing English songs; making wall posters; having a handwriting exhibition, spelling contests, speech competitions and dialogue performances; and using gramophone records, tape recorders, slides and microphones.

The last suggestion may indicate the influence of Audiolingualism that was entering China at the time — and was also hinted at in Series Four. Gramophone records and tape reels produced by companies such as Linguaphone were popular means of promoting self-study in foreign languages, most notably through the use of pattern drills. There were also pedagogical experiments using Linguaphone and similar materials for secondary school English teaching (Price, 1979), and David Crook, Isabel Crook and Margaret Turner, three of the consultants for Series Five, were instrumental in introducing this pedagogy to China, according to Liu Daoyi.[11] However, the only drills in Series Five are phonetic drills, not sentence drills that are most commonly associated with Audiolingualism.

It appears, therefore, that the focus on oracy was in keeping with contemporary international trends, but Audiolingualism itself was not adopted in Series Five. The mimetic pedagogy of Series Four remains, but is extended to include a greater amount of student practice which is not just recitation but also freer communication. The aim to develop oracy is in accordance with the recommendations of the report produced prior to the development of the new curriculum, and is supported by contents of different passages that touch on pedagogy, such as Book 3 Lesson 1:

> Chang :   ... Have you got the new English text-book?
> Li   :   Yes. Here it is. Look, there are lots of pictures in it.
> Chang :   Then there must be a lot of stories.
> Li   :   I hope there are some poems and plays, too.
> Chang :   So do I. I'm sure the lessons will be very interesting.
> Li   :   Yes. Now how shall we improve our English this term?
> Chang :   Our teacher says speaking helps a lot. So let's try to speak English whenever we meet.
> Li   :   That's a good idea. (Series Five Book 3: 1–2)

Another feature of the recommended pedagogy, the use of question and answer routines involving the teacher and the students, is exemplified in Book 2 Lesson 13, 'An English Lesson'. Learning strategies are also reinforced:

> Chang :   ... Can you tell me how you learn the new words?
> Wang :   Well, I learn them this way. When I read a new text, I pay a lot of attention to the pronunciation and spelling of the new words. At the same time I try to remember their meaning in the sentence. I put them down in my notebook, and carry it about with me. In this way I can go over the words from time to time. (Series Five Book 3 p. 46)

The messages concerning intended pedagogy in the syllabus and the textbooks are consistent: they bring out the importance of oracy as well as literacy, and the need for students to take responsibility for their own learning by developing effective strategies.

Series Five thus follows the trends towards oracy in most of the previous series, but sets out, for the first time, a coherent description of the intended pedagogy in the syllabus. This encompasses a specific approach to spoken skills (deep learning through recitation and free practice), plus the familiar combination of the Structural Approach and the Grammar-Translation Method.

Grammar

1. **What** is ↘this?
   It is *a* ↘chair.

2. What ↘is it, then?
   It is a ↘star.

3. Compare:

   1) **What** is **this**?

   这 是 什么?

   2) This **is not** a bag.

   这 不 是(一个)书包。

   3) **Is this** a cap? 这是(一顶)帽子吗?

4. **This** is *the* earth.   This is *a* pen.
   That is *the* sky.   That is *a* book.
   That is *the* sun.   That is *a* star.
   That is *the* moon.   That is *a* lamp.

Exercises

I. Read; then say in Chinese:

   box   pen
   not   bed
   cook   desk
   what   then

II. Change these into negative and interrogative sentences:

   1. This is a desk.   2. This is the earth.
   3. That is a chair.   4. That is the sky.

III. Answer these questions:

   1. What is this?

· **20** ·

Figure 4.2   Extract from Series Five

The grammar section of this lesson shows the use of the mother tongue for contrastive linguistics (e.g. the word order in Chinese is the reverse of the English 'What is this?') and for vocabulary reinforcement. Students are introduced to English grammatical terms (e.g. 'negative' and 'interrogative') from an early stage of the series (Series Five Book 1, p. 20).

Linguistic components

The linguistic components of Series Five are organized according to established patterns, but with some variations at the early stage of the series. The series has a linear progression, which includes the alphabet, the International Phonetic Alphabet (IPA), oral production of vocabulary, single sentences, questions and answers, simple dialogues, and reading passages. This contrasts with the more complex and somewhat muddled progression of linguistic components in Series Four Book 1. The sequence of tenses in Series Five is: present simple, present continuous, future simple, past simple, past continuous, present perfect and past perfect. This is basically the same sequence as in Series Four (although that series did not have a focus on the past continuous, and also extended the range of tenses to include the future-in-the-past). Series Five starts with demonstratives, the verbs *to be* and *to have*, pronouns, comparison of adjectives and various kinds of clauses and sentence structures. Again, the range of grammar points is less comprehensive than Series Four, and more than half of the lessons in Series Five do not have an explicit grammar focus. This reduction in the learning load is consistent with the materials developers' decision to respond to teachers' criticism of the heavy demands and steep learning curve of Series Four, and to provide an easier progression for students from learning the alphabet to producing simple sentences in English. However, there is an increase in the new vocabulary specified for lessons in Series Five (2,106) compared with Series Four (1,272). According to Tang Jun, this arises from the use of more realistic reading passages in Series Five, particularly in Books 5 and 6, and from more time being available for English in the timetable for schools operating the twelve-year schooling system (for which Series Five was intended).[12]

Content

Series Five is relatively less politicized than Series Four, and also contains a lower percentage of moral messages. Of 165 examples of discourse identified in the series, more than half have no obvious political or moral message (Table 4.6). The percentage of political messages is the lowest in any series since Series One.

Table 4.6   Political and moral messages in Series Five

Discourse total	Messages total	Nil	Moral	Political	Political (attitude)	Political (information)	Political (role model)
165	167	85 (50.90%)	26 (15.57%)	56 (33.53%)	30	3	23

The political messages are similar to those in Series Four, which had passages with a strong patriotic or socialist message. One notable difference, however, is that the passages about communes in Series Four are replaced by political tracts in Series Five (e.g., 'Imperialism Will Not Last Long' in Book 5 Lesson 2; 'Imperialism and All Reactionaries Are Paper Tigers' in Book 6 Lesson 1; and 'The Revolutionary Tradition of the Good Eighth Company' in Book 6 Lessons 7 and 8). These themes reflect the political climate of the time: the People's Communes were a product of the Great Leap Forward at the end of the 1950s, but the results in the early 1960s disappointed many Chinese leaders. Also, by 1963, the war in Vietnam was exacerbating tensions between China and the USA. This accounts for the positive portrayal of North Vietnam in Book 6 Lesson 12, which tells of a young supporter of Ho Chi Minh, the leader of the communist forces:

A Letter from South Viet Nam

Can Tho Town
March 30, 1963

Dear Chieu,

....

On April 7 last year, we cadres were holding a meeting in a village near the town. We had sent Little An out on a secret mission and were waiting for his return.

Coming back from the mission, Little An found the village surrounded by the U.S.-Diem clique. He took off his coat and wrapped two hand-grenades in it.

Suddenly a shout was heard behind him: "Stop, boy!"

Little An ran at full speed along the path. The pursuit went on, the enemy following him closely. Whistles were heard. The boy ran, holding in his arms the torn black coat. He headed for the other side of the village opposite to the place where the meeting was being held. The enemy was thus put on the wrong track.

Now an old wall about two metres high crossed his path and blocked his way. The fourteen-year-old boy stopped and stood with his back up against it. From three different directions the enemy soldiers advanced towards him. He calmly took the pin of a grenade out with his teeth and waited.

The boy threw the grenade at the first group when they were about four metres from him. Three were killed. When the second group on his left came close enough Little An threw his second and last grenade at them. Some staggered in the cloud of smoke. The third group on his right crept slowly towards him, joined by the survivors from the first two groups. He rolled up his coat, making believe that he was wrapping a grenade in it.

> The sun was already high and shining on his face. He threw out his little sunburnt chest, and faced the enemy, so that it looked as if he were ready to throw a third grenade at them. White as death they stopped short. Two gun shots rang out. Wounded in the chest Little An staggered and his coat fell down at his feet. He looked at his enemies calmly. Another shot. Little An shouted in a broken voice: "Long live ... Uncle Ho ... !" "Down with ... U.S. imperialism!"
>
> Little An died a heroic death. When we heard of it, a fire of anger burnt in our hearts. We are determined to avenge him. We are determined to do everything we can for the liberation of our south and unification of our motherland. Little An will always live in our memory.
>
> Quang
> (Series Five Book 6: 43–5)

It also accounts for the negative portrayals of the USA and its allies, as in 'The Miner and Coal' in Book 2 Lesson 14, about an unemployed miner impoverished by capitalism, and the description of an English town in Book 3 Lesson 4, which includes the following:

> On the south side of the town there is a river. It runs from east to west. It is not very wide but it is quite deep. And the water is not at all clean. Along the river there are many small and shabby houses. The streets in this part of the town are narrow and not at all straight. The poor working people live here. (Series Five Book 3: 11–2)

The moral messages focus on familiar themes, such as having good work attitudes and study skills, being an active and helpful member of society, being determined in the face of adversity and always doing one's best.

The relative mildness of the political messages in Series Five is also emphasized by the fact that only about 50 of the 781 non-Thorndike words have strong political connotations. The rest are related to everyday words, names of relatives, animals, sports, food, sickness, places and specific vocabulary items arising from a reading passage. The selection of passages reflects the recommendations of the syllabus, that realistic materials should be used as far as possible, even if they are neutral in terms of political and moral messages, but unsuitable passages (i.e., which promote a 'decadent capitalist' lifestyle) should be avoided.

Summary

The second phase of curriculum development described in this chapter was set against a backdrop of national policies that were primarily oriented towards national economic construction and of relative openness towards English-speaking nations. An existing portrayal of this period describes it as a 'renaissance' for English Language teaching (Tang Lixing, 1983). In terms of the curriculum development process, this second phase was certainly a time of innovations that sought to improve upon the muddling-through of the previous phase. The higher official status of English and the relatively low degree of politicization in the socio-political environment allowed for changes in the processes and products of curriculum development which aimed at improving the quality of pedagogy and lessening the political content. These changes were started for Series Four and extended for Series Five. They included: strengthening research prior to curriculum development; the formation of a centrally-dominated pluralistic structure for curriculum development with clearly defined responsibilities; a willingness to look beyond China and the USSR for pedagogical ideas (although the influence of new foreign trends is not strongly evident in the pedagogy of either series in this phase); an increased sensitivity to the needs of grassroots teachers of English; a wider range of published resources, such as a syllabus, teacher's handbooks and tapes; and a more elaborate organization of textbook content, which saw a shift towards an amalgam of oracy and literacy-oriented pedagogies, thereby extending the main skills focus from reading to also embrace listening, speaking and writing.

Three factors in particular contributed to this attention to educational quality. Firstly, at the macro-level, the socio-political climate became relatively depoliticized, with backlashes against the USSR, following the schism, and against politicization after the failure of various political campaigns. English had a higher official status in China than in the late 1950s, although there were still international tensions, for instance over Vietnam. Secondly and thirdly, at the meso-level, the PEP and, at the micro-level, teachers had garnered useful experience from the first phase of curriculum development, which had revealed various shortcomings. The process of curriculum development in this phase is characterized by a move away from the pragmatic, expedient and relatively incoherent 'garbage can' approach that was a feature of the first phase to one of greater pluralism, or 'democratic centralism', to use Leung's (1991) description and a higher degree of curriculum coherence, which was achieved by the establishment of a mechanism with clearly defined roles for the PEP, outside agencies and teachers. This move was facilitated by the wider availability of suitable personnel and the acquisition of appropriate expertise. The PEP now possessed the personnel to design and produce the syllabus and materials in-house, with input from a consultative editorial committee and from teachers. The functions of the outside agencies and teachers were not mere rubber-stamping; the influence of the outside agencies, through members serving on the editorial committee, and of the teachers, through their suggestions and feedback, was evident in the incorporation of their input in the finalized syllabuses and textbook resources.

There was still some political content, supporting current policies, but this was considerably reduced from the three series in the first phase. The PEP appeared to have struck an acceptable balance of political, economic (as reflected in the concern for 'expertise' in English Language) and pedagogical influences in the second phase, as neither series was completely rejected by teachers (who did, nevertheless, criticize Series Four) or political leaders until 1966, when the radical leftists regained power and the Cultural Revolution started.

One result of the greater attention to pedagogical quality was the longer lifespan of Series Four compared to previous series, although this was helped by the relatively stable political environment in China until 1966. Series Four was used until the Cultural Revolution, five years after its initial publication. It was also influential in the development of post-Cultural Revolution series, as shown in Chapter 6. However, the series was not free from criticism. Teachers complained to the PEP that the vocabulary load was heavy for students throughout the series and, in the early stages, the move from the alphabet to extended discourse (i.e., the reading passages) was too rapid for the students. These comments were taken into account when Series Five was produced. Series Five reflects the relative depoliticization of the period in the reduction of political content, and also reflects the pluralistic nature of the development process by demonstrating a range of pedagogical influences — views on domestic and international trends in language learning from the consultants, as well as the grassroots concerns of junior secondary school teachers. Despite this attention to quality, Series Five lasted for just three years: it was published by the PEP for use in schools from September 1963 onwards, and was used until 1966, when the Cultural Revolution began. Materials to extend the course for use in senior secondary school were prepared for introduction in 1966 but they were never published. Tang Jun recalls that, as the politicization that marked the Cultural Revolution got underway, Series Five was discarded as 'useless' by the Ministry of Education.[13] As a result of the chaos of the Cultural Revolution, it was not until 1982 that this sophisticated system of curriculum development was eventually emulated and further strengthened.

5 The Cultural Revolution, 1966–76

The heyday of English in China's schools was brief. The two political lines (i.e., ideology-oriented and economics-oriented) which could be discerned in the CCP as early as the mid-1950s came into sharp conflict once more in the mid-1960s, as Mao Zedong felt his political power base under threat from economic reformers. Mao responded to the reforms of the early 1960s by launching the Great Proletarian Cultural Revolution, as the movement was euphemistically called, through an editorial published by the *Liberation Army Daily* on 18 April 1966 (Hsü, 1990). The agenda for the Cultural Revolution adopted at the Eleventh Plenum of the Eighth CCP Central Committee on 8 August 1966 was summarized in sixteen points in the 'Decision of the Central Committee of the Chinese Communist Party Concerning the Great Proletarian Cultural Revolution'. The movement was designed to 'criticize-struggle-transform', in particular 'to struggle against and overthrow those persons in authority who are taking the capitalist road, to criticise and repudiate the reactionary bourgeois academic "authorities" and the ideology of the bourgeoisie and all other exploiting classes and to transform education, literature and art and all other parts of the superstructure not in correspondence with the socialist economic base' (quoted in Li, 1995: 411).

The Cultural Revolution was the largest and longest lasting of the political movements that Mao launched in China. Mao's aims were to re-establish class struggle as the main thrust of policy and social action, to eradicate feudal customs, culture and ideas, and to place the country under his supreme leadership. These were to be achieved by politicizing the masses and mobilizing the youth as the vanguard of the movement (Hsü, 1990). One of the sixteen points was the formation of the *hong weibing* (Red Guards) as leaders of the revolutionary movement against capitalist tendencies and traditional aspects of Chinese society. This move confirmed earlier indications that education would be one of the focal points of the Cultural Revolution. In a letter to Defence Minister, Lin Biao, dated 7 May 1966, Mao Zedong wrote:

> While the students' main task is to study, they should also learn other things: that is to say, they should not only learn book knowledge, they should also learn industrial production, agricultural production, and military affairs. They should also criticise and repudiate the bourgeoisie. The length of schooling should be shortened, education should be revolutionised, and the domination of our schools and colleges by bourgeois intellectuals should not be tolerated any longer. (Quoted by Löfstedt, 1980: 124)

The Red Guards initially went about their task with violent zeal. Anarchy broke out in schools in many places, with gangs of Red Guards abandoning their schooling to undertake journeys around the country to carry out political campaigns that often involved struggle sessions, *chaojia* (ransacking homes) and beatings. In 1967, the PLA entered those schools that remained open to give military and political training to teachers and students engaged in revolutionary activities. Many educational organizations, including the PEP, were closed down and staff were rusticated or assigned to manual labour — PEP staff were sent from Beijing to work on farms or as shop assistants in rural towns. Intellectuals were not the only group to suffer: the class struggle involved anyone suspected of harbouring bourgeois or capitalist sentiments. English Language teachers were major targets because of the connotations of capitalism, privilege and other forms of political undesirability associated with English. They were criticized, vilified and persecuted.

The plan for educational reform published by the Central Committee of the CCP in January 1967 called for a reorientation of the foreign language curriculum: 'Destroy and abolish all old textbooks; compose and publish new ones. Foreign language textbooks should be reviewed and rewritten, and Chairman Mao's works, anti-revisionist articles or similar materials incorporated in them' (cited in Löfstedt, 1980: 128). Popular slogans at the time were 'I am Chinese. Why do I need foreign languages?' and 'Don't learn ABC. Make revolution!' (Qun and Li, 1991). Understandably, teachers were very reluctant to teach English Language classes at this time. For students, too, there were no inherent benefits: proficiency in English would not lead to improved career or study prospects in the contemporary political climate. English ceased to be taught throughout China. As an English Language teacher, Tang Lixing recalls:

> The effects of the political movement and nationalist sentiment upon foreign language teaching [were] almost disastrous. All the textbooks were banned and criticized. Foreign language teachers were falsely accused of being spies of foreign countries or flunkeys of Imperialism or worshippers of everything foreign. [Teaching English] was so affected by distrust and dislike of all things foreign that even when such subjects as Chinese, maths [and] history were resumed, English was still widely rejected. This author [Tang Lixing] had the experience when he was first assigned to a secondary school as an English teacher in 1968, he was told by the school authorities that English was not

taught and for more than one year he had to teach politics and history. (Tang Lixing, 1983: 44)

The anarchy of the early phase of the Cultural Revolution caused disquiet even amongst the leaders who had been particularly active in creating the mass mobilization. Thereafter, the Red Guards were urged to return home. Schools were reopened from 1968 onwards, although they were drastically remodelled as centres for political indoctrination and radicalization (Löfstedt, 1980; Pepper, 1996). Educational policy and practices reversed many of those that were features of the early 1960s. Where the economic reformers had preferred the teaching profession to comprise a body of educators with limited political functions, cleansed of the stigma of class labels and equipping the new generation to contribute to national economic development, the Maoists wanted to turn the classroom into a microcosm of revolutionary society, with teachers leading students in class struggle and critical reassessment of the current social and political order. The reforms in education were wide-ranging. The school year was shortened. Formal examinations and tests were abolished — instead, correct revolutionary attitudes became the credentials for higher study. Students' credentials for graduation were likewise determined on the grounds of ideological suitability. Work-study programmes proliferated. Workers, peasants and soldiers took control of schools and taught lessons. They organized military training, farm work and factory experience. Rustication policies for students and secondary school graduates were introduced, and urban teenagers were assigned to rural communes far from home. The time in the curriculum allocated to laodong (physical labour) increased (Löfstedt, 1980; Pepper, 1996).

A turning point in the fortunes of English came when Mao told Red Guard leaders at Peking University in 1968 that he regretted not learning English early in life:

> It is good to know English. I studied foreign languages late in life. I suffered. One has to learn foreign languages when one is young. ... It is good to learn English. Foreign language study should be started in primary school (quoted in Unger, 1982: 282).

Soon after Mao made this statement, which was published in national newspapers, English Language started to reappear on the school curriculum. The English Language textbooks produced by local committees in 1969 and 1970 were highly politicized, and paid scant attention to pedagogy:

> Textbooks always began with "Long live" and ended with "Quotations" [from Chairman Mao]. Throughout the book, there was not a single text dealing with a foreign theme or foreign culture. To teach textbooks like this, ... [the teacher] never had to worry about teaching methods; he did not even have

to prepare his lessons. All he had to do was teach the new words, read the text, and translate the text into Chinese. ... No tests or evaluations were given, because tests and examinations were condemned as treating students like enemies. ... [There were] crises of motivation and discipline. The profession ... had undergone its most severe winter. (Tang Lixing, 1983: 44–5)

Factionalism and instability continued to characterize the Cultural Revolution, even after the mass mobilization had ceased. For instance, Mao's once trusted ally, Lin Biao, was killed in the aftermath of an apparent coup attempt in 1971. However, the status of English improved in the early 1970s as the political and economic climate shifted. Premier Zhou Enlai, who appeared to be a constraining influence on the political zeal of the Cultural Revolution, issued a directive in 1972 that educational work should be more concerned with quality than productive labour. Examinations, abhorred and abolished by the Maoists, were re-introduced for university entrance. At this time, there were signs of *détente* with the instigation of 'ping-pong diplomacy' through sporting contacts with the USA and other capitalist countries and the visit of the US President, Richard Nixon, in 1972. Such changes were short-lived, however, for a new radical political group known as the 'Gang of Four' came to prominence in 1973. The group, comprising Mao's wife, Jiang Qing and three supporters from Shanghai, Zhang Chunqiao, Yao Wenyuan and Wang Hongwen, espoused policies that emphasized struggle against opposing groups, and a new period of political persecution began. One campaign, the 'Pi Lin Pi Kong' ('Criticize Lin Biao, Criticize Confucius') movement, was directed against the traditional values of Confucian education, *inter alia*. The Great Education Debate that followed in 1974–76 brought into sharp conflict the two competing views of education. The radical political group predominated until the death of Mao in September 1976 seriously eroded the Gang's power base, and they were arrested the following month. Their demise ultimately cleared the way for more moderate leadership and a shift from 'politics to the fore' to an emphasis upon economic modernization under Deng Xiaoping.

During the Cultural Revolution, English was so politically sensitive that few regions of China promoted the subject; and many English Language teachers taught other subjects. If a school did offer English Language, it was often taught by untrained 'worker-peasant' volunteers (Tang Lixing, 1983). Where textbooks were produced (in major cities and some provinces), they were discarded once the Cultural Revolution ended and the PEP reopened. No copies were kept in the Ministry archives. The data for this chapter is therefore fragmentary, as I was only able to obtain some components of English Language textbook series for secondary schools produced in Beijing and Shanghai (three textbooks of each), and Tianjin and Shaanxi (one of each) during the early to mid-1970s.

The features of the English Language curriculum during the Cultural Revolution are shown in Table 5.1.

Table 5.1   Features of the English Language curriculum of the Cultural Revolution

	Various Cultural Revolution Series
Genesis	produced during periods of relative calm in time of politicization; Mao Zedong and Zhou Enlai encouraged study of English
Role and status of English	political transmission; low official status
Role of agencies PEP (Ministry of Education): Consultants: Teachers (grassroots):	inoperative inoperative designers and producers of teaching materials
Process	teams working in isolation
Syllabus	no specific syllabus
Resources	various regional textbooks
Organization	various; commonly including sentence and dialogue drills — reading passage — grammar exercises
Discourse	progression from weak to strong realism
Linguistic components	standard tense sequencing; controlled vocabulary
Intended pedagogy	Structural Approach, Grammar-Translation and Audiolingualism
Political and moral messages	mainly politicized messages; few moral messages

With the PEP closed down, the Cultural Revolution completely disrupted the curriculum development work of the early 1960s. Although it has not been possible to trace those concerned with local curriculum development during the early to mid-1970s, the dates of first publication of three of the series — the Shaanxi textbook in September 1973, the Shanghai series in December 1973, and the Beijing series in June 1976 — were linked to the move towards academic quality instigated by Zhou Enlai in 1972. The Tianjin series was first published in January 1972, suggesting that it was the product of an earlier move, maybe instigated by Mao's positive comments about learning English, to restore some teaching of English Language to the junior secondary school curriculum. The series were written by groups organized by the local education bureaux: the Shanghai series (which, confusingly, was also used in Tianjin) by the Shanghai Secondary and Primary Teaching Materials Editing Team; the Beijing series by the Beijing Municipal Education Bureau Teaching Materials Editing Team; the Shaanxi series by the Shaanxi Provincial Secondary and Primary Teaching Materials Editing Team and the Tianjin series by the Beijing Municipal Education Bureau Teaching Materials Editing Team.

Clues to the process of development are given in the introduction to the Shanghai series:

> According to the teaching of our Great Leader Chairman Mao that education must undergo thorough reform, the editorial team of Xuwei District in Baoshan County formed the English Language Education Group. This volume is an amendment of the teaching materials that underwent reform a few years ago. In the process of editing, the support of the worker-peasant-soldier masses and revolutionary teachers and students was sought. We also had support and assistance from relevant departments in Jiangsu Province, Zhejiang Province and Shandong Province. Editing new teaching materials for the proletariat is a difficult and long-term mission which requires continuous trial-and-error and adjustments. Regarding the problems that exist in these materials, we hope you comrades will put forward your valuable suggestions and criticisms. (Shanghai Series Book 7: 77, in translation)

The work of curriculum development was carried out by teachers at the grassroots, as it would be extremely unlikely that outside agencies (such as university scholars) would be available to work in a county district such as Xuwei. The editorial team states that it consulted teachers, students and the key revolutionary groups, the workers, peasants and soldiers, in compiling the textbooks, but it is difficult to ascertain the extent to which there was a genuine consultation process or whether the statement is rhetorical. The Tianjin series contains a similar introduction:

> One of the important aspects of the proletarian revolution in education is the thorough reform of the old teaching materials and the editing of new materials for the proletariat. Under the guidance of Chairman Mao's revolutionary educational thought, and with the assistance and support of the worker-peasant-soldier masses and the revolutionary teachers and students of our municipality, we edited this volume, which is for junior secondary three, semester two. Since we do not claim to have a thorough comprehension of the revolutionary educational thought of our Great Leader Chairman Mao, this teaching material is bound to have many mistakes and shortcomings. I hope the worker-peasant-soldier masses and the revolutionary teachers and students will point them out and criticise them. (Tianjin Series Book 4, preface, in translation)

The cautious comments in the final two sentences indicate the highly politicized climate of the Cultural Revolution and the nervousness of any groups entering the realms of public discourse, as publishing English language materials clearly had highly sensitive political implications at the time. The comments are also reminiscent of those made in the introductory notes to textbooks produced during the Great Leap Forward, an earlier period of politicization.

Analysis of the contents of the four series (Table 5.2) shows that the curriculum developers made reference to materials produced by the PEP before the Cultural Revolution, although some adaptations were made and new content introduced. There are also indications that the Shanghai and Beijing series writers referred to Chinese Language materials.

Table 5.2   Antecedents of some passages in Cultural Revolution English Language series

Passage in CR Series	Title	Antecedent
Shanghai Book 7 Lesson 3	At the Library	Series Four Book 1 Lesson 27
Shanghai Book 8 Lesson 5	Don't Forget Who Dug the Well	Series Five Book 3 Lesson 7
Shanghai Book 9 Lesson 5	Doctor Bethune and the Wounded Soldier	'Chinese Language Primary Readers' Book 5 Lesson 34 (1964)
Shanghai Book 9 Lesson 8	Lenin and the Guard	'Chinese Language Primary Readers' Book 7 Lesson 19 (1964)
Tianjin Book 4 Lesson 1	Lo Sheng-chiao	Series Two Book 3 Lesson 13
Tianjin Book 4 Lesson 3	Friendship Trees	Series Four Book 3 Lesson 9
Tianjin Book 4 Lesson 5	Yu Kung Removed the Mountains	Series Two Book 3 Lesson 17
Beijing Book 2 Lesson 2	My Family	Series Two Book 1 Lesson 13
Beijing Book 2 Lesson 3	A Dialogue	Series Two Book 1 Lesson 15
Beijing Book 2 Lesson 5	Our Classroom	Series One Book 1 Lesson 30
Beijing Book 5 Lesson 5	A Wolf in Sheep's Clothing	Series Three Book 9 Lesson 16
Beijing Book 5 Lesson 8	The Year	Series Four Book 3 Lesson 6
Beijing Book 6 Lesson 7	Chairman Mao and the Wounded Soldier	Series Three Book 10 Lessons 4 and 5
Beijing Book 6 Lesson 2	The Farmhand and the Snake	'Chinese Language Primary Readers' Book 9 Lesson 33 (1964)
Shaanxi Book 1 Lesson 1	Read and Write	Series Two Book 1
Shaanxi Book 1 Lesson 4	Map and Flag	Series Two Book 1 Lesson 4
Shaanxi Book 1 Lesson 7	I Am A Pupil	Series Two Book 1 Lesson 6

It has not been possible to obtain the syllabuses or guidelines appertaining to the series published during the Cultural Revolution, and no key informant can recollect seeing any. It is doubtful whether any were published. No new national syllabus was issued at this time, because the PEP had been closed down, so the series of textbooks that appeared were probably based on syllabuses or guidelines drawn up by the writing team for their own reference. Each series contains an introductory statement. As noted above, the Shanghai and Tianjin series state that the materials are for the 'proletariat', and have been written in accordance with Mao Zedong's ideas about revolutionary education. They do not mention how English could be put to use in contemporary Chinese society. However, an elaboration is found within the main body of the Shanghai series, in a dialogue between an old docker (Sung) and some junior secondary school pupils (Book 8 Lesson 1):

> Sung   : ... Try to tell me why you're learning English.
> Pupil B : We're learning English for the revolution.
> Sung   : That's right. We want to learn from the revolutionary people of other countries in the world. We also want to tell them about our country. (Shanghai Series Book 8: 2)

The four series that are analysed in this chapter comprise the following components: the Beijing series has six books for junior secondary school, and also caters for senior secondary level; the Shanghai series contains fourteen books, six of which are intended for junior secondary schools; the Shaanxi series has three books for junior secondary school level; and the Tianjin series has six books. For those series containing six books, each book covers the syllabus for one semester, while each of the Shaanxi books is designed to cover one year's syllabus. It is not known if other components (such as teacher's handbooks or tape recordings) were provided. Technically, the textbooks in all four series are simple productions (Figures A.6–9, pp. 212–3), especially the Shaanxi series, which is printed on poor quality paper and has a soft paper cover with a coloured band and a two-colour illustration of Yan'an. This is likely to be because Shaanxi Province was poorer than the major cities that produced the other series. All books are the same size, measuring 18.42 cm x 13 cm ($7\frac{1}{4}$ inches x 5.12 inches). Shanghai series has a strong paper cover, coloured front page and a line drawing of Shanghai waterfront, while the Beijing series has a soft white cover, with a two-colour picture of Tiananmen Square. The Tianjin series has a soft cover in cream with a coloured band, but no illustration.

Pedagogy

The limited amount of material available from the Cultural Revolution and the degree of decentralization of curriculum development in this period restricts the analysis that is possible with regard, in this case, to pedagogical concerns. Nonetheless, there is sufficient evidence for trends to be discerned.

The Shanghai series has, as a preface, a set of quotations (given in English) from Marx, Lenin and Mao Zedong about language:

> A foreign language is a weapon in the struggle of life. – Karl Marx
>
> Language is the most important means of human intercourse. – V.I. Lenin
>
> Why do we need to study language and, what is more, spend much effort on it? Because the mastery of language is not easy and requires painstaking effort. – Mao Tsetung (Shanghai Series Book 7, preface)

The main body of each book is made up of 'lessons': each lesson contains sufficient materials for several days' classes. The lessons start with a passage, which is usually an anecdote, description or a dialogue. In some cases, there is a brief dialogue at the end of the anecdote or description. This next section is a sentence pattern, followed by the vocabulary list (with phonetic transcription and Chinese translation). Next come notes on the passage, with an explanation in Chinese, some model utterances for oral practice, grammar points and exercises. The exercises cover a range of types, including phonetic recognition, substitute drills, fill-in-the-blanks, guided writing and open questions (e.g., 'Is there a library in your school? Where is the library?'). There is a general review at the end of each book. Later books (e.g., Book 8 and Book 9) have supplementary reading passages, and all books have appendices: a phonetics table and a vocabulary list in Book 7, and a list of irregular verbs and a vocabulary list in Book 8 and Book 9.

The series is based, at least as far as the available books are concerned, around the passages. The vocabulary appears to have been chosen according to the contents of the passage (as most of the discourse is quite realistic), although there is an element of control: each passage has a limited number of new words. There does, however, appear to be a graded grammar syllabus. For instance, in Book 7, the future simple and the use of *going to* for referring to future events are presented in consecutive lessons. This suggests that the writers chose the passages for their messages, but tailored the content so that the new language items would not be too numerous and would adhere to some structuring. The approach is predominantly Structural Approach and Grammar-Translation, but there are elements, such as the oral practice and open questions, that also suggest a more holistic communicative approach. This mixture is reflected in Shanghai Book 8 Lesson 1, in which a student of English describes his way of learning the language:

> I listen attentively in class and practise a lot. I read and write English every day. With the help of my teachers and comrades I've overcome a lot of difficulties. Now I can speak a little English. But I must go on working hard. (Shanghai Series Book 8: 2)

The approach in the Beijing series quite strongly reflects Audiolingual pedagogy, as each lesson starts with pattern drills for oral repetition. In the grammar sections, there are similar transformation and substitution drills to practise the grammatical structure. For instance, the substitute drill in Beijing Book 5 Lesson 6 is:

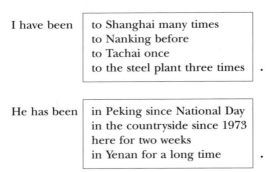

I have been | to Shanghai many times
to Nanking before
to Tachai once
to the steel plant three times | .

He has been | in Peking since National Day
in the countryside since 1973
here for two weeks
in Yenan for a long time | .

(Beijing Series Book 5: 43)

However, the reading passages are initially intended for intensive study according to Grammar-Translation principles, as no comprehension exercises are provided in Book 2 and Book 5 (but they do appear in Book 6). Thus the Beijing series, as with the Shanghai series, shows eclecticism, but is inclined more towards Audiolingualism than Grammar-Translation.

The Shaanxi series also displays eclecticism. The reading passages are the initial component in each lesson, followed by vocabulary study and a focus on the key grammatical structures. However, there are elements of Audiolingualism in the substitution drills that are used to practise the grammar. For instance, in Shaanxi Book 1 Lesson 11, the drill is:

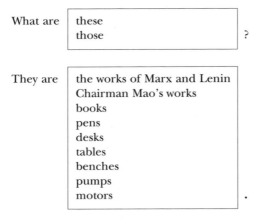

What are | these
those | ?

They are | the works of Marx and Lenin
Chairman Mao's works
books
pens
desks
tables
benches
pumps
motors | .

(Shaanxi Series Book 1: 52)

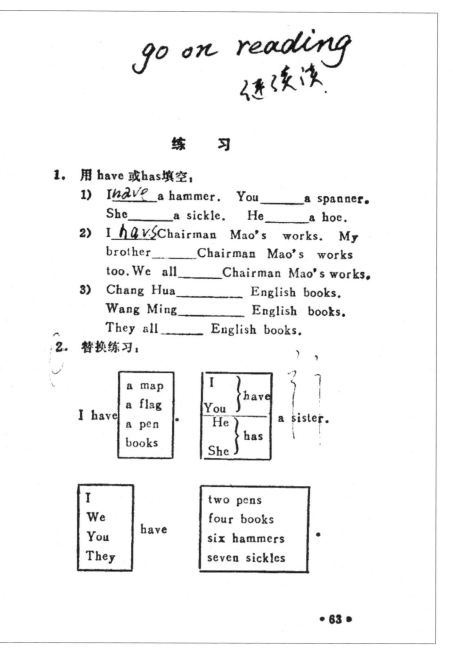

Figure 5.1   An exercise from the Shaanxi series, practising the verb *to have*

The handwritten notes are by the teacher, who formerly taught Russian and was trying to keep ahead of the students in his English Language classes (Shaanxi Series Book 1: 63).

This eclecticism is not evident in the book from the Tianjin series, which has a strong orientation towards Grammar-Translation. This series is also divided into lessons, with a general review, a revolutionary song ('The Internationale'), a list of irregular verbs and a vocabulary list. Each lesson starts with a reading passage — the central focus of each lesson — that is usually a story, followed by notes on the passage. The next section comprises exercises, including questions on the passage, phrases to learn by heart, sentences for reading aloud, composition topics and passages for translation from English into Chinese and vice versa. There is a specific grammar section in only three of the ten lessons in the available textbook, but the items covered (the passive voice, the infinitive, simple, compound and complex sentences, and adverbial clauses) appear in approximately the same order as they do in other series, such as the Beijing series (Book 6). This suggests a degree of control over the linguistic level of the contents, which is reinforced by the generally consistent amount of new vocabulary items per lesson.

From the limited evidence available, the Cultural Revolution series contain a mixture of Structural, Grammar-Translation and Audiolingual pedagogy. The use of Audiolingualism was seen to a small degree in Series Five, but there were no pattern drills, such as the ones above, in that series. Thus the main impact on the pedagogy of some Cultural Revolution series was the strengthening of features of Audiolingualism. This is an interesting development for the period, as Audiolingualism was associated with Western pedagogy. However, the series that contain Audiolingualism were produced during a relatively less politicized time as the Cultural Revolution was ending. Such pedagogy probably could not have been used when the movement was at its height in the late 1960s.

The Beijing series is divided into lessons, with appendices in each book. In Book 1, the appendices are a general review, a revolutionary song (once again, 'The Internationale'), a list of irregular verbs and a vocabulary list. All books have similar appendices, except that, in Book 2, 'Classroom Language' replaces the list of irregular verbs. The lessons start with sentence patterns, which are drilled, and then there is a passage. The exercises that complete the lesson are related to grammar practice. The linguistic components appear to be controlled, with the grammar following a set sequence, and the number of new vocabulary items in each lesson is evenly distributed.

The Shaanxi series starts with a quotation by Mao Zedong (in Chinese), which states 'Study can teach us things we did not understand before'. The early lessons are concerned with the alphabet and orthography. Each lesson has a set of vocabulary items or a passage as the course develops. These are followed by sections on grammar, pronunciation, classroom English and exercises. The grammar focuses mainly on the present simple tense, and the amount of new vocabulary is likewise controlled. At the end of the book, there are appendices on phonetics, orthography, vocabulary, the alphabet and military English:

(I)
rifle
hand-grenade
machine-gun
gun
mine
plane
tank
warship

(II)
Fall in!
Line up!
Attention!
Eyes right!
Eyes front!
Count off
Left turn!
Right turn
March off!
Double march!
Halt!
At ease!

Dismiss! (Shaanxi Series Book 1: 83)

Commonalties across the series include an emphasis on reading, with the passage providing the central, organizing focus of each unit, and a controlled language syllabus, which restricts the number of new words per unit and incorporates a graded progression of grammatical items. This accords with the Structural Approach and the Grammar-Translation Method, while the sentence patterns for drilling are associated with Audiolingualism.

What is noteworthy about all the textbooks is how closely they resemble the series produced by the PEP at times when politicization was not prevalent. As noted above, the Cultural Revolutionary series have features of pedagogy and patterns of general organization that were present in Series One, Two, Four and Five. This was not the case during an earlier period of politicization, namely the Great Leap Forward. Then the textbooks (Series Three) were built around passages that showed little evidence of control of linguistic content. There are several possible reasons for this. Firstly, the various teams of curriculum developers who wrote the Cultural Revolution series would probably have been unaware of Series Three, which did not get beyond the piloting stage, so the alternative approach would not have been within their experience. Secondly, in the early 1960s the PEP had built up a fixed team of curriculum developers who had established and consolidated a clear style of textbook organization in the various editions that appeared at that time. The Cultural Revolution series were therefore working intertextually within the established tradition.

Generally speaking, the discourse in the Cultural Revolution series is oriented towards a medium to strong degree of realism. In the early stages of some series, the realism is weaker, because the message of the discourse is closely delimited by the controlled linguistic syllabus: with few linguistic resources to play with, the textbook writers are constrained in the kind of passages that they can produce. However, as the series develop, the increasing range of available linguistic resources facilitates the use of more realistic passages.

Linguistic components

Analysis of the language contents of the textbooks indicates careful attention to aspects such as grammar and vocabulary. The Cultural Revolution series have some of the features of Series One, Two, Four and Five (to which the writers appear to have referred), in that efforts have been made to structure the language content and to limit the amount of new items introduced in each new lesson. This contrasts markedly with the experimental series (Series Three) that was published during the politically-charged Great Leap Forward. At that time, the textbooks mainly included political passages with little regard paid to the demands placed on the students by the large amount of new language items in each lesson.

In the Shanghai series, tenses are taught in a sequence: future simple tense; future with *going to;* past simple tense; past continuous tense; present perfect tense. In the Beijing series, there also appears to be some form of sequencing in Book 5 and Book 6, with the present perfect tense being followed by the passive voice in the present simple, past simple, future simple and present perfect tenses (in that order). The sequences are similar to those found in Series One, Two, Four and Five. The Shaanxi series starts in familiar mode, with demonstratives, *to be* and *to have:* components that are found in the early stages of Series One, Two, Four and Five. The available book in the Tianjin series pays less attention to grammar, with a grammar focus in only three out of ten chapters.

In terms of vocabulary, the number of new words presented in each lesson seems to have been controlled, at least to some extent. The number of new vocabulary items is linked to the realism of the text: the more realistic the text, the more likely it is to require a higher number of new vocabulary items. Thus to control the level of difficulty of the vocabulary, the textbook writers would have to strike a balance by not including an excessive number of new items while not sacrificing too much realism at the same time. One would expect to find a greater degree of control in the earlier stages of a series, when realism is weaker. The Shaanxi Book 1 averages 9.33 new words per lesson, with a range of nil to 19. Beijing Book 2 averages 12.9 new words per lesson, with a range of 11 to 15. These figures are similar to those in Series One.

As the realism increases, so the degree of control over the vocabulary would be likely to lessen. In the Shanghai series, Book 7 has an average of 15.70 new words per lesson, ranging from 12 to 22; Book 8 has an average of 16.25, ranging from 9 to 23; and Book 9 has an average of 17.62, ranging from 13 to 23. Tianjin Book 4 averages 17.70, with a range of 14 to 24, while Beijing Book 5 and Book 6 average 18.78 (range: 15 to 22) and 19.00 (range: 12 to 28) new words per lesson respectively. These figures are comparable to those of books for the later stages of series produced before the Cultural Revolution.

Content

All the Cultural Revolution series contain strong political messages, a clear reflection of the socio-political climate of the time, although no series has as high a percentage of political messages in the discourse as Series Three (96.80%). The details are shown in Table 5.3.

Table 5.3   Political and moral messages in the Cultural Revolution series

Shanghai series

Discourse total	Messages total	Nil	Moral	Political	Political (attitude)	Political (information)	Political (role model)
39	39	4 (10.26%)	4 (10.26%)	31 (79.48%)	11	1	19

Beijing series

Discourse total	Messages total	Nil	Moral	Political	Political (attitude)	Political (information)	Political (role model)
62	63	25 (39.68%)	3 (4.76%)	35 (55.56%)	17	10	8

Tianjin series

Discourse total	Messages total	Nil	Moral	Political	Political (attitude)	Political (information)	Political (role model)
19	20	1 (5%)	4 (20%)	15 (75%)	4	3	8

Shaanxi series

Discourse total	Messages total	Nil	Moral	Political	Political (attitude)	Political (information)	Political (role model)
15	15	1 (6.67%)	0 (0%)	14 (93.33%)	8	0	6

In the Shanghai series, the discourse is centred initially around the daily life of students. These include reports of activities, dialogues, and descriptions of places. Most of the activities are 'revolutionary' in nature, such as Shanghai Book 7 Lesson 2, 'Our School'), which contains a reference to the students' work on a farm or in a factory. Later, stories and anecdotes are introduced. Another type of passage is a scientific description, such as 'The Earth' (Shanghai Book 9 Lesson 1), which corresponds to the view in China that English was an important medium for science:

The Earth

The earth is like a big ball. It moves all the time. It rotates once every twenty-four hours. At the same time the earth moves around the sun. It takes a little over 365 days to make one revolution. This makes one year.

The sun shines on the earth. It gives us warmth and light. There is air all around the earth. When the air moves, we call it wind. Little drops of water in the air make clouds. As the clouds move about, they bring us rain and snow. Nothing can grow on the earth without air, water and sunlight.

The surface of the earth is not even. There is land and sea; there are mountains and rivers.

On the earth there are a lot of useful things. We must use them for the good of people. (Shanghai Series Book 9: 1)

Overall, however, the Shanghai series has two main themes: revolutionary action pervading daily life, and role models. Several passages describe pupils in political activities (of a non-violent nature), such as following Mao Zedong's teaching, as in Shanghai Book 7 Lesson 1, for example:

Going to Middle School

I am fourteen. I go to middle school this term. I am very happy.

Grandpa says to me, "My child, you are a middle school pupil now. Before liberation your father and I were too poor to go to school. Thanks to the Party and Chairman Mao, all the children of the working people can go to school now. You must study hard for the revolution."

I will keep Grandpa's words in mind. I must always follow Chairman Mao's teaching, **"Keep fit, study well and work hard."** (Shanghai Series Book 7: 1)

Other revolutionary actions include helping the army (Shanghai Book 7 Lesson 10):

We are very busy here. Beside farm work, we have political study twice a week. We stand guard day and night with the PLA men. We must guard against any surprise attack on our country by Soviet revisionist social-imperialism. (Shanghai Series Book 7: 61–2)

Various role models are presented, including the writer, Lu Xun (Shanghai Book 7 Lesson 9), the altruistic soldier, Lei Feng (Shanghai Book 8 Lesson 4; Shanghai Book 9 Lesson 7), some Canadian women who rescued a child from a frozen pond (Shanghai Book 8 Lesson 6), the Canadian doctor, Dr Norman Bethune, who assisted in the revolution (Shanghai Book 9 Lesson 5) and Red Army soldiers (Shanghai Book 9 Lesson 6). The story of Dr Bethune relates how he donated blood — although he himself was very sick — to help a wounded soldier:

> Soon the blood of the Canadian doctor flowed into the veins of the Chinese soldier. The soldier got saved.
>
> Doctor Bethune has set us a fine example. We must learn from his spirit of internationalism and communism. (Shanghai Series Book 9: 29)

Moral messages in the series include encouragement to lead a healthy lifestyle (e.g., getting up early, playing sports), to be helpful to others (e.g., repairing a light for an old lady) and to avoid waste of food, old clothing or, as in the following example from Shanghai Book 9 Lesson 2, equipment:

A Good Lesson

> Last Thursday I was working with Master Worker Wang in the workshop. My job was to nail up boxes. A nail was bent. I pulled it out and threw it away. Soon I threw away another bent nail.
>
> Master Worker Wang picked up the nails and hammered them straight. Then he nailed a lid on a box with them.
>
> I felt uneasy. I didn't know what to say. How could I waste nails like that? It was wrong. We must make full use of every bit of material.
>
> What a good lesson it has taught me! I shall always remember it. (Shanghai Series Book 9: 7)

The Beijing series also includes a focus on revolutionary activities. As well as encouraging students to work on a farm or in a factory and to study Mao's works, some passages advocate class struggle. Although the use of violence is not openly advocated, it is hinted at. For example, the passage in Beijing Book 6 Lesson 2 concludes:

> Chairman Mao teaches us: **"Who are our enemies? Who are our friends? This is a question of the first importance for the revolution."** We have already won great victories in the Great Proletarian Cultural Revolution. But there are still class enemies at home and abroad. They are ready to attack us in different ways. We must carry the revolution through to the end, and we must never take pity on snake-like scoundrels. (Beijing Series Book 6: 10)

As well as including role models for emulation, such as Chairman Mao or the highly productive agricultural commune at Dazhai, the series also vilifies people, including a stereotypical pre-revolutionary landlord; the sage, Confucius; Mao's ally-turned-opponent Lin Biao; and, as a post-Cultural Revolution addition (the book is a third edition published in June 1978), the Gang of Four. Confucius (who used positive and negative role models in his own teaching) is criticized as a 'parasite' and 'reactionary thinker' who 'looked down upon labour'. The attack on Confucius in the series is linked to the political campaign that sought to eradicate 'feudal' thinking, dating back to March 1973 (Li, 1995). However, this campaign — the 'Criticize Lin Biao, Criticize Confucius' movement — was primarily directed at Mao's political opponent Lin Biao, who was accused of being a counter-revolutionary.

The Beijing series, like the Shanghai series, often reminds students of how life has changed since the 1949 revolution. In Beijing Book 6 Lesson 9, the narrator buys his daughter a watch and tells her how his father relied on the stars to tell the time at night, so he could wake the narrator in time for work:

> My daughter was deeply moved by the story. She said: "Father, you have given me not only a watch, but also a very good lesson in class education. The bitter past of the working people will always help me tell good from bad, right from wrong. I'll work with all my energy and devote my whole life to the cause of communism." (Beijing Series Book 6: 62)

The focus of the extant book from the Tianjin series is more international in its orientation. It contains passages with positive portrayals of a Chinese soldier losing his life saving a Korean boy, of CCP policies in Tibet, and of Karl Marx. Friendship with Albania, a steadfast friend of China since 1949, is celebrated through the planting of trees (Tianjin Book 4 Lesson 4). The passage starts with a quotation from Mao Zedong.

Friendship Trees

"China and Albania are separated by thousands of mountains and rivers but our hearts are closely linked. We are your true friends and comrades. And you are ours."

In China, one of the most cherished symbols of this friendship is the 'China-Albania Friendship Tree'. Thousands of Albanian olive trees have been presented to the Chinese people. These trees were planted in south China. The Chinese people looked after their friendship trees with great care. The first of these were given to Premier Chou En-lai by Comrade Mohmet Shehu. Two trees were planted by them personally. They blossomed in 1868 and bore fruit. By 1970 many more Albanian olive trees were strong and bearing olives. Now more and more olive trees are growing up in our country. These flowers of Chinese-Albanian friendship will blossom all over China.

Long live Chinese-Albanian friendship! (Tianjin Series Book 4: 16)

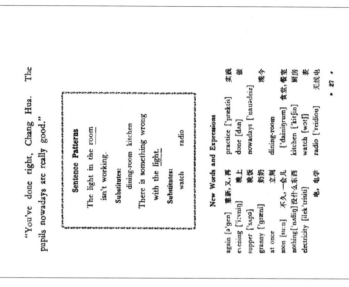

Lesson Five

The Light Is Working Again

It is evening. Chang Hua is having supper. Granny Wu from next door comes in.

"Chang Hua, the light in my room isn't working. I think there's something wrong with it. Can you help me?"

"Oh, yes, Granny. I'll come at once."

*

*   *

In Granny Wu's room, Chang Hua is busy working at her light. Very soon the light is on again.

"Oh, that's a good boy. Thank you very much, Chang Hua."

"It's nothing, Granny. We learned something about electricity at school. And we have a lot of practice, too."

26

"You've done right, Chang Hua. The pupils nowadays are really good."

Sentence Patterns

The light in the room isn't working.

Substitutes:

dining-room kitchen

There is something wrong with the light.

Substitutes:

watch radio

New Words and Expressions

again [ə'gen] 重新,又,再
evening ['i:vniŋ] 晚上
supper ['sʌpə] 晚饭
granny ['græni] 奶奶
at once 立刻
soon [su:n] 不久,一会儿
nothing ['nʌθiŋ] 没什么东西
electricity [ilek'trisiti] 电学

practice ['præktis] 实践
done [dʌn] 做
nowadays ['nauədeiz] 现今
dining-room ['dainiŋrum] 食堂,餐室
kitchen ['kitʃin] 厨房
watch [wɔtʃ] 表
radio ['reidiou] 无线电

27

Figure 5.2   Extract from the Shanghai series

Chang Hua serves as a role model, and young people receive a compliment from the older generation. The linguistic difficulty of the passage is controlled, and the sentence patterns are linked to the passage, indicating integration of form and meaning (Shanghai Series Book 7: 26–7).

There are also negative portrayals of other countries, which is not evident in the available textbooks in the other series. The USA is criticized for aggression in the Korean War in one passage ('Lo Sheng-chiao', which had appeared in Series One, Two and Three), and for racial discrimination in another ('Eddie Lewis', which had previously appeared in Series Four).

From the limited evidence available, the Shaanxi series is very strongly politicized, even though the edition is a 1978 reprint of the original 1973 textbook. New words in Shaanxi Book 1 include *hammer, sickle, Marx, Lenin, cadre, revolution, comrade: P.L.A.,* and *commune,* so even at a very early stage of the course, vocabulary items have political connotations. As with the Beijing and Shanghai series, the students are encouraged to engage in revolutionary activities in their daily lives, such as by helping on a farm or by studying the works of Mao, Marx and Lenin. CCP leaders are praised in a passage (Shaanxi Book 1 Lesson 9) that is illustrated with portraits of Mao Zedong and Hua Guofeng, again indicating that the passage is a post-Cultural Revolution addition:

We Love Chairman Mao and Chairman Hua
We Love Our Party

Chairman Mao is our great leader and teacher.
Chairman Hua is Chairman Mao's good pupil and good successor. He is our Party's wise leader.
We love Chairman Mao.
We love Chairman Hua.
We love our Party. (Shaanxi Series Book 1: 42)

Although the evidence is fragmentary, it is clear that the textbooks during the Cultural Revolution phase had a strong degree of politicization and also maintained a degree of moral education. A number of the themes, such as praise for Chairman Mao, racial discrimination in the USA, the improvement in life since 1949 or the heroism of role models, are found in pre-Cultural Revolution series, but, with the exception of the highly polemic Series Three from the Great Leap Forward, to a lesser extent. Clearly, therefore, there is a link between politicization in the socio-political climate of China and the themes and contents of English Language textbooks, although the details of the themes and contents depend upon the teams producing the textbooks. For instance, the Shanghai series appears to be less aggressive than the Beijing series, which advocates class struggle. The most political content is in the Shaanxi series. Liu Daoyi suggests that, with regard to the Cultural Revolution series, 'the more professional the writers, the less political the contents': in other words, some writing teams probably had better training and more experience in materials writing than others, and were thus more able to balance the political imperatives with pedagogical concerns.[1]

Summary

The Cultural Revolution series were produced towards the end of a period of heightened tension concerning English Language teaching. Some of the main targets at the time were capitalism and imperialism, with which English was strongly associated. Intellectuals had also been attacked, which had serious consequences for schooling and curriculum development. The vulnerable position of English in the school curriculum was particularly evident in this period, when it was subjected to political attack. The teaching of the language virtually stopped during the mass mobilization phase of the Cultural Revolution. When English did reappear in the school curriculum, with encouragement from Mao Zedong and Zhou Enlai (who linked English to national development), syllabuses and resources were produced on a local basis by teachers, as the PEP had been closed down and many of the outside agencies were no longer engaged in English Language teaching. It is this decentralization of responsibility to local teams and the dismantling of the elaborate, pluralistic consultative mechanisms that had been the hallmark of the previous period which marks the Cultural Revolution curriculum as a distinct phase.

However, while many aspects of education in China were radically revised during this phase, including the curriculum development process, English Language textbook series did not alter in fundamental character. It seems that the 'renaissance' in English Language teaching in the early 1960s still retained some influence, once the political climate permitted English to be restored to the school curriculum. This intertextuality indicates that, by the end of Series Five, a tradition had been established in the organization, content and pedagogy of textbook series that was not totally destroyed by the early stages of the Cultural Revolution.

Without the centralized and relatively pluralistic process of curriculum development, the local curriculum developers were placed in an exposed position of responsibility. They had to produce politically acceptable textbooks in a highly sensitive subject at a time when political mistakes could have very serious consequences. The developers tried to maintain some balance between political and pedagogical goals, depending upon their skill and experience, by referring to earlier PEP series for models of linguistic organization and pedagogy, but incorporating more political content. The concern for pedagogy is further reflected in the use of Audiolingualism in some of the Cultural Revolution series — this was not strongly evident in previous series. The attention to linguistic progression and pedagogy is very different from Series Three, which was produced during the previous period of politicization, the Great Leap Forward, but it should be remembered that the Cultural Revolution series appeared at a time of relative political calm and international *détente*.

For this reason, many of the findings in this chapter contradict those of an existing portrayal in the literature by Tang Lixing, who writes:

> When English finally reappeared on the curriculum around 1969 or 1970, it was distorted. The English of the textbooks was not the English of any English-speaking country. Textbooks were not compiled according to any linguistic theory or within any teaching methodological limitations, but rather according to instructions from the then authorities. Textbooks always began with "Long live" and ended with "Quotations". Throughout the book, there was not a single text dealing with a foreign theme or foreign culture. (1983: 44)

Attention had obviously been paid to linguistic theories and pedagogy in the four series analysed in this chapter. The series are not as strongly political as Tang Lixing's portrayal suggests, but it is possible that other, more political and less carefully constructed series were published, matching Tang Lixing's description.

After the Cultural Revolution came to an end in 1976, with the death of Mao Zedong in September and the arrest of the 'Gang of Four', the reestablishment of the PEP in the following year brought about another phase of English Language curriculum development, with the return to centralized processes.

6 Modernization under Deng Xiaoping, 1977–93

The demise of the Cultural Revolution marked the end of a period of relative isolation, both political and economic, for China. Mao's designated successor was Hua Guofeng, who was viewed as a conciliatory figure, capable of bringing together the factions that had polarized in the latter years of the Cultural Revolution (Short, 1982). He reactivated a number of economic policies, most notably the Four Modernizations Programme, first elucidated by Lin Biao in 1959, which targeted agriculture, science and technology, defence and industry. In the event, Hua's tenure of power proved to be just a brief interregnum and in 1978 Deng Xiaoping took control as the paramount leader of China and instigated economic reforms. The new directions in policy were boosted by *rapprochement* with the USA. The exchange of ambassadors was announced on 16 December 1978, and shortly afterwards, Deng visited the USA. According to Philip Short, a journalist stationed in Beijing at that time, Deng's visit triggered an upsurge of interest in the USA:

> As though at the turn of a giant switch, the Chinese press, which a few months earlier had been depicting American life in terms of alcoholism and divorce, strikes and racial tension, printed stories about Disneyland, and photographs of Deng and his entourage disappearing under ten-gallon stetsons at a Texas rodeo. Through television, John Denver, Shirley MacLaine and the Harlem Globetrotters made their way into Chinese homes and community centres. A documentary on American life showed ... a wedding party in a Chinese restaurant in New York, at which the young Chinese bride, looking shyly at her American husband, said she hoped relations between the two countries would prosper as her own new Chinese-American marriage. For a country where, a year earlier, Deng had had to intervene personally to authorise the first marriage between a foreigner and a Chinese for more than a decade, it would be hard to find a more emotion-charged symbolism for the new attitudes being created. (Short, 1982: 296)

Education was perceived by the CCP as playing a crucial role in the Four Modernizations, as the government embraced human resource development.

The objectives for education were both qualitative and quantitative, with moves to improve academic and vocational quality being paralleled by the development of mass education. The teaching of English was a particular problem after the Cultural Revolution. It had re-emerged in the curriculum sporadically and tentatively around the country in the early 1970s, especially following Nixon's visit, but for many teachers, the subject was too politically sensitive to teach at that time. This situation led to a shortage of qualified, practising English Language teachers at the end of 1976. A recruitment drive, facilitated by the availability of people returning home after displacement during the previous decade, resulted in those with previous English Language or Russian Language teaching experience being eligible for assignment to teach English.

Deng remained the dominant force in Chinese politics until his death in 1997. One of his strategies to kick-start economic development was the establishment of Special Economic Zones, situated mainly in coastal areas, to create a concentration or critical mass of resources in favourable fiscal conditions that would enable the zones to act as the pioneers of economic modernization. Another strategy was the Open Door Policy, designed to encourage foreign companies to invest in China in the form of joint ventures with Chinese companies, and thus facilitate the transfer of technological expertise. Deng was cognisant of the political and cultural problems that the policy could produce, and, in a statement at the Twelfth Congress of the CCP in August 1982, stated:

> We will unswervingly follow a policy of opening to the outside world and actively increase exchanges with foreign countries on the basis of mutual equality and benefit. At the same time we will keep a clear head, firmly resist corrosion by decadent ideas from abroad and never permit the bourgeois way of life to spread in our country. (Cited in Hayhoe, 1984: 206)

Similar reservations to those raised by traditionalists in imperial and republican China resurfaced in the early 1980s, as CCP political hard-liners felt that the Open Door Policy threatened not only Chinese cultural integrity but also socialist values. In 1983 and 1984, the 'Campaign against Spiritual Pollution' was launched, mainly targeting pornography and 'harmful' works of art and literature (Li, 1995). However, this campaign was short-lived, but served as a reminder that there were still factions within the CCP that resisted economic reforms.

All the same, the Open Door policy increased people's dealings with English speakers and was a further significant boost to both the status and role of English. The development of international trade and the tourist industry led to the creation of well-paid jobs for translators and interpreters. Language study also became a form of entertainment, fuelled by the increasing wealth of the urban Chinese, who could afford television sets, fees for night school courses, educational materials and, latterly, access to the Internet.

'English Corners', a congregation of learners conversing in English, appeared in many towns and cities in the late 1970s. As a result, as Tang Lixing observes:

> English learning has become a mania for the nation. Television courses, radio lessons, part-time or night schools have offered an almost unlimited variety of educational opportunities for people to learn English or further their education. The CCTV [China Central Television], for example, has been running a series of English programmes for beginners, intermediate learners, English teachers, ESP [English for Specific Purposes] learners, and even children. Three most popular TV programmes nowadays are "Sunday English", "Follow Me (BBC)", and "Ying Ying Learns English" (for children). (Tang Lixing, 1983: 46)

However, the government also faced the question of political liberalization, which culminated violently around Tiananmen Square on 4 June 1989. The CCP was also under pressure from the purist members of its own ranks, who viewed the changes brought about by economic modernization, such as the increasing influence of imported ideas and the dilution of ideological propagation, with growing disquiet. The CCP was able to resist the pressure from both sides through repression with force on the one hand, and appeasement through brief rhetorical campaigns promoting ideological purity, such as the Anti-Bourgeois Liberalization movement of 1986 and 1987, or the removal of reformers, such as Zhao Ziyang and Hu Yaobang, from their key posts.

The 1978 curriculum

The English Language curriculum that appeared in 1978 and which remained in force until 1982 was part of the national recovery that took place after the turbulence and destruction of the Cultural Revolution. The development of the new curriculum was a vehicle for creating the new English Language section of the reformed PEP, and also marked the formal restoration of English in junior secondary schools on a nation-wide basis. Curriculum development was fraught with uncertainties in 1977, when work started, because the institutional framework within the Ministry of Education was lacking, schooling was still in the process of recovery, and the political situation was unclear. The socio-economic climate was one of tentative depoliticization and national economic reconstruction, but while there were indications that the 'expert' aspect of the 'red and expert' equation would be emphasized once more, the outcome of the political struggle to be Mao's successor was still not settled and the new government policies had yet to bed down.

The CCP held its Eleventh Congress in August 1977, and decreed, *inter alia*, that new school textbooks were urgently required to support the new policy of national economic development (Löfstedt, 1980). In September, the Ministry of Education triggered the process of developing the curriculum for primary and secondary schools, as schooling returned to a semblance of the system that operated immediately prior to the Cultural Revolution. In January 1978, the Ministry of Education announced plans to allow a choice of two courses for English and other foreign languages, especially Russian, Japanese and French, to be instituted the following September. One course would start in Primary 3, and last for eight years up to the second year of senior secondary school. However, this would be limited to major cities that possessed sufficient primary schools teachers and resources to teach English in primary schools. In the rest of the country, the course would be a five-year programme covering junior and senior secondary school. Foreign language education at the tertiary level was also developed. In 1978, Beijing Foreign Languages Institute and Shanghai Foreign Languages Institute reopened. Opportunities became available for foreign language undergraduates to study overseas, and native speaker teachers were recruited to work in tertiary institutions. From 1980, the proportion of marks from the foreign language test that counted for the purposes of university entrance was increased from 30% to 100% in 1983 (Qun and Li, 1991).

The PEP was re-established in December 1977, but could not take on all the work of producing new syllabuses and accompanying textbooks, as many of the former members of staff had been rusticated or dispersed during the Cultural Revolution and had yet to return. Being short-staffed, the PEP therefore relied heavily on commissioned assistance, and was not fully operational until the end of the decade, when it moved into new premises in Sha Tan Hou Street in Beijing. Tang Jun returned to her post in charge of the English Language section in 1977 and was involved in recruiting new staff or arranging for the recall of former staff dispersed during the Cultural Revolution. For instance, she recruited Liu Daoyi from Beijing Foreign Languages Institute in 1977, to work on the primary English Language curriculum, and Liu Jinfang from Zhengzhou University, who joined the PEP in early 1979 after a chance meeting with Tang Jun.[1]

The PEP's task was to publish textbooks for the primary section of the eight-year course, and a standard set of textbooks for the secondary section of the eight-year and five-year courses. The Ministry allowed schools to select supplementary materials, especially if they judged that the PEP series did not meet the needs and abilities of their students. The syllabus would set out the fundamental attainment targets in terms of language skills, size of vocabulary and grammatical forms to be covered. A complicating factor was the ability of teachers. At this time, there was a massive recruitment drive, and the number of full-time English Language teachers shot up to 113,866 from the 19,751 teachers recorded before the Cultural Revolution. The quality of these teachers was variable, as many had basic qualifications (graduation from junior secondary school) and most would not have had opportunities to maintain their English skills in the previous decade.

In 1977, the PEP mobilized a group of professors, experienced teachers and textbook writers to produce a new syllabus and accompanying textbooks (Series Six) for English. The features of the curriculum which emerged in 1978 are shown in Table 6.1. The group was drawn from two major institutions: teachers from the English Department of the Beijing Foreign Languages Institute, including two respected scholars, Professor Zhou Muzhi and Professor Xia Zuhui, and teachers from the English Department of the Shanghai Foreign Languages Institute. Much of the actual textbook writing was carried out by Tang Jun, who acted as project director, with assistance from other writers such as Liu Yan (from Tianjin Foreign Languages Institute) and Dong Weijun (a cousin of Ying Manrong) as more staff were recruited or returned to the PEP. The other team members helped to draft the syllabus, gave feedback on drafts of the textbooks and supplied materials for the writers' use.[2]

Table 6.1   Key features of the English Language curriculum, 1978–82

	1978: Series Six
Genesis	commitment to economic modernization after Cultural Revolution
Role and status of English	means of access to scientific and technical information; low/medium official status
Role of agencies PEP: consultants: teachers:	writing syllabus and textbook resources some participation in writing syllabus and textbook resources negligible input; some arbitration over disputes about textbook content
Process	team formed to write syllabus and textbooks under pressure of time
Syllabus	published after textbooks; stresses balance between knowledge and usage of language; advocates integration of political, moral and language education
Resources	six textbooks (Series Six)
Organization	sentence and dialogue drills — reading passage — grammar exercises; traditional sequence of grammatical items
Discourse	progression from weak to strong realism
Linguistic components	phonetic alphabet; 1,250 vocabulary items; established grammar items
Intended pedagogy	mainly Audiolingualism and Structural Approach; some Grammar-Translation
Political and moral messages	strong presence of moral messages; weak presence of political messages

A draft version of the syllabus was produced and circulated to provincial teaching researchers and education bureaux for comments. Conferences on the draft syllabus involving the editing team, teachers and English Language specialists were held in Wuhan, Shanghai, Nanjing, Jinan and Beijing, and provoked lively discussions on how the textbooks should be organized. An issue that split the editorial team was when to teach the International Phonetic Alphabet (IPA), and this question was only resolved when the books were being drafted. According to Liu Daoyi, Zhou Muzhi strongly advocated starting Book 1 of the course with the IPA, before introducing the orthographic alphabet.[3] The Shanghai delegates did not agree, arguing that it was unnecessary to teach the IPA separately and that the IPA symbols could be incorporated in the lists of new vocabulary. Zhou was insistent, citing his own experiences in improving his pronunciation in the 1950s, under the influence of Soviet methodology. The Project Director, Tang Jun, was unable to break the deadlock, and referred the matter to the Chief Editor of the PEP, Ye Liqun. Ye asked Tang to produce a draft of Book 1 using Zhou's methods. Then, Ye invited a group of teachers from Beijing to arbitrate. As a result, as Liu Daoyi recalls,

> ... meetings were held, ... and some of the experienced teachers were quite straightforward. They said "If this book will be imposed on us, I would like to retire!" Zhou Muzhi had to change his mind, so there was a compromise approach to developing the new materials, so first we taught the students the English letters, and in the second semester, the English phonetic symbols were taught.[4]

As the pressure to produce textbooks mounted, the writers were installed in the Xiyuan Hotel in Beijing and later in the Xiangshan Hotel in the Fragrant Hills on the outskirts of the city for a year until the PEP's new office was opened in 1980. According to Liu Jinfang, they worked seven days a week on the project to complete Books 4, 5 and 6.[5] Producing materials from scratch was a problem, given the decade-long hiatus caused by the Cultural Revolution. The time constraints meant that they were not able to collect many ideas from teachers when compiling the series, other than in the incident quoted above. For the reading passages, they used whatever resources were available provided that they had appropriate political, moral or generally educational themes. Liu Jinfang felt that the political climate had lightened by the time she joined the project in 1979 (by which time Deng Xiaoping had affirmed the CCP's commitment to economic modernization), so the passages in later books in the series had less political content.[6] A few passages were resurrected or adapted from passages in Series Five, such as the story of the cock and the fox in Book 4 Lesson 18, and 'The Seasons' in Book 2 Lesson 31. Another passage, 'Lenin and the Guard' in Book 3 Lesson 11, appeared in the Shanghai Cultural Revolution series, although it had its origins in primary Chinese Language readers. The majority of the passages were new, some created by

Tang Jun and Liu Jinfang, others taken from simplified reading books (such as Aesop's Fables), magazines, encyclopaedias, or from materials supplied by the consultants, and adapted to meet the constraints of grammar and vocabulary. The antecedents of some of the passages are shown in Table 6.2.

Table 6.2   Antecedents of some passages in Series Six

Passage in Series Six	Title	Antecedent
Book 1 Lesson 1	The ABC Song	Series Five Book 1 Lesson 1
Book 4 Lesson 18	The Cock and the Fox	Series Five Book 4 Lesson 4
Book 2 Lesson 31	The Seasons	Series Five Book 4 Lesson 37
Book 3 Lesson 11	Lenin and the Guard	Shanghai Series Book 9 Lesson 8

The uncertain socio-political climate is evident in the English syllabus of 1978, as the PEP utilized the rhetoric of both the politics-oriented and economics-oriented camps:

> English is a very widely used language throughout the world. In certain aspects, English is a very important tool: for international class struggle; for economic and trade relationships; for cultural, scientific and technological exchange; and, for the development of international friendship.
>
> We have to hold high the great banner of Chairman Mao Zedong, and effectuate the policies initiated by the Party under Hua Guofeng's leadership, so that by the end of this century, we can achieve the Four Modernisations of industry, science and technology, agriculture and defence and make China a strong socialist country. To uphold the principle of classless internationalism and to carry out Chairman Mao's revolutionary diplomacy effectively, we need to nurture a large amount of "red and expert" people proficient in a foreign language and in different disciplines. That is why we have to strengthen both primary and secondary teaching. (PEP, 1978: 1) (In translation)

This statement quotes from a speech by Hua Guofeng at the opening of the Eleventh CCP Congress on 22 August 1977, when he said, 'We must hold high the great banner of Chairman Mao and resolutely defend it' (cited in Short, 1982: 216). The reference aligns the rhetoric of the syllabus with the prevailing Party line. A similar quotation is in the passage in Series Six Book 2 Lesson 32: 'We hold high the great banner of Chairman Mao, and Chairman Hua is leading us on a new Long March.' Tang Jun recalls that, after the Cultural Revolution, people had a feeling of *xin you yu ji*, which is an idiom with an intense meaning of 'once bitten, twice shy', and they were very cautious in the statements made in the syllabus.[7] The rest of the syllabus is concerned with how the general policies may be operationalized within the subject area. English is portrayed as an ideal vehicle for fostering desirable political attitudes:

> [English teaching] should be guided by a Marxist standpoint and methodology, integrate political and ideological contents into the textbooks and teaching so that the students can receive political and ideological education when they learn English. (PEP, 1978: 2, in translation)

To this end, reading passages need to be chosen carefully:

> The selected passages should be helpful in educating students to love Chairman Mao, the Party, socialism, labour and science; to inherit and carry forward the fine traditions and manners of our Party, and to establish a conscious will to serve the people of China and all over the world heart and soul. (PEP, 1978: 3, in translation)

However, despite the emphasis on political and ideological training, the syllabus stresses that the fundamental task of teaching English 'is to enable students to lay a sound foundation in learning a foreign language' (PEP, 1978: 2, in translation). It advocates that the initial stages of the course

> ... should be arranged according to the simplest grammar, and the most commonly used vocabulary and most familiar topics in the daily life of children and teenagers. The selection of topics should be expanded in accordance with the improvement in the students' language ability. (PEP, 1978: 4, in translation)

This resembles the 1963 syllabus (see Chapter 4), which was produced under similar conditions, in that China was emerging from a period of politicization. Other goals of the new syllabus, such as international friendship and the development of scientific knowledge, could be met by including in the textbooks 'a selection of materials that reflect the situation in Britain and America, some simplified or revised original English materials, and a number of simple scientific articles' (PEP, 1978: 3, in translation). As for genre,

> Passages at the earlier stages are dominated by dialogues or short passages reflecting students' daily life. There is also a small number of poems. Passages in the later stages are mainly stories, fairy tales, fables, short plays, diary and letter extracts, and short passages about general scientific, technological, historical and geographical knowledge. (PEP, 1978: 27, in translation)

The syllabus sets each year's requirements in detail. The syllabus covers the two courses: one starting at primary level, and the other at junior secondary school, although the textbooks are written mainly for the latter. General, graded targets are given for six areas: the alphabet, phonetics, handwriting, vocabulary, grammar and passages, and by the end of the third year of junior secondary school, the students are expected to master the following:

1. to distinguish, read, recite and write the letters of the alphabet;
2. to read aloud the passages fluently with virtually correct pronunciation, intonation, sentence stress, rhythm and pauses;
3. to copywrite skilfully and clearly in italics with correct capitalisation, format and punctuation;
4. to spell the previously learned words (about 1,250 in total) and to identify the part of speech and meaning; identify pronunciation of words that conform with basic spelling rules; tell the part of speech and meaning of a word from the root and prefix or suffix; to be aware of idiosyncrasies in English, such as a word with multiple meanings or parts of speech, short phrases, phrasal verbs and expressions;
5. to analyse the structure of uncomplicated and complex sentences and to tell the type and role of the clause; to know and differentiate the usage of the five common tenses; to have a knowledge of all grammar items covered, and to use them correctly in speech and writing;
6. to read the passage according to meaning and phonetic knowledge; to recite and retell parts of the passage; to ask and answer questions about the passage in speech and in writing; to write down by dictation materials less difficult than the passage; to read materials of a similar level of difficulty to the passage using a dictionary, and to translate some parts into Chinese.[8]

As far as the goal of nurturing 'red and expert' students is concerned, the 1978 syllabus places greater emphasis on the latter. Reference is made to the political role of English, but as the syllabus was written at a time of uncertainty, as noted above, the rhetoric was cautiously politicized. The detail of the language aspects of the syllabus shows a concern for pedagogy and language learning. The relationship is expressed in a section of the syllabus that outlines the role of the teacher:

> A teacher should be devoted to the educational policies of our Party, strive academically for the best, and to teach English well for the Revolution. Teachers should ensure that they have accurate pronunciation and grammar, and neat handwriting. They should constantly try to improve their oral proficiency and try to conduct classroom teaching in English. They should consider the characteristics of their students, improve their teaching methods, prepare lessons carefully and constantly improve teaching quality. They should show concern for the healthy development of the students in morality, study and physical education. They should educate students as to the purpose of learning English, make them upright in their attitude towards learning, and teach them to learn English well for the Revolution. (PEP, 1978: 4–5, in translation)

Series Six, entitled 'English', comprised six books, one for each semester of the three years' junior secondary course. The technical quality of the textbooks is similar to that of previous series. The size of the books is 18.42 cm x 13 cm ($7\frac{1}{4}$ inches x 5.12 inches); they have a thin paper cover, with a single pastel colour on woven design incorporating four line drawings, and while Book 1 has two pages of colour illustrations, all books have black and white illustrations (Figure A.10, p. 213). The number of lessons in each pair of books corresponds to the allocation of class periods for the year. Thus Book 1 (19 lessons) and Book 2 (13 lessons) have a total of 32 lessons for the 160 allocated class periods in Year 1. There are 24 lessons in Book 3 (12 lessons) and Book 4 (12 lessons) for the 128 class periods in Year 2, and a similar number in Book 5 and Book 6 for a similar allocation. Each book has a contents page which sets out the main features of each lesson, including the specific phonetic, grammar and structure points to be covered.

Pedagogy

The most striking feature of the general organization of Series Six is the similarity to previous series, with an initial focus on oral skills shifting to attention to reading skills, with the blend of the Structural Approach, Audiolingualism and the Grammar-Translation Method. The series starts with the alphabet and simple vocabulary — everyday objects or those likely to appeal to students' interests, such as *plane* and *gun*. Simple dialogues are introduced in Book 1, as are short reading passages and the phonetic symbols. From Book 2 onwards, reading passages become the central focus of the lessons, but there is still considerable attention to oral drills. By the end of the series, the reading passages have reached short-story length, sometimes encompassing two lessons, while the oral drills have become substitution dialogues of several lines in length.

However, unlike Series Five, for example, the contents of Series Six are not integrated in terms of topic, as there is no strong connection between the various components of each lesson. Every lesson in the series starts with drills, which present either fragments of dialogues or sentence structures, or both. The pedagogy implied by these drills is the use of repetitive learning as a means to develop oral skills. The attention to oral skills through drilling is consistent with the behaviourist Audiolingual approach. The other major components of each lesson are the reading passages and grammar practice. The passages are followed by comprehension questions, sometimes in the form of multiple choice questions, which implies that understanding should be taught through leading questions that draw the students' attention to key elements of the passage. The arrangement of the grammar-focused exercises, placed between the reading passage and the comprehension questions, indicates that the students should first meet and practise the grammar items before moving on to investigating the meaning of the passage. As indicated in the syllabus, the exercise types include blank-filling (such as providing the correct form of the verb), transformation (changing an element of a sentence) and translation (English to Chinese and Chinese to English) exercises. This is consistent with the view that one purpose for the passage is to serve as a vehicle for the presentation of new linguistic items, which are then practised through manipulation exercises. After the practice of the linguistic items comes a focus on the comprehension of the passage. This approach ensures that attention is paid to the linguistic aspects of the passage before its overall meaning and content is considered. Such pedagogy reflects the Grammar-Translation Method, which also places a primary emphasis upon grammar and reading.

All this points to a lack of integration, but there is some degree of cohesion. For instance, in Book 4 Lesson 22, the drills are about personal information, past experience, and the closure of public facilities; there is a dialogue about how a boy got a black eye, and a reading passage about Franz Liszt's kindness to a piano teacher. The grammar section focuses on interrogative sentences; the spelling and pronunciation section has words that are not connected with other sections of the lesson, and the pronunciation and intonation section is related to the drills. However, a common thread running through the drills, dialogue, the grammar section and the pronunciation and intonation section is the use of disjunctive questions (such as 'He is a teacher, isn't he?') This grammar-based link as the unifying element of the lesson is quite tenuous and symptomatic of the lack of time for careful structuring. The emphasis on dialogues reflects the concern in the syllabus to foster oral communicative skills, and the passages serve a similar purpose for developing reading skills.

In accordance with the syllabus, Series Six has a variety of discourse genres, with everyday dialogues in Book 1 and Book 2, and then short stories and factual passages. A few examples of discourse in the earlier books in the series are relatively weak in terms of realism: instead, the intention is to practise specific grammatical elements. For instance, in Book 1 Lesson 14, one dialogue (or to be precise, monologue) presents the contracted form of the second person singular of the verb *be:*

> You're a boy.
> You're thirteen.
> You're a student.
> You're in Grade One. (Series Six Book 1: 63)

It would be a rare situation in which these sentences could be used in real life, because the addressee is presumably already aware of the information. An example of a slightly more realistic drill is in Book 2 Lesson 26, where the dialogue presents different forms of the present continuous tense:

Teacher : Stand up, Li Pin. You're standing now, aren't you?
Li Pin   : Yes, I am.
Teacher : You're not sitting, are you?
Li Pin   : No, I'm not. (Series Six Book 2: 51)

In this case, there is a degree of realism in that Li Pin actually obeys the teacher's instruction to stand up, which would be a common classroom instruction. However, the questions and answers that follow are unrealistic, as it is obvious to both speaker and hearer that Li Pin is standing. A more realistic example of a drill is found in Book 5 Lesson 3:

A : Excuse me, can you tell me

how I can get to the railway station?
where the No. 3 bus stop is?
when the train will arrive?
why the train is late?

B : Certainly.

Take a No. 3 bus.
It's on the other side of the street.
It'll arrive in half an hour.
Something is wrong with the bridge up the line.

A : Thank you.
B : It's all right. (Series Six Book 5: 23)

This drill could be transferred to a real-life situation, although the repetition of the question formula is a little unnatural. Overall, though, the discourse in Series Six is mainly oriented towards strong realism. By the end of the series, reading passages and dialogues presented for oral practice are all strongly realistic. In this respect, Series Six resembles previous series in incorporating Audiolingual drills and a structurally-based linguistic syllabus.

Tang Jun describes the intended pedagogy as following these principles: *ting shuo ling xian, du xie gen shang, zhong he xun nian, zhuo zhong yuan du* ('listening and speaking first; then reading and writing; integrated training, emphasizing reading').[9] These principles suggest that the course would be made up of distinct phases, such as an oral-aural phase followed by a reading and writing phase, which may need different pedagogies. The syllabus states the overall aim of teaching English is to enable the students to use the language, rather than just to know the grammar. The general pedagogical strategy involves both explanation by the teacher and practice by the students:

> In order to develop practical ability to use English, it is necessary to explain some relevant rules and uses. However, explanation is for the purpose of

guiding practice. Whether it be phonetics, grammar or vocabulary teaching, we should follow the objective law of consciousness-raising: practice — theory — practice. When teaching a new linguistic item, we usually begin with oral exercises. When the students have some awareness of the item after some practice, a summary can be made. Sufficient exercises and an appropriate summary can effectively guide practice so as to ensure the students' mastery of the item. (PEP, 1978: 3, in translation)

This pedagogy reflects the Structural Approach, in that it proceeds from one linguistic structure to the next. The role ascribed to oral drilling in this regard means that the influence of Audiolingualism, first noted in Series Four, also remains in Series Six.

The syllabus advises on teaching individual language areas. For phonetics, imitation is recommended, as training in pronunciation 'is, to a large extent, a process of habit-formation' (PEP, 1978: 5, in translation), which again echoes the tenets of Audiolingualism. Vocabulary, it suggests, is best taught through drilling and memorization, but teachers can give guidance on spelling and word formation rules. Grammar teaching should follow the practice–theory–practice steps, with pattern drills providing an appropriate means for focusing on a particular structure. Reading passages 'provide material for comprehensive training in listening, speaking, reading, writing and translation' (PEP, 1978: 9, in translation), and teachers should explain points of interest concerning linguistic items. However, 'what is more important is to conduct exercises in reading aloud and reciting the passage, questioning and answering, retelling both orally and in writing, and translating the passage into Chinese' (PEP, 1978: 9–10, in translation), which are features of the Grammar-Translation Method. Caution is advised for reading passages from foreign sources: 'we should use a Marxist-Leninist standpoint and view to give a brief and appropriate analysis' (PEP, 1978: 10, in translation). Extracurricular reading is encouraged, as are performances, story-telling, exhibitions, wall newspapers, displays and other activities to create a foreign language environment.

Unlike some of the previous series, Series Six does not contain any passages that describe how a typical English lesson is conducted. There are hints on pedagogy. For example, in Book 2 Lesson 32, the passage suggests that teachers are expected to use English when teaching, and that students should learn to listen and speak, as well as read and write:

> We work hard at English, and many are doing well. We can speak a little. We understand the teacher when he speaks to us in English. We can read a little English, too.
>
> ... When we are back at school in autumn, we will have a new English textbook. We will learn to speak better and read more. (Series Six Book 2: 113–4)

Taken holistically, however, the intended pedagogy for the 1978 curriculum is an amalgam of (mainly) the Structural Approach and Audiolingualism, with a later incorporation of the Grammar-Translation Method. Real-life language is presented in many instances throughout Series Six and the stress is clearly placed upon students' usage of language, which is attained through practice in oral and written production. The production of language is controlled, in that there is little scope for creativity in language use by the students: they are not expected to generate new language, but to master the contextualized language items, which is consistent with the Structural Approach. The practice–theory–practice steps and the use of habit-forming drills and manipulation exercises, which is the predominant pedagogy, are consistent, to a large extent, with an Audiolingual approach. The influence of Grammar-Translation is evident in other aspects of Series Six, such as the reading passages, but this influence is smaller than that of a structuralist communicative approach, through Audiolingualism in the oral domain and, in the written domain, a blend of exercises focusing on discrete linguistic components supporting the production of longer discourse. This eclectic blend follows trends established since Series Four, when greater attention was paid to oracy. The curriculum development process, involving specialists with different opinions on pedagogy, resembles a melting pot (or, given the time constraints in Series Six, a pressure cooker). The blend shows that overseas ideas are not embraced wholeheartedly by the PEP, but are absorbed and adapted through synthesis with more traditional Chinese English-Language teaching methods.

Linguistic components

The syllabus sets out the linguistic components that are expected to be taught in each year of the course. These are summarized in Table 6.3.

The syllabus was written in order to prescribe the arrangement of linguistic components in Series Six. The order of the items and the setting of a number of words to be covered correspond with the practices prescribed for earlier series. The arrangement of the grammar items shows the continued influence of Professor Zhang Daozheng's ideas on grammatical sequencing that was first noted in Series One. It was also present in Series Four and Five, which, according to Liu Jinfang, were main points of reference for the writers of Series Six.[10]

As noted above, Series Six is not a topic-based course, unlike Series One for example. Without the constraint of attempting to integrate the linguistic items too closely with the contents of the reading passages and other elements of a lesson, the textbook writers were able to follow the set order of linguistic components. This presentation of discrete linguistic items in a prescribed sequence is a feature of the Structural Approach (see Table 1.1, p. 10). As

Table 6.3   Linguistic components to be covered in Series Six (adapted from PEP, 1978)

	Year 1	Year 2	Year 3
Vocabulary	about 400 words and a few expressions	about 400 more words and a few more expressions	about 450 more words and a few more expressions
Phonetics	1. phonetic transcriptions 2. consonant liaisons 3. basic spelling rules 4. word stress, sentence stress and rhythm 5. loss of plosive 6. falling and rising tones	1. liaisons 2. division of sense groups and pauses 3. intonation in long sentences	nil
Grammar	1. parts of speech 2. plurals; possessive forms of nouns 3. pronouns 4. prepositions of time and place 5. ordinals and cardinals 6. simple present, present continuous, 'to be going to' 7. simple and co-ordinate clauses; statements, general and special questions; imperatives	4. definite and indefinite article 5. comparison of adjectives and adverbs 6. modal verbs 7. future, past, present perfect tenses 8. alternative and reflective questions 9. adverbial and objective clauses	1. infinitives 2. passive voice 3. past continuous, past perfect, future in the past tenses 4. indirect speech 5. attributive clauses

the syllabus explains: 'The arrangement of grammatical items in the textbooks is that a grammatical item appears in the passage or exercises before it is formally taught, so as to make it easier for the students to master' (PEP, 1978: 8, in translation). The vocabulary component reflects a certain lack of linguistic control. The total number of vocabulary items presented in Series Six is 1,737. The average of new words per lesson is relatively high, compared with previous series: it resembles Series Three in this respect. Book 1 averages 12.89 new words per unit, and this rises to 32.33 in Book 3; the overall average is 21.75 (in Series Three, it was 20.12; in Series One, just 9.26). However, the percentage of non-Thorndike vocabulary (33.97%) is comparable with most other series.

Content

As noted earlier, the syllabus acknowledges the contribution that the English Language curriculum can make to political education, although Liu Jinfang observes that this role weakened as the development of the curriculum went on.[11] Table 6.4 shows the breakdown of political and moral messages in 159 examples of discourse identified in Series Six.

Table 6.4   Political and moral messages in Series Six

Discourse total	Messages total	Nil	Moral	Political	Political (attitude)	Political (information)	Political (role model)
159	163	86 (52.76%)	46 (28.22%)	31 (19.02%)	18	3	10

Several messages in Series Six do have explicit political import, although there are fewer (31, or only 19.02%) than in previous series. The presence of moral messages is relatively quite strong, but the largest proportion of messages has neither moral nor political connotations. The political messages are dispersed throughout drills and passages, including references to the late Chairman Mao Zedong, and to his immediate successor, Hua Guofeng. For instance, the passage in Book 1 Lesson 19, which is a pupil's description of her class, concludes:

> We study for the people. We love the people. We love the Communist Party. We love Chairman Hua. (Series Six Book 1: 104)

Some passages promote loyalty to the CCP, its leaders and its ideology. Book 2 Lesson 32 includes a quotation about Chairman Hua leading the

Chinese people on a new Long March. A further example is found in an exhortatory lecture given by a scientist to a class of junior secondary students in Book 3 Lesson 4. After comparing his pre-1949 childhood with the students', he encourages the students to work hard and to keep fit: 'I needn't tell you that good health is a must for building socialism.' He adds, 'Above everything else, study Marxism. It's an important guide to the study of science.' Throughout the series, there is a subtext suggesting that positive features of society are the result of socialism following the 1949 revolution. Comparisons between pre- and post-1949 China are made on several occasions. For instance, in Book 3 Lesson 5, the drill states:

> There were no schools in the village before liberation, but now there are quite a few.
>
> There were no doctors in the village before liberation, but now there are quite a few. (Series Six Book 3: 53–4)

In the same lesson, the reading passage presents a description of a town, accompanied by line drawings showing a contrast between former poverty and modern prosperity:

> Our town is not big. There are about one hundred and sixty thousand people in it. It is on a new railway line. The streets are wide and straight, and there are many new houses and shops along them. There are trees everywhere. There is a big modern hospital and some fine schools. (Series Six Book 3: 55–6)

Another theme, also evident in previous series, is the negative portrayal of foreign countries. Six passages could be construed as serving propaganda purposes. The treatment of coloured people is a major aspect of the theme. Book 3 Lesson 9 and Lesson 10 feature a story of a coloured boy being bullied by classmates. In another passage, in Book 4 Lesson 23, a black girl writes defiantly of the discrimination she faces; however, Book 6 Lesson 14 ends with the somewhat back-handed compliment that, 'Today, at least in the eyes of the law, blacks and whites in America are equal.' In Book 6 Lesson 23, democracy is criticized, being lampooned in a story about a mythical country where only people who can afford to buy golden trumpets (represented in the USA by the owners of the mass media) are able to make their voices heard. The story was adapted from the original version written by an American writer, Mike Quin, in 1940:

Golden Trumpets

> Mr Hornsnagle, an American news reporter, asked the ruler of Yap Yap whether free speech was allowed under his rule.
>
> "Yes, indeed," said the ruler. "My people enjoy complete freedom of speech. We decide everything according to public opinion."

"But how do you find out what the public thinks?" asked Mr Hornsnagle.

"That's very simple," said the ruler. "Whenever any policy has to be decided, we get all the people here in my palace. Then we decide our policy by just listening to the Golden Trumpets."

"What are the golden trumpets, please?" asked Mr Hornsnagle.

"Golden Trumpets," said the ruler, "are used to express public opinion here. I raise my right hand above my head and shout: 'All those in favour, blow.' Immediately all those who are in favour of the proposal blow their golden trumpets. Then I raise my left hand and say 'All those against, blow.' This time those who are opposed blow theirs. The side which makes the bigger and louder noise is naturally the majority and the policy is decided in their favour."

"That," said Mr Hornsangle, "is the most complete democracy that I have ever heard of. I would very much like to see one of these meetings."

On the next afternoon, the people of Yap Yap, both rich and poor, were called into the palace to decide an important matter. There were only four rich men. The rest were poor.

When everybody was there, the ruler stepped forward and raised his right hand.

"All those in favour, blow," he shouted.

The four rich men all lifted their golden trumpets and blew hard.

Then the ruler lifted his left hand. "All those against, blow," he shouted. Not a sound came from the poor people. Thus the policy was decided and the meeting was over.

Mr Hornsnagle asked the ruler why only the four rich men blew trumpets.

"Because they are the only people who have golden trumpets," said the ruler. "The others are all poor working people."

"That doesn't seem very much like free speech to me," said Hornsnagle.

"And how do you do it in America?" said the ruler.

"In America," said Hornsnagle, "instead of golden trumpets, we have newspapers, magazines and radio stations."

"That's very interesting," said the ruler. "But who owns all these newspapers, magazines and radio stations?"

"The rich," said Hornsnagle.

"Then it's the same as Yap Yap," said the ruler. (Series Six Book 6: 108–11)

Industrial relations in Britain are portrayed in a poor light in Book 6 Lesson 15 in a story called 'Dustmen on Strike'.

On the other hand, some foreign characters appear as role models: not just those who assisted the CCP, such as the Canadian doctor, Norman

Bethune, who is mentioned in Book 2 Lesson 3, but also people who stood up for their beliefs or acted against injustice. An example is the story of Nathan Hale, in Book 5 Lesson 3. Hale was an American spy who was captured by the British in the war of independence; he died heroically, declaring patriotically, 'I only regret that I have but one life to lose for my country.' Sir Rowland Hill is praised for his invention of the postage stamp in Book 6 Lesson 24, particularly as he provided poor people with an affordable means of communicating with each other. There are two stories about famous Western scientists demonstrating their ingenuity: Galileo in Book 5 Lesson 11, and Edison in Book 6 Lesson 19. International understanding is portrayed as being encouraged through the use of satellites in Book 4 Lesson 20, and sports in Book 5 Lesson 9.

A very common moral theme is desirable behaviour. Young Pioneers are depicted cleaning the house of a grandmother who was hospitalized in Book 3 Lesson 8 and Lesson 9, and being chastised for failing to offer their seats on a bus to some old people in Book 3 Lesson 6. Other values are presented through fables, such as the story of the hare and the tortoise in Book 2 Lesson 22, and of the Arab who allows his camel to take over his tent in Book 3 Lesson 12.

As far as the vocabulary is concerned, there is a large amount that does not appear in Thorndike (590 out of 1,737, or 33.97%), but this does not represent a high level of politicization. As with Series Five, the majority of the non-Thorndike words are derived from the use of realistic English in the passages, and not from any real attempt at political indoctrination. This reflects the influence of Tang Jun and Liu Jinfang, who drew up a word-list based on the particular needs of the Chinese students.[12] The number of non-Thorndike words increases when the discourse is drawn from original sources, such as in Book 5 and Book 6, while the instances of words specifically related to communism, socialism and the CCP are small.

Overall, the discourse in Series Six presents an image of hard-working, helpful students with aspirations to further the common good. China is portrayed as a developing, harmonious country, which has seen great improvements since the CCP came to power. Western countries are depicted as defective in race and industrial relations, as well as in democratic processes, but international understanding is presented as desirable. The contribution of some individual Westerners to science and music is acknowledged. Overt political slogans are rare, but there are references to Chairman Mao Zedong and Chairman Hua Guofeng in the early books in the series. The rhetoric of the syllabus is more explicitly politicized than the textbooks in Series Six, because of the political climate at the time of its production, and, of its other priorities, international class struggle is not reflected strongly in the textbooks. However, Series Six does correspond to the syllabus' emphasis on international understanding, and scientific and cultural exchange.

A RHYME

My Book

I will not spoil this little book,
Nor drop it on the floor.
I will not turn its corners down,
To spoil it more and more.
My book's a little friend to me,
And so a friend to it I'll be.

mai ⟍buk

ai 'wil nɔt 'spɔil ðis 'litl ⟋buk
nɔ: 'drɔp it ɔn ðə ⟍flɔ:
ai 'wil nɔ(t) 'tə:n 'its 'kɔ:nəz ⟋daun
tu 'spɔil it 'mɔ:r ən(d) ⟍mɔ:
mai 'buks ə 'litl 'fren(d) tu ⟋mi:
ənd 'səu ə 'fren(d) tu it 'ail ⟍bi:

110   a hundred and ten

Figure 6.1   Extract from Series Six Book 1 Lesson 19

This poem constitutes an *envoi* for the book. The repetition of the poem in IPA indicates the influence of scholars such as Professor Zhou Muzhi who advocated teaching phonetics at an early stage of the course (Series Six Book 1: 110).

The end of the Cultural Revolution had two significant influences on the 1978 English Language curriculum. Initially, the political climate was characterized by uncertainty, although it became increasingly more favourable for the promotion of English Language teaching in the junior secondary school curriculum than during the previous decade. The second major influence was time: the curriculum was put together in great haste, as it was needed to fill a vacuum caused by the collapse of national education systems and the widespread abandonment of English Language teaching during the Cultural Revolution. The political uncertainty of the Hua Guofeng era is reflected in the rhetoric and cautionary asides of the English syllabus, such as the call to teachers to adopt a Marxist-Leninist standpoint when handling passages written by foreigners. A few passages contain negative portrayals of Western countries, but, overall, Series Six contains more moral than political messages. The uncertainty was reflected mainly at the rhetorical level, and some explicit political statements ultimately contributed to the demise of Series Six when the climate became more depoliticized.

Although the trigger for curriculum change was the familiar linkage in periods of relative depoliticization with economic development, the process of curriculum development in this phase does not show the same degree of research, planning and consultation that was a feature of the early 1960s. One result is that the organization of the contents is more confused than in Series Four. The reasons were mainly the short time frame, the unavailability of adequate resources in the aftermath of the Cultural Revolution and the differences of opinions between the two principal groups of specialists. The PEP was still handicapped by a lack of staff, and it had to rely heavily on outside agencies at first, although the PEP project leader, Tang Jun, made the final decisions. A few members of teachers, such as teachers from Beijing, were consulted only on a small number of issues: time and resources did not permit nation-wide canvassing of grassroots opinions, for instance. The writers of Series Six were left to their own devices, adapting and using any suitable materials that they could find from severely limited sources, and creating new materials as necessary. In this regard, the development process was poorly planned, lacked a clear conception of purpose (other than seeking to achieve a cautious balance between 'redness' and 'expertise') and was characterized by pragmatic expediency, thus resembling the 'garbage can' approach that was also a feature of the first phase of curriculum development identified in this study.

Series Six was basically a compromise — in terms of the process of development, of content and of organization. It appeared during a transitional period, but, like Series Four, it was published at a time of transition from politicization to economic modernization, rather than vice versa, as was the case with Series Two. In some respects, Series Six resembles previous series produced during times when state policies were oriented towards economic goals, such as Series Four and Five. The rationale for the curriculum sets out the link to economic modernization; outside agencies were consulted; and attention was paid to pedagogical concerns, but, at the same time, Series Six shares features of earlier series produced in times of politicization: references in the syllabus and/or reading passages to CCP leaders and to ideological goals, and a rushed process of curriculum development. Overall, this fourth phase of the EFL curriculum has similarities to the first phase: the socio-political climate was in a state of flux; mechanisms for piloting the textbook series were not in place; there were severe time constraints on the developers; and political and pedagogical aspects were later deemed inappropriate.

Given these constraints and the rapid political, economic and social changes that occurred after Deng Xiaoping became the paramount leader in 1978, it is not surprising that this curriculum did not last long. Series Six was unpopular with many teachers, who complained that the books were too difficult to teach. This was viewed by the PEP staff as arising from the loose structural organization of the lessons — which meant that the linguistic components were not strongly integrated with the reading passages[13] — and also to the shortage of teachers qualified to handle the textbooks with autonomy.[14] The explicit references to Hua Guofeng in the syllabus and the textbooks created a particular problem for the PEP after his fall from power in 1978. The need to revise the curriculum was an urgent consideration as recent history had shown the grave consequences for those who had published positive references to a fallen politician. Indeed, the PEP had had to recall and dispose of an entire series of Chinese Language textbooks produced in 1978 soon after publication, because the large amount of political content — including praise of Hua Guofeng — was no longer appropriate (Lai, 1994). This proved a salutary experience for the PEP, which had a bearing on subsequent developments of the English Language curriculum.

The 1982 curriculum

By 1982, China had embarked upon a further series of wide-ranging economic reforms that were internationalist in outlook, and dissipated many of the tensions which afflicted curriculum development in the periods when Mao Zedong and, to a lesser extent, Hua Guofeng were the paramount leaders. Unlike the two previous phases, the 1982 curriculum was produced during a period of relatively low politicization and of favourable conditions, in terms of the expertise and time that were available. The status of English continued to rise at this time: this was the era of English learning as a 'mania for the nation' (Tang Lixing, 1983: 46). The Open Door Policy, which had been instituted since the introduction of the 1978 curriculum, raised many Chinese people's interest in interacting with foreigners, and had led to a blossoming interest in spoken as well as written English. English Corners — congregations in public places where participants conversed in English — and imported television programmes teaching English, such as BBC Television's 'Follow Me' series, became very popular (Short, 1982).

The 1982 curriculum had two specific aims: to correct the orientation of the previous curriculum, which was viewed as problematic; and to prepare an educated élite to play a pioneering role in economic modernization in the context of the Open Door Policy. The political content of Series Six, especially the eulogies of ex-Chairman Hua Guofeng and the rhetoric left over from the Cultural Revolution, was unsuitable for the strong economic orientation of state policies. In schools, teachers complained that the learning load in terms of linguistic components overburdened students, particularly as the time allocated in 1978 (656 hours) was just over half the time (1,238 hours) allowed for a similar curriculum in 1963 (Tang Jun, 1986). The revision to the allocation of hours for English teaching in 1982 — up by 112 hours to 768 hours for junior and senior secondary schooling — meant that the adjustment to the syllabus would not have to be quite so severe. Another factor to be taken into account was people's heightened interest in oral English and Western culture.

The genesis of the 1982 curriculum resembles the system that operated before the Cultural Revolution. The main trigger for the 1982 curriculum was the Ministry of Education's decision to provide teaching resources for the newly created multi-track education system. In reality, as Liu Daoyi explains, this entailed paying particular attention to *zhongdian* (key) secondary schools, which catered for academically more able students and which were allocated more resources and better qualified teachers than mainstream schools.[15] The curriculum development process reflects the centrally-dominated pluralistic approach of the early 1960s. The PEP wrote and co-ordinated the publishing of Series Seven and the syllabus, in consultation with both outside agencies (the tertiary specialists) and teachers. What was new about the planning process was the depth of consultation with teachers, most notably through the conference held in 1981 and the collection of comments on the draft version. Not all suggestions were acted upon, if they fell outside the scope of the PEP's policy for handling the dilemma concerning mass versus élite education, but some were accepted.

By 1981 the PEP was much stronger than in 1977. It occupied new premises, which were larger than before, with a purpose-built office block. The staff continued to be strengthened. Liu Daoyi underwent training in English Language teaching pedagogy in the United Kingdom in 1981 and, on her return, worked with Tang Jun, Wang Meifang and Liu Jinfang as editors and writers of the 1982 curriculum. A group of specialists from Beijing Foreign Languages Institute were appointed as consultants to provide feedback, suggest materials and polish the drafts of the textbooks. A key figure in this regard, acknowledged with a credit in the textbooks, was Professor Deng Yanchang (Frank Tang), an American-born Chinese. Thus there were two main channels — Liu Daoyi and Deng Yanchang — for access to Western ideas of pedagogy.

The time scale for producing the new curriculum was less pressing than for the 1978 curriculum, as planning began eighteen months in advance, and Series Six was available for reference and adaptation. The PEP, recognizing the importance of feedback from teachers, held a national conference at the Summer Palace in Beijing in September 1981, at which delegates — principally teachers, but also some specialists from tertiary institutions — discussed the new curriculum. According to Liu Daoyi, the conference called for the removal of political themes from the textbooks, more attention to listening and speaking, and a wider range of resources to cater for the different levels of students.[16] The last point was a major tension facing the curriculum developers. On the one hand, the introduction of key schools meant that the syllabus and Series Seven should be sufficiently challenging so as to suit the academically more able students. To ignore them would be counter to the thrust of current policy. On the other hand, Series Six had been criticized as too difficult for average students. Catering for key school students would run the risk of making the curriculum too difficult for the majority of students. In handling this classic élite-mass education tension, the PEP set the linguistic demands of the core materials (i.e., the textbooks in Series Seven) at a level below that of key school students, but catered for the latter by providing supplementary materials such as more reading passages, listening exercises and optional extra vocabulary.

The features of the 1982 English Language curriculum are summarized in Table 6.5.

Table 6.5   Key features of the English Language curriculum, 1982–93

Genesis	development of multi-track education, especially the establishment of key secondary schools; supporting economic modernization in a period of low politicization and high official status for English
Role and status of English	international transfer and communication; access to higher education and lucrative employment; high official status
Role of agencies PEP: consultants: teachers:	designers and writers of syllabus and Series Seven feedback and advice piloting, feedback and advice
Process	research into English Language teaching in China and abroad; team established to develop syllabus and materials; piloting in some schools; advisory consultative editorial committee reviewed materials
Syllabus	stresses communication; lists targets in pronunciation, vocabulary, grammar; provides hints on pedagogy
Resources	Series Seven: textbooks, cassette tapes of reading passages and practice drills, teacher's books, wall charts
Organization	sentence and dialogue drills — reading passage — vocabulary — grammar exercises (extra reading passage)
Discourse	progression from weak to strong realism
Linguistic components	phonetic alphabet; 1,250 vocabulary items; traditional sequence of grammatical items
Intended pedagogy	predominantly Structural Approach; with Audiolingualism, Grammar-Translation and Functional/ Notional Approach
Political and moral messages	strong presence of moral messages; weak presence of political messages

The contents of Series Seven show strong intertextuality, in that the writers made reference to previous series, principally to Series Six. Both series have similar organization, linguistic components, reading passages and, in places, identical illustrations, but there are sufficient differences in the process and product of curriculum development to suggest that Series Seven is more than just a revision of Series Six. In terms of passages, Table 6.6 includes those that appear in both series.

Table 6.6   Antecedents of some reading passages in Series Seven

Title	Location	Origin
I Can Say My ABC	Book 1 Lesson 5	Series Four Book 1 Lesson 1; Series Five Book 1 Lesson 1; Series Six Book 1 Lesson 1
My Class	Book 1 Lesson 20	Series Six Book 1 Lesson 19 (adapted)
On a Bus	Book 2 Lesson 7	Series Six Book 3 Lesson 6 (adapted)
A Letter	Book 2 Lesson 11	Series Six Book 1 Lesson 14 (adapted)
The Cock and the Fox	Book 2 Lesson 12	Series Five Book 4 Lesson 4 (adapted)
The Crow and the Fox	Book 2 supp. reading 2	Series Five Book 3 Lesson 10 (adapted)
The Seasons	Book 2 Lesson 15	Series Four Book 3 Lesson 6 (adapted); Series Five Book 4 Lesson 11 (adapted); Series Six Book 2 Lesson 31 (adapted);
The New School Year	Book 3 Lesson 1	Series Six Book 3 Lesson 1 (adapted)
At the Library	Book 3 Lesson 3	Series Five Book 3 Lesson 17 (adapted); Series Six Book 3 Lesson 3 (adapted)
Lenin and the Guard	Book 3 Lesson 13	Series Six Book 3 Lesson 11 (adapted)
The Monkey and the Crocodile	Book 4 Lessons 2 and 3	Series Six Book 4 Lessons 14 and 15 (adapted)
It's Unfair	Book 4 Lessons 4 and 5	Series Six Book 4 Lessons 16 and 17 (adapted)
What's Wrong with Tom?	Book 4 Lesson 8	Series Six Book 4 Lesson 17 (adapted)
An Australian Boy in Beijing	Book 4 Lesson 10	Series Six Book 4 Lesson 21 (adapted)
The Piano Concert	Book 4 Lesson 11	Series Six Book 4 Lesson 22 (adapted)

(continued on p. 154)

Table 6.6   (*Continued*)

Title	Location	Origin
The Universe and Man-Made Satellites	Book 4 Lesson 12	Series Six Book 4 Lesson 20
Why the Bat Comes Out Only at Night	Book 5 Lesson 1	Series Six Book 5 Lesson 1 (adapted)
Nathan Hale	Book 5 Lesson 2	Series Six Book 5 Lesson 3 (adapted)
A Question of Pronunciation	Book 5 Lesson 3	Series Six Book 5 Lesson 5 (adapted)
The Pyramids	Book 5 Lesson 7	Series Six Book 5 Lesson 4 (adapted)
Once a Thief Always a Thief	Book 5 Lesson 8	Series Six Book 6 Lesson 17 (adapted)
Edison's Boyhood	Book 5 Lesson 9	Series Six Book 6 Lesson 19 (adapted)
The Fisherman and the Genie	Book 5 Lesson 11	Series Six Book 5 Lessons 7 and 8 (adapted)
Joe Hill	Book 6 Lesson 2	Series Four Book 3 Lesson 5 (adapted); Series Five Book 4 Lesson 12 (adapted)
Dustmen on Strike	Book 6 Lesson 3	Series Six Book 6 Lesson 15 (adapted)
Water, Steam and Ice	Book 6 Lesson 4	Series Six Book 6 Lesson 16
Look Carefully and Learn	Book 6 Lesson 9	Series Six Book 6 Lesson 22 (adapted)

Many of the passages were adapted. Some were simplified, through the rewriting of complex sentences; others had their political content toned down. The following is an example of a rewritten passage. In the original form, in Series Six Book 1 Lesson 19, it reads:

> I'm a middle-school student. My name is Wei Fang. I'm in Class 9, Grade 1, of the No. 15 Middle School.
>
> There are fifty-three students in my class. Thirty of them are boys. The others are girls. We study politics, Chinese, English, maths, geography and other lessons. We work hard at them.
>
> Many of us are good at English. English is easy, but we like it.
>
> We love science, too. We make model planes, model ships and transistor radios. Some of us like singing and dancing, others go in for sports.

We study for the people. We love the people. We love the Communist Party. We love Chairman Hua. (Series Six Book 1: 103–4)

In Series Seven Book 1 Lesson 20, this passage appears as follows:

I'm a middle-school student. My name is Wei Fang. I study at Yu Ying Middle School. I am in Class 3, Grade 1. There are twenty boys and twenty-three girls in my class.

I come to school at seven thirty. Classes begin at eight. We have four lessons in the morning and two in the afternoon. At three fifty we have sports.

We study Chinese, maths, English and other lessons. We like maths. We like English, too. Some of us are good at it.

We work hard. We study for the people. (Series Seven Book 1: 118–9)

In the new version, references to Hua Guofeng, the CCP and politics as a school subject are omitted.

Series Seven was published progressively between January 1982 (Book 1) and May 1984 (Book 6). The series was not piloted in schools, but a draft version was published and distributed to specialists in tertiary institutions and teachers in different parts of the country (most notably Haidian district of Beijing) for feedback, which was then incorporated into the final version of the textbook resources. The contribution of these outside agencies and teachers is acknowledged in the preface to textbooks in Series Seven:

The draft version of this series has been commented upon by educational bureaux, lecturers in teacher training colleges and secondary school teachers in many provinces, cities and autonomous regions. We are grateful for their suggestions. (Series Seven Book 1: I)

Liu Jinfang recalls that one recurrent message from teachers in key secondary schools was a request for more conversational dialogues.[17] The PEP decided not to act on this suggestion, as they felt it would make the series too difficult for most students. They advised these teachers to prepare their own supplementary resources.

The syllabus did not appear until 1986. This reflects the established tradition that there was a symbiotic relationship between the PEP textbook resources and the syllabus: Series Seven represented the official embodiment of the syllabus. As there was only one publisher (and this publisher was closely involved in the development of the syllabus), it was not thought to be necessary to make a syllabus publicly available before the preparation of textbook resources. The publication of the syllabus merely served to reinforce the legitimacy of Series Seven. The delay allowed reference to be made in the syllabus' introduction to a significant statement by Deng Xiaoping. Invited to produce a calligraphic inscription for Jingshan Secondary School in Beijing in 1983, Deng wrote 'Orient education towards modernization, the outside world and the future.' This statement, known as *sange mianxiang* ('Three Orientations'), served to legitimize current trends in education that might be viewed as politically sensitive, such as the move in the English curriculum towards more listening and speaking to facilitate communication with foreigners.

Other than this allusion to Deng Xiaoping's statement, the syllabus makes no mention of leading political figures in its introduction. Instead, the introduction concentrates on the economic benefits accruing from the study of English:

> A foreign language is an important tool for learning cultural and scientific knowledge; to acquire information in different fields from around the world; and to develop international communication. "Orient education towards modernisation, the outside world and the future." Our country has adopted the Open Door Policy; the reforms of our country's economics, politics, technology and education are being wholeheartedly implemented; throughout the world, new technological reforms are booming. In order to construct our country as a modern socialist nation, with a high level of civilisation and democracy, we have to raise the cultural and scientific quality of all people in the country. We need to nurture a large number of experts who are goal-oriented and ethical, possessing culture, discipline and, to different extents, competence in various aspects of foreign languages. Under these circumstances, the value of foreign languages as important tools becomes greater. Therefore, foreign languages are listed as a basic subject in our country's secondary schooling. (PEP, 1986: 1, in translation)

In many respects, Series Seven followed the established tradition of English Language textbooks in China: they were inexpensively produced (basically, so they could be affordable for consumers from a range of socio-economic backgrounds across the country). The size is the regular 18.42 cm x 13 cm ($7\frac{1}{4}$ inches x 5.12 inches); the books have a thin paper cover, with a single pastel colour design incorporating coloured drawings, and the illustrations are mainly line drawings, with a few colour pictures at the front of each book (Figure A.11, p. 214). However, there were some technical innovations, with a greater array of components making up the textbook resources. They included teacher's books and cassette tapes of the reading passages and pattern drills. Supplementary reading and listening exercise books were also available. These extra resources reflect greater attention to the development of students' oral skills and to providing pedagogical support to the teachers.

Pedagogy

In common with previous syllabuses, the 1986 syllabus sets out the general learning targets and rationale, teaching principles, and the specific linguistic components to be covered at each year level. The learning targets do not contain a political dimension, unlike the syllabus for the previous curriculum, but stress that developing competence in English is the priority and, at the same time, it is important to provide the students with a good moral education (PEP, 1986: 2–3). The teaching principles stress the primacy of oral language, as the basis for competence in listening, speaking, reading and writing. This is a regular theme of previous syllabuses, which was reflected in earlier textbook series by the emphasis on oral development in the early stages of the course (through the use of Audiolingualism, for instance), before shifting towards greater concentration on reading and writing skills (with an increase in the use of Grammar-Translation). The 1986 syllabus encourages the use of songs, stories, conversations (such as in 'English Corners'), spelling bees and other extracurricular activities to strengthen students' oral competence.

The syllabus discusses teaching principles in considerable depth (at 84 pages, this syllabus is more substantial than its predecessors). It recommends the judicious and gradually declining use of the mother tongue (unlike the previous syllabus that allowed for more use of Chinese in English lessons). It suggests a foundation built on pronunciation, vocabulary and grammar, but it also stresses communicative principles. For instance, for reading passages, it says that it is important to let the students grasp the idea of the whole passage before examining the details ('otherwise they will not see the wood for the trees'), and even then, the details should be examined in the context of their relationship to the whole (PEP, 1986: 9). This technique departs from the Grammar-Translation Method and reflects more communicative approaches. The linguistic components are set out for each year group under the usual categories of the alphabet, pronunciation, handwriting, vocabulary, grammar and reading passages. The 1986 syllabus follows its predecessors in terms of its symbiotic relationship to the textbook resources, its organization and general content, but it does contain some innovations. It suggests a more communicative approach and is less political in tone than earlier syllabuses.

As with Series Six, each book in Series Seven is designed to cover one semester. The number of lessons in each pair of books does not correspond directly to the allocation of hours in the syllabus. Books 1 and 2 contain a total of 38 lessons for the 170 class periods allocated to English in Secondary One; Books 3 and 4 contain 29 lessons for a similar allocation; and Books 5 and 6 contain 22 lessons for 160 periods. The lower ratio of lessons to class periods in Secondary Two and Secondary Three is explained by the increased learning load that is included in Books 3 to 6, as these books devote more attention to reading passages.

Each book has a contents page, which sets out the main linguistic components and the title of any reading passage. There is a consolidated vocabulary list at the end of the books, as well as a collection of supplementary reading passages, which is an innovation. Book 1 also contains an appendix listing the phonetic symbols, together with examples and a diagram showing the position of the vocal organs for producing the individual sounds. Book 1 starts with the alphabet and letter formation, and also introduces simple, everyday vocabulary items that have relevant vowel sounds. Another feature, which runs through Books 1 and 2, is 'Everyday English'. This section presents a functional usage, such as greetings or asking the date. After presenting the alphabet, Book 1 teaches simple sentence structures in conjunction with common vocabulary items. A typical lesson is organized as follows: a pattern drill introduces the structure; a dialogue or, later, a reading passage presents the structure in a more realistic context; the new vocabulary is tabulated; any new grammar is presented; exercises practise various aspects, including pronunciation and intonation, vocabulary, spelling, grammar and handwriting; and the lesson concludes with 'Everyday English'. The phonetic symbols are printed as an appendix, and they are given in the consolidated vocabulary list at the end of the book, but they are not taught in the main body of a lesson until Book 2 Lesson 1 and Lesson 2. Thereafter, the lessons in Book 2 have the same basic organization as Book 1, with the addition of some rhymes after 'Everyday English'. From Book 3 onwards, the reading passage becomes more of a central focus. An extra section, notes on the reading passage, is added and exercises on reading comprehension are included in some lessons after the grammar exercises. 'Everyday English' is discontinued. This organization is followed, with minor variations, for the rest of Series Seven.

The lessons in Series Seven are loosely structured, in that there is not always a strong theme connecting all the components. For instance, in Book 3 Lesson 12, the drills present reflexive personal pronouns (e.g. 'I can repair it *myself*). The grammar section and one of the exercises practise reflexive pronouns but the reading passage, about friendship, has no examples of this grammatical item. There is, however, a tenuous thematic link, in that the context of the drills is people helping one another or participating together in an activity, which is similar to the reading passage. In other instances, the link is stronger, with the reading passage containing examples of the sentence patterns and also having a thematic link. In Book 4 Lesson 10, the sentence patterns are about past experience related to the present, mainly using the present perfect tense. These include questions about students' experience of learning English. The reading passage is a letter written by an Australian boy, describing his life in China to date, including his experiences of learning Chinese. Overall, however, such cohesive links are not a strong feature of Series Seven.

Is your mother a doctor, too?
No, she isn't. She's an English teacher.
What's your sister?
She's a nurse.

TEXT(课文)

My Family

I am an English boy. My name is Mike. I am twelve. My sister's name is Rose. She is fourteen. Rose and I are students. We like school.

My father is a teacher. He is a teacher of English. My mother is a nurse. They work hard. My little brother's name is Jack. He is only four. We all like Jack.

page seventy-seven 77

B

What's your name?
My name is Li Ping.
How old are you?
I'm twelve.
Are you a middle-school stud[ent]
Yes, I am.
Are you in Grade Two?
No, I'm not. I'm in Grade O[ne]

C

Are you middle-school studen[ts]
Yes, we are.
Are you in Grade Three?
No, we aren't. We're in Grad[e]
Are you Young Pioneers?
Yes, we are.

D

Is your father a doctor?
Yes, he is.
76 page seventy-six

Figure 6.2   Extract from Series Seven Book 1

Dialogues and reading practice on the topic of personal information. Passages about foreigners like this one were rare in previous series (Series Seven Book 1: 76–7).

This does not mean that there is little control over the contents. The linguistic components of the more realistic elements, such as dialogues and reading passages, are controlled so that they do not include many unfamiliar items that have not been covered beforehand. For example, no dialogues or reading passages contain past simple tense verbs until *was* and *were* are introduced in Book 3 Lesson 4. However, the control is not rigid: the dialogue includes two examples of regular past simple tense verbs, *called* and *asked*, which are not covered until the grammar section of the following lesson.

The organization and cohesion of Series Seven resembles that of Series Six (and therefore Series Two, Four and Five), in that the alphabet is taught before the phonetic symbols, and the early focus on oral skills is complemented in later stages by a growing emphasis on reading skills. The arrangement of the various sections of a lesson — basically, drills, dialogues and reading passages, presentation and practice of linguistic components, reading comprehension exercises and miscellaneous tailpieces — is likewise similar to Series Six. There are two innovations, the supplementary reading passages and the functional 'Everyday English', which reflect, respectively, the need to provide extra materials for the key schools and the greater attention being paid to communicative oral competence. As with Series Six, the organization reflects an amalgam of pedagogies. Drilling is linked with Audiolingualism; the focus on grammatical items is a feature of the Structural Approach; and the arrangement of the passages and related exercises is characteristic of the Grammar-Translation Method, but with a more communicative twist, as mentioned earlier. Another pedagogy, the Functional/Notional Approach is apparent in the brief examples of everyday English.

As noted above, there are a number of similarities between Series Six and Series Seven in the way in which the contents are organized. Likewise, the degree of realism of various components of discourse is similar. For instance, in both series, the pattern drills or dialogues that are placed at the beginning of many lessons display a weak or medium level of realism, in that they are included mainly in order to present and practise individual linguistic items, rather than to provide contextualized examples of realistic English usage. Also, in both series, the reading passages show a strong level of realism: their *raison d'être* is to present a story or information for instructive and/or entertainment purposes. The principal difference between the two series in terms of discourse is the addition in Series Seven of extra, strongly realistic, discourse components.

In Series Seven, the preliminary dialogues and drills in a lesson focus on a particular sentence pattern or grammar item. In the first two books, and in a few instances in Book 6, these have 'weak' realism, as the meaning of the sentences or dialogues is relatively insignificant; they simply demonstrate the grammatical form in question. For example, in Book 6 Lesson 1, the drill comprises pairs of sentences, including:

Many people speak English.
English is spoken by many people.

We often use a recorder in our English class.
A recorder is often used in our English class. (Series Seven Book 6: 1)

These sentences are uncontextualized — they are not placed in any sociolinguistic setting — and their purpose is just to show how the passive voice is formed. However, most of the preliminary dialogues from Book 3 onwards can be classified as 'medium' realism in that, although the communicative value of the dialogues is less important than the mastery of the structure, the language can be transferred directly to a real-life context. For example, in Book 3 Lesson 3, all the drills are transformation dialogues containing examples of the modal verbs *can*, *may* and *must*. An option in one of the drills is the following exchange:

A :   Excuse me, may I have a look at that book?
B :   Certainly. Here you are. (Series Seven Book 3: 21)

In practising this drill, the pupils use realistic, communicative language — and even may make reference to an actual book — but the main purpose is to practise a specific linguistic item.

Series Seven also contains situational dialogues that may be used for role-playing. These dialogues are strongly realistic, because their central focus is on everyday social interaction rather than on demonstrating grammatical usage. An example is in Book 3 Lesson 4, which contains a complete telephone conversation between Mary and Mrs Black. The conversation demonstrates the conventions in English for starting a call:

Mrs Black :   Hello!
Mary   :   Hello! May I speak to John?
Mrs Black :   Sorry, John isn't in. (Series Seven Book 3: 32)

Mrs Black then takes a message for John and the call ends with appropriate valedictions. By studying and practising this dialogue, students would be equipped with the necessary and appropriate language to use the telephone and leave or take a message in English.

The genres in Series Seven are similar to those of previous series — stories, anecdotes, informational passages and dialogues. One innovation in the discourse of Series Seven is the section entitled 'Everyday English', which is found in Book 1 and Book 2. This section presents functional items, such as asking for information or greeting people. These items are strongly realistic, as they are intended to be directly and holistically transferred to communicative situations. For example, in Book 2 Lesson 13, the section has the following exchange:

Shall we go and play pingpong?
That's a good idea.
Are you ready?
Not yet. Wait a minute, please. (Series Seven Book 2: 99)

This exchange is not meant to be studied for its grammatical components, such as the use of *Shall* or the imperative *Wait*. Instead, the focus is on real-life English in a given situation. As with the telephone dialogue quoted earlier, by learning these set phrases, the students will be better able to handle social interactions in English.

Another innovation in Series Seven is extra attention to reading. Two formats of reading passage are used. The first format is strongly realistic, as the main purpose is to enhance the students' ability to comprehend a complete piece of realistic discourse. Reading passages in the traditional position as the focal point of lessons from the latter stages of Book 1 onwards are complemented by the supplementary reading passages at the end of each book and also occasionally by an extra reading passage inserted at the end of the lesson. For example, Book 5 Lesson 10 has a second reading passage, 'A Story about Thomas Edison'. The second format of new reading material has 'medium' realism because the passages are also used for grammatical exercises. In Book 6 Lesson 5, for example, the lesson ends with a story called 'Give and Take', an Arabian fable about a rich man who falls into a river. He is so mean that he refuses to 'give' his hand to rescuers, and only responds when someone says, 'Take my hand.' The story is presented with eight blanks for students to fill in with appropriate prepositions.

Overall, there is a shift in Series Seven towards more realistic discourse in both oral and written language. The oral discourse has more sentence drills in the form of dialogues than previous series, and a new section, 'Everyday English' presents communicative language. The written discourse includes extra reading passages at the end of each book and within some lessons. This shift shows that, in terms of discourse, Series Seven embraces some of the tenets of the Functional/Notional Approach, especially in its use of dialogues with a medium or strong level of realism. However, the pedagogical approach implicit in Series Seven is broadly similar to Series Six, which in turn resembles that of Series Four, dating back to before the Cultural Revolution. The intended pedagogy is predominantly the Structural Approach, but there is also an amalgam of Audiolingualism, the Grammar-Translation Method and the Functional/Notional Approach. The spine of the course is the grammatical syllabus, broken down into individual items, and ranked from what is perceived as the easiest or most useful to the most difficult or less common items. In the early stages of the course, the focus is on short dialogues and sentence patterns for oral drilling — features consistent with Audiolingualism. As the course develops, the reading passage assumes greater prominence, and some exercises focus on the grammar of the passage and English-Chinese and Chinese-English translation, in accordance with the Grammar-Translation Method. Features of the Functional/Notional Approach, as noted above, are also evident. This approach presents and practises realistic English within its appropriate sociolinguistic setting. In Series Seven, there are fragments or complete dialogues that are directly transferable to everyday situations, and thus provide scope for communicative activities such as role plays. However, the functional/notional aspects are limited, because other features of the approach are lacking. For instance, students are provided little opportunity for creative or personal language use. Generally speaking, the kinds of oral and written production expected of the students by the exercises are heavily controlled and textbook-centred rather than student-centred. Opportunities for genuine, personalized communication — for instance, in the form of students exchanging information or writing their own letters to pen-friends — are not included, although a skilful teacher might be able to adapt some of the existing exercises to suit such a purpose.

Linguistic components

The provision of extra class periods for English in the junior secondary curriculum meant that the syllabus could prescribe longer lists of linguistic components to be covered. These targets are summarized in Table 6.7 (see p. 164).

The grammatical components in Series Seven, particularly the tenses, generally follow the arrangement of previous series. The verb *to be* is covered first, along with some common verbs in the present indefinite tense. Later the series introduces *to have*, before moving on to the present continuous, future, past continuous, present perfect and future-in-the-past tenses. Series Seven also follows the order of Series Six by presenting the alphabet before the phonetic symbols. The loose integration of the grammatical components with the other elements of the lessons in Series Seven stems from the writers' adherence to the fixed ordering of the grammatical syllabus in accordance with the Structural Approach. The grammatical components exert a strong controlling influence over the contents of the series. In a lesson, the amount of grammar previously covered, plus the new grammatical items for that lesson, determine the grammatical complexity of the reading passage.

For vocabulary, however, the opposite pertains: the contents of the reading passage generally determine the new vocabulary to be presented in the lesson. This accounts for the fact that Series Seven follows the prescribed grammatical syllabus very closely but is able to incorporate a two-tier vocabulary comprising core words which are deemed to be required learning, and non-core words which are relevant to specific reading passages, and are optional learning. The

Table 6.7 Linguistic components in the 1986 syllabus (adapted from PEP, 1986)

	Year 1	Year 2	Year 3
Vocabulary	about 450 words and a few expressions	about 450 more words and a few more expressions	about 350 more words and a few more expressions
Phonetics	1. phonetic transcriptions 2. consonant liaisons 3. basic spelling rules 4. word stress, sentence stress and rhythm 5. loss of plosive 6. falling and rising tones	1. liaisons 2. division of sense groups and pauses 3. intonation in long sentences	nil
Grammar	7. parts of speech 8. plurals; possessive forms of nouns 9. pronouns 10. prepositions of time and place 11. ordinals and cardinals 12. present simple, present continuous, *to be going to* 13. simple and co-ordinate clauses; statements, general and special questions; imperatives	4. definite and indefinite article 5. comparison of adjectives and adverbs 6. modal verbs 7. future, past, present perfect tenses 8. alternative and reflective questions 9. adverbial and objective clauses	1. infinitives 2. passive voice 3. past continuous, past perfect, future in the past tenses 4. indirect speech 5. attributive clauses

two-tier system is an innovative way to address the tension between linguistic control and the achieving realism in the reading passages. It also caters for the wide ability range for which the series is designed. The figures for vocabulary are distorted by the system if the grand total of 1,825 words is used as the basis for the average per lesson (20.51). However, only 806 words are identified as core words (an average of 9.01 words per lesson) — although the number of core words falls below the target of 1,250 words set out in the syllabus. This flexibility demonstrates attention to different students' needs, which was one of the requests of teachers attending the conference at the Summer Palace.

Content

The messages in Series Seven focus more on moral than on political themes — even more so than Series Six. Table 6.8 shows, however, that the majority of the discourse examples do not have a clear moral or political connotation.

Table 6.8   Political and moral messages in Series Seven

Discourse total	Messages total	Nil	Moral	Political	Political (attitude)	Political (information)	Political (role model)
168	169	108 (63.91%)	47 (27.81%)	14 (8.28%)	6	1	7

The moral messages are conveyed either through traditional fables, such as 'The Cock And the Fox' (Book 2 Lesson 12) or 'The Fox and the Crow' (Book 2 Supplementary Reading Passage 2); modern stories or everyday anecdotes and dialogues. In Book 2 Lesson 6, two Young Pioneers exhibit exemplary behaviour by handing in a lost watch to the police; and in Book 2 Lesson 7, Young Pioneers offer their seats to an old woman (unlike in Series Six, when they are chided for failing to do so). Some passages offer the children advice on appropriate behaviour, such as the one about good manners (Book 6 Lesson 8), which covers a variety of social situations, including forming an orderly queue, using a handkerchief, not spitting, standing up when speaking to an older person and not making too much noise in public. It goes on to cover the classroom:

> As a student, it is bad manners to come late to class. If you are late, you should make an apology to the teacher either at the time or after class. It is also bad manners to keep silent when the teacher asks you a question. If you do not know the answer, say so immediately. If you do know, answer in a loud enough

voice so that all the class may hear. It is polite for the students to help the teacher. Sometimes students can help their teachers to clean the blackboard, to close or open the door or windows. Sometimes there are papers to collect or hand out. This kind of help is always appreciated. (Series Seven Book 6: 80–1)

Book 6 Lesson 1 stresses the diligence and its rewards, in terms of intellectual benefits:

Ping :   ... But, Dad, English is so hard!
Dad :   It is hard, but when you've learned it, you'll find it a bridge to so much knowledge. And you'll find you can enjoy so many more books, if you know English.
Ping :   Well, I'll try harder. (Series Seven Book 6: 4)

In previous series, a prevalent feature of the political messages conveyed by the reading passages was the negative portrayal of other countries, particularly Western, capitalist nations. In Series Seven, however, there are very few reading passages that give a bad impression of foreign countries. The only notable examples are the passage about a dustman's strike (Book 6 Lesson 3), which is retained from the 1978 series, and the story of Joe Hill (Book 6 Lesson 2), a trade unionist in the USA. Even the latter is placed within its historical perspective, as the passage states that Joe Hill moved to USA at the turn of the century: 'At that time, things were hard for the workers.' Two stories, 'Once a Thief, Always a Thief?' (Book 5 Lesson 8) and 'It's Unfair' (Book 4 Lessons 4 and 5), which have a moral message conveyed through a negative incident, are set in a Western country, but a recurrent theme in previous series, the poor treatment of blacks in the USA, is not found in Series Seven.

Indeed, there are several passages that contain a positive portrayal of other countries and their people. For instance, 'My Family' in Book 1 Lesson 14 describes a happy, hard-working family from England. Likewise, an American girl's letter in Book 2 Lesson 11 describes her apparently contented family life, and expresses an interest in finding out more about China. The actions of foreigners deemed praiseworthy include the medical assistance given by Dr Norman Bethune to the CCP's Eighth Route Army in the Anti-Japanese War (Book 5 Lesson 10), Franz Liszt helping a struggling piano teacher (Book 4 Lesson 11), Nathan Hale's patriotic speech before his execution (Book 5 Lesson 2), Thomas Edison's practical ingenuity (Book 5 Lesson 9) and a woman's self-sacrifice during the sinking of the *Titanic* (Book 4 Lesson 13):

People had to leave the ship. Women and children were the first to get into the lifeboats. Suddenly a woman shouted, "Please make room for me. My children are in that boat. I must go with them! Please!"

"There's no more room here," someone shouted back. The children heard their mother and began to cry.

A young woman was sitting near the poor children. She stood up. "Here," she shouted. "Take my place! I'm not married and I have no children."

She got out and the thankful mother joined her children in the lifeboat.

Soon after that, the ship went down. More than 1,500 people lost their lives. Among those was the young woman.

Who was she? Her name was Miss Evans and she was going home to Boston. But nobody knew more about her than that. (Series Seven Book 4: 127–8)

Overtly pro-CCP political content is less evident but not totally absent from Series Seven. In the same lesson as the passage about Joe Hill (Book 6 Lesson 2), there is the story of Li Dazhao, a CCP founder-member who was captured and killed during the Civil War in 1927. According to the passage:

While he was in prison, he would not give in and fought bravely. Just before he was killed, he made a speech. These were his last words: "You can kill me, but you can't kill all the communists. Communism is sure to win."

Comrade Li Dazhao is not dead! He will never die! His name will be remembered by the Chinese people for ever. (Series Seven Book 6: 24)

However, this example is exceptional. No passages mention any CCP leader by name — not even Mao Zedong. The emphasis on moral messages is evidenced not only by the small amount of discourse devoted to political messages, but also by the vocabulary. The number of non-Thorndike words (501, or 27.45%) is relatively low, and of these, vocabulary with direct political connotations is in a small minority: *Young Pioneer* is introduced in Book 1 Lesson 14, and Book 6 Lesson 2 includes *the PLA*, *liberation* and *Chinese Communist Party*.

The low political content and the positive portrayal of foreigners corresponds with the economic orientation of the nation at the time, including the Open Door Policy, as is reflected in the 1986 syllabus. The shift from generally negative to generally positive references to other countries mirrors the significant change in the Chinese media that took place after Deng Xiaoping's visit to the USA. Also, the lack of references to political leaders may be explained by the PEP's determination to learn from the mistakes of the 1978 curriculum, whose glowing references to Hua Guofeng in Series Six rendered it obsolete and politically incorrect by his fall from power. The 1982 curriculum lasted for 11 years, until funding and partners were secured for a large-scale revision to the curriculum that was a significant reflection of China's economic development and internationalization.

Summary

The English Language curricula of 1978 and 1982 resembled but extended the approach to curriculum development that prevailed between 1960 and 1965 when the syllabus was oriented towards economic rather than political goals. The PEP re-established itself as the central curriculum development agency, while outside agencies contributed to the production of the syllabus and accompanying textbooks by acting as consultants and materials writers, and teachers also played a significant role in the process. The intended pedagogical approach of this phase also resembled that of the early 1960s, moving away from the traditional, teacher-centred methodology of the textbooks that appeared during the Cultural Revolution.

New features of this phase include the amalgamation of a range of pedagogical approaches, and a gradual depoliticization of contents, marked by a defrosting in the portrayal of Western societies. These changes can be attributed to two factors: to the role of the outside agencies, the specialists in top institutions in China, who had knowledge of different approaches to English Language teaching around the world; and to the less stringent political restraints of the Dengist era, which made it acceptable to appropriate pedagogical ideas from Western countries and economically desirable to promote cross-cultural understandings.

7 *Integrating with globalization, 1993 onwards*

Despite the political uncertainties of the late 1980s, economic reforms such as the Open Door Policy continued unabated, which ensured that the trends towards pedagogical developments in the English Language curriculum that stressed communicative competence remained in place. The new curriculum that appeared in 1993 was marked by major innovations that took seven years to materialize for various logistical reasons, so the genesis lay in events that pre-dated the Tiananmen Square incident and the curriculum development was hindered but not stopped by the political turmoil.

The Open Door Policy increased people's dealings with English speakers and was a further significant boost to both the status and role of English. The development of international trade and the tourist industry led to the creation of well-paid jobs for translators and interpreters. Language study also became a form of entertainment, popularized by the increased access to electronic goods and to various forms of mass media in English produced either domestically or imported from overseas. There were increasing opportunities for foreign travel for business, study and, latterly, tourism. More educational institutions were able to import native-speaker teachers, initially at tertiary level and then increasingly at secondary level. China hosted international events such as the Asian Games in 1990 and the International Women's Conference in 1995, put in bids for the Olympic Games (failing in the attempt to win the 2000 Games, but winning the 2008 Games to be held in Beijing), and achieved entry into the World Trade Organization in November 2001. By the turn of the century, English had become a prerequisite for university entrance and for many posts in the civil service. Taxi drivers in major cities had to pass proficiency tests.

An interesting phenomenon that emerged in the late 1990s was Li Yang's 'Crazy English' learning method, which employs various techniques to overcome reticence in speaking English, such as chanting exhortatory slogans. Participants in 'Crazy English' classes are encouraged to 'speak as loudly as possible', 'speak as quickly as possible', and 'speak as clearly as possible'. Li links English learning to a patriotic message that the language will help China to exercise economic hegemony over the USA, Japan and Europe — this message resonates with the role of English in contributing to nation-building that lay behind the establishment of the Tongwen Guan in 1861. As Bolton observes,

> ... Li Yang's approach appears to give voice to the material hopes of millions of Chinese in a variety of brash English that twangs American but rings global with its exhortation 'Make the voice of China be widely heard all over the world!' (Bolton, 2002: 196)

It was estimated that, in 1995, about 50 million junior secondary students were studying English, 350,000 were studying Russian and 160,000 Japanese (Liu, 1995). The number of full-time junior secondary English language teachers was 374,454 in 1994, having risen from just 73 in 1957 (State Education Commission, 1995). The study of English was a compulsory subject for all tertiary students, regardless of their major, and led to the College English Test, a nationwide examination that attracts around 5.5 million candidates annually (Yang, 2001).

A series of major reforms in education were undertaken from the mid-1980s onwards. They addressed problems that had either surfaced or not disappeared since the Four Modernizations and the Open Door Policies had begun in 1978. The reform programme was multi-faceted, but two policies had a particular impact upon the development of the English Language curriculum. The first aimed at improving the provision of mass education, as there were areas of China that had yet to achieve this goal, which had social equity implications. The Nine-Year Compulsory Education Law was promulgated in 1985. The second was the policy of decentralization that was designed to cater for the specific educational needs of different localities. The impact on the English Language curriculum was the wider range of teaching and learning situations that it would have to serve, and the opportunity for agencies at a local level to develop and publish their own textbook series in competition to those produced by the PEP, although the PEP remained responsible for publishing the syllabus.

The 1993 curriculum

A national survey of secondary school students in 1986 carried out by the State Education Commission (SEdC) — as the Ministry of Education was then called following its upgrading in 1984 — revealed severe problems in secondary school students' language competence and concluded that Grammar-Translation teaching methods, out-of-date language material, the shortage of qualified teachers and equipment, and the rigid format of written exams had hampered the effectiveness of teaching and learning English. As a result, the SEdC undertook reforms of the secondary school curriculum, textbook production, pedagogy, teacher education and examination systems. These initiatives were then linked to the broader educational policies regarding mass education and decentralization. A further stimulus to reform was the promise of funding from the United Nations Development Programme (UNDP), which encouraged the PEP to undertake a large-scale project of curriculum innovation. The features of the 1993 curriculum are summarized in Table 7.1.

Table 7.1   Key features of the English Language curriculum from 1993

Genesis	Nine-year compulsory education; strengthening of English language teaching; national economic modernization; strengthening of the Open Door Policy; decentralization of decision-making
Role and status of English	Economic development — international transfer and communication; access to higher education and lucrative employment; very high official status
Role of agencies PEP: consultants: teachers:	Collaboration in researching and producing Series Eight Advice and (foreign agency) co-producers Consultants; feedback from piloting and post-implementation use
Process	(Series Eight) research in China and abroad; collaboration with foreign publisher, specialists and teachers; extensive piloting; teacher training; continuing revisions in the light of post-implementation feedback
Syllabus	Produced by CTMRI, published by the PEP; stresses communicative competence; lists function/notions, as well as vocabulary and grammar
Resources	Series Eight, plus other textbooks produced by various regions. Series Eight includes: Student's Books, Teacher's Books, Workbooks, Reading Practice Books, cassettes, wall pictures, videos, CD-ROMs, etc.
Organization	Integrated topic-based, cyclical progression with regular revision
Discourse	Anecdotes, stories, everyday dialogues, scientific and cultural passages
Linguistic components	Focus on realistic oral skills; functions, notions; traditional arrangement of grammatical components
Intended pedagogy	Eclectic: Structural-Functional/Notional, with some Audiolingualism
Political and moral messages	Some moral messages; very weak political content

In response to the crisis of quality in students' English language skills, the Curriculum and Teaching Materials Research Institute (CTMRI) — a unit of the SEdC founded in 1983 — turned to international solutions, and noted, in recent decades, that 'there have been significant developments in the theory and practice of English language teaching in the world. More emphasis has been put on the use of the language for purposeful communication' (Liu, 1995: 2). The SEdC also decided to improve the technical quality of primary and secondary school textbooks, and set up a joint venture with a foreign publisher to produce the new national English Language textbook series. The commission also decided to allow greater local autonomy in curriculum development: in a notable change from previous practice, three English Language syllabuses were permitted — the national syllabus, and syllabuses for local use developed by Shanghai Education Commission and Zhejiang Education Commission. Regional publishers were also permitted to submit textbook resources for the national syllabus to the newly set-up National Evaluation Committee of Primary and Secondary School Textbooks (NECPSST), a bureau within the SEdC, for approval.

The composition of the CTMRI actually formalized a relationship between the PEP and outside agencies that has been identified in previous instances of curriculum development, such as Series Four, Five, Six and Seven. The members were drawn from the PEP and consultants from tertiary institutions, and their role was to carry out research in curriculum and pedagogy in order to draw up the syllabus and also to help to develop Series Eight. The CTMRI also appointed overseas consultants, such as Professor Deng Yanchang (Frank Tang), the American-born Chinese language specialist (by then working at the University of Hawai'i) who had worked on Series Seven, to advise on specific projects. The leader of the team was Liu Daoyi, who was the head of the English section and also Deputy Chief Editor of the PEP. Liu Daoyi had spent one year from 1985–86 studying in Australia under linguistics specialist Michael Halliday, and was influenced by contemporary ideas relating to English Language teaching. Halliday was noted for his work on functional grammar, which emphasized the importance of contextualizing features and pragmatic intentions that govern language in use, rather than language rules *in vacuo*. This work had informed the Functional/Notional Approach to foreign language teaching that had been developed in many Western countries since the mid-1970s, and which had had an influence on Series Seven.

A more communicative approach was seen by the CTMRI as the way to improving what Hymes (1972) terms the 'communicative competence' of students, and a new syllabus was to be drafted accordingly in 1987 (although it was not published until 1993). It was a novel approach for China:

> It is the first time in the history of EFL in China that the actual use of the language for communication should be placed in such a prominent position.

This indicates that schools will no longer teach students about the language but teach them how to use it. (Liu, 1995)

Alternative textbooks to the PEP's Series Eight were produced by different agencies, including the South East Normal University (for use in the Guangdong region); Beijing Normal University; Sichuan Educational Science Institute and the South West Normal University; and a team from Jiangsu Province. Selection of textbooks was carried out at the provincial level (or municipal level in the major cities), but in the event, most provinces selected Series Eight, which took over 70% of the market share (Liu, 1995). This is understandable given the PEP's resources, experience and prestige as part of the SEdC. Because of this dominance, the analysis of textbook content in this chapter will be restricted to the PEP series.

The English syllabus for the new secondary school curriculum introduced in 1993, prepared by the CTMRI and published by the PEP, sets out the official role for foreign languages:

> A foreign language is an important tool for making contact with other countries and plays an important role in promoting the development of the national and world economy, science and culture. For the purpose of meeting the needs of our Open Door Policy and speeding up socialist modernisation, efforts should be made to enable as many people as possible to acquire certain command of one or more foreign languages. (PEP, 1993: 1, in translation)

English was by far the most common foreign language because of its importance in examinations to higher levels of schooling. The guidelines issued by the CTMRI for the compilation of teaching materials stipulate that 400 class hours were to be devoted to English in three-year junior secondary schools and 530 hours in those which offer four-year courses (PEP, 1989). The syllabus states that the curriculum should not be politically overt, but materials should be chosen which, as noted earlier, focus on moral education, and also foster patriotism and socialism (PEP, 1993). The ambit of English study was expanded to include foreign culture. Overall, the aims of the syllabus go beyond the development of communicative competence. Besides giving basic training in the four linguistic skills, the curriculum should also strive to:

> ... develop [students'] thinking ability; help them acquire more knowledge of foreign culture; strengthen international understanding; arouse their interest and study, and form correct methods and good habits of study so that an initial foundation can be laid for their further study of English as well as future work. (PEP, 1993: 1, in translation)

The guidelines acknowledge the value of learning from past experience and experiments to develop an effective new curriculum:

174   China's English: A history of English in Chinese education

> We must pay attention to our efficient traditional teaching experiences, such as knowing the history of English teaching and secondary school textbook compilation in our country, studying and summarising the experiences and lessons of using the current teaching syllabus and teaching materials, as well as the experiences of teaching experiments in all parts of the country. Those experiences suit the features of teaching English in our country and play an important role in our English teaching work. (PEP, 1989: 5)

To develop communication, the syllabus advises that time devoted to students practising using the language must exceed teacher-centred instruction and drilling should not be stressed too much. Teachers were encouraged to use a variety of teaching strategies to create situations for communicative activities:

> Language form has to be combined with its meaning and with what the students think and want to say. Special attention should be paid to turning the language skills acquired through practice into the capacity of using the language for the purpose of communication ... . When the students realise that they can communicate in English they will go on learning with more interest and motivation. (PEP, 1993: 6, in translation)

The learning targets of the new syllabus are summarized in Table 7.2. The targets are divided into two levels to allow for flexibility. Level One is for students to cover in the first two years; Level Two is for the third year (for those areas operating a three-year junior secondary programme) or for the third and fourth year (for those areas operating a four-year junior secondary programme).

Table 7.2   Summary of learning targets for the 1993 curriculum (adapted from PEP, 1993)

Level One	Targets
Listening	understand simple classroom English and give simple answers; understand the main idea of a passage read by the teacher using familiar patterns and vocabulary
Speaking	carry out simple classroom routines; do question-and-answer exercises in the textbook; use some of the 'Daily Expressions in Communication'
Reading	understand a reading passage with less than 2% new words with a dictionary
Writing	have neat handwriting and basic orthographic skills; write a dictation based on a familiar passage at a speed of five to seven words per minute; answer questions in the textbook in writing; make simple sentences based on models

(continued on p. 175)

Table 7.2   *(continued)*

Pronunciation	use the International Phonetic Alphabet and reading rules to pronounce new words; read aloud the reading passage with basic accuracy
Vocabulary	have an active oral and written command of about 350 common words and 100 common expressions; passive command of about 300 other words; use phonics
Grammar	master the inflections and 3 basic sentence structures; use the present simple, past simple, future simple and present continuous tenses orally and in writing
Level Two	**Targets**
Listening	understand classroom English and give answers; understand the main idea of a passage read by the teacher using familiar patterns and vocabulary; understand with 70% correctness after listening three times to native speakers' recording of familiar materials at a reading speed of 100–110 words per minute
Speaking	do simple classroom routines; do question-and-answer exercises in the textbook; use 'Daily Expressions in Communication'; retell passages in simple English
Reading	read for gist with a dictionary; read aloud and recite coherently; understand a reading passage with less than 2% new words with a reading speed of 40–50 words per minute (3-year programme) or 50–60 words per minute (4-year programme) with 70% correctness
Writing	have neat handwriting and orthographic skills; write (at around 10–12 words per minute) a dictation based on a familiar passage read at a speed of 100–110 words per minute; answer questions in the textbook in writing; make simple sentences and communicative discourse (such as messages) based on models
Pronunciation	use the International Phonetic Alphabet and phonics to pronounce new words; read aloud the reading passage accurately; use correct pronunciation and intonation
Vocabulary	have an active oral and written command of around 600–700 frequently used words plus 200 common expressions; have a passive command of around 400–500 other words; use the rules of reading to remember the spelling of words; tell the meaning and parts of speech of derivatives and compounds; identify the meaning and parts of speech of polysemants in context
Grammar	master inflections and 5 basic sentence structures; use present simple, past simple, future simple, present continuous, present perfect, past perfect and future-in-the-past tenses orally and in writing; master passive voice in present simple and past simple tenses and in sentences containing modal verbs; master usage of infinitives functioning as the object, object complement and adverbial; understand usage of infinitives as subject or attributive

The syllabus follows the pattern of its predecessors by setting out the rationale, requirements and content of the programme, as well as the language items to be covered. One innovation is a list of phrases for 30 functional/notional situations, labelled 'Daily Expressions in Communication'. It also draws its vocabulary list from the Cambridge English Lexicon, rather than the lists compiled by Thorndike or Michael West. The Cambridge English Lexicon list of frequently used English words incorporates vocabulary such as *pioneer, league* and *comrade*, which enables the CTMRI to include *Young Pioneer, Youth League* and *Comrade* in the syllabus, but these are the only distinctively political terms.

The contents of the syllabus reveal of synthesis of new and old approaches that were also evident in the development of Series Eight. There continues to be a strong presence of discrete linguistic components, both grammatical and lexical, and an attempt to quantify the learning load (for instance, in the number of new words to be learnt and the percentage of correctness expected). These features were present in previous syllabuses. The new approach, the stress on communicative discourse in the four skills or listening, speaking, reading and writing, is grafted on to existing practice. The threshold for understanding spoken and written discourse is quantified: for listening, it is to achieve 70% correctness in understanding after listening three times to native speakers' recording of familiar materials at a reading speed of 100–110 words per minute, and there is a similar threshold for reading skills. Speaking and writing skills include the production of discourse using simple structures.

The seven-year delay between initiating curriculum change and producing a new curriculum occurred because of the time-consuming processes of securing funding and tendering the international co-operative aspects of the textbook project. Liu Daoyi wanted to enter into a collaborative project with a foreign publisher who could provide the expertise in communicative materials writing and technical production that the PEP lacked, while the PEP would carry out supervisory and editing work. Following discussions that began in the course of Liu's visit to the Educational Book Fair in Beijing in 1986, a foreign publisher based in Europe was engaged. After several months, however, problems emerged in executing the contract — one reason being the PEP's dissatisfaction with the draft materials — and the project was discontinued. Liu Daoyi then met a representative of UNDP in Beijing, and, in 1987, both parties entered into an agreement, with the UNDP undertaking to finance a project involving the PEP and a foreign publisher in the production of a new textbook series for junior secondary English, as well as supporting teacher education workshops. The contract for a foreign publisher was put out to tender, and Liu Daoyi went to UNDP headquarters in Paris to consider the proposals. A publisher based in Australia was initially considered by Liu Daoyi to be the most acceptable, but in the event, the designated writer was not available for the amount of time that Liu Daoyi considered necessary for the project. Finally, Longman International from the United Kingdom won the contract. According to the agreement, Longman International would provide input in terms of materials writing, design and production skills, and in supporting the teacher education programme. Longman International supplied a consultant (L.G. Alexander, whose work, including the television series, 'Follow Me', was well-known in China), two writers (Neville Grant and myself), editorial support and technical training. Liu Daoyi was the Chief Editor of the project. The PEP staff were responsible for editing the textbooks, producing supplementary materials, and overseeing the design, production and dissemination of all the components of the series, which was entitled 'Junior English for China'.

The project commenced with a six-month research period, in which Grant, the chief writer from Longman International, met with teachers and discussed issues relating to English Language pedagogy in China. In the project guidelines, the CTMRI invoked the process of *zhongxue weiti xixue weiyong* (grafting Western practices on to Chinese culture) to allow a marriage of overseas theories of language acquisition and language teaching with the practical realities of language education in China:

> We should make further researches into all the pedagogic schools, rejecting the dross and assimilating the essence, and make them serve us according to our national conditions. (PEP, 1989: 5)

Grant, an experienced textbook writer who had been involved in projects in Africa, the Middle East and the Caribbean, preferred to build on local practices, rather than to import new methods without reference to the local context, as he recalls:

> I was very much swayed (in different directions!) by the meetings I had in Beijing, Chengdu and elsewhere with teachers and researchers — and of course by my interactions with my colleagues in the PEP. Among the salient memories I have are the deeply felt urge for change among many of my informants — by the desire for English to be learnt in a more practical and communicative manner — even if questions were begged as to what 'communicative' might mean; conversely the voices of caution expressed by the PEP — who, commendably kept their ears very close to the ground on their many visits to schools across China. (A very positive feature of the PEP's *modus operandi*.) The PEP were only too well aware of the deeply conservative forces within the rank and file of the profession ... The PEP's caution was reinforced by visits to schools, where at times I saw abysmal English lessons! ... All in all I was swayed by all this and similar experiences to attempt to synthesise what was regarded as best practice in China with what was considered to be acceptable elements of communicative pedagogy. The approach evolved ... through extended negotiation between the PEP and myself.[1]

To achieve an appropriate balance between the traditional Structural Approach and more communicative pedagogy was, at times, a hit-and-miss affair, as Liu Daoyi comments:

> We had to make ... revisions for the first book. ... The first time [Grant] made things very interesting, but he couldn't control the language load, so we said "This is very good, very interesting, but the teachers wouldn't be able to accept your material. Try to make it easier." The next time, he seemed to be more structural, making things a little bit less interesting. So we said, "Well, this is closer to the old book." So we were not very pleased! We had to revise it. The last version, we said "Good! Just right!"[2]

Generally, however, the view of blending the Structural Approach with a more communicative pedagogy was shared by the PEP team and Grant, who comments:

> [The PEP] had a strong (in my view fully justified) belief in a carefully graded structural programme; their talk was of grammar forms, seldom of functions ... I had no difficulty with this; I have long held the view that grammatical grading according to the quasi-logic of the language, with the grammatical items practised in a communicative manner was a good way of synthesizing old and new.[3]

In this respect, Liu Daoyi's experience proved complementary:

> As I studied linguistics in Sydney, I didn't study the new methodology very thoroughly — only one year — but I really got the essence of the new ideas, but my knowledge of the methodology and my knowledge of the English language is limited, so we needed assistance from Neville [Grant]. For his part, he was very strong at using the new methods because he had already written textbooks using the new methods. Whereas we had knowledge, we had theories, we wrote books using an approach that was very much influenced by the Structural Approach ... but we put our effort into the books, because we think we know our students, how Chinese students can develop their English, their linguistic ability, what kind of pedagogical situations there are in China, so when we adopt the new ideas, we are very careful; when we take a step forward, we have to be very cautious not to go too far.[4]

One important influence upon pedagogical approaches adopted in the new curriculum was the experiments that had been conducted in different parts of China, most notably since 1983, when key schools were re-established. In some places, such as Beijing, Shanghai and Guangzhou, key school teachers were supplementing Series Seven with textbooks imported from Hong Kong or the West, including the 'New Concept English' series by L.G. Alexander. The approaches in these series, often with an emphasis on realistic communication, stimulated interest in foreign pedagogical ideas, and assisted some scholars in China in the design of their own pedagogical approaches. One example cited by Liu Daoyi was the 'Global Teaching' approach developed by a group of Hubei scholars led by Liu Zhaoyi. It shifted the focus from grammar to reading for communication, according to Liu Daoyi:

> Teachers used to do reading aloud, explanation, then memorisation when they dealt with a reading passage, and they spent several hours analysing the text, citing all the examples from reference books, getting the students to translate from Chinese into English. The students had to take notes. They ignored the information in the texts. And then, with the 'Global Teaching' method of texts, [the scholars] want teachers to concentrate on the global meaning; they must pay more attention to the content, the information, so they asked the teachers to go over the text quickly, within one class period. That worked very well.[5]

Once drafted, the textbooks were piloted. The piloting was more extensive than for any previous series, both in terms of time and location. It took place over a three-year period in different environments: in major cities, such as Beijing, county towns and small towns, so that a broader range of feedback could be collected from teachers. Although only minor adjustments were subsequently made to the series (such as revising some of the teaching notes), the PEP responded to teachers' requests by producing extra supplementary materials, such as wall charts, collections of alternative lesson plans, a book showing stick figures for teachers to copy on the blackboard, and a new edition of the Teacher's Books with notes in Chinese to replace the interleaved pages from the Student's Books. The PEP also published materials contributed by teachers, such as facemasks of the characters in the series for use in role plays. Teacher education videos showing model lessons were also produced.

My role in the development of Series Eight was concerned with teacher education, and involved collaborating with Liu Daoyi in writing the Teacher's Books and presenting workshops to teachers in the areas that were piloting Series Eight. These workshops, which were carried out in major cities such as Beijing and Wuhan, remote cities in Inner Mongolia, Xinjiang, Dandong (on the border with North Korea), as well as small towns in Anhui and on the Yangzi River, formed part of a series involving three or four teams of trainers (one trainer from overseas and one from the PEP) that took place between 1990 and 1993. The Teacher's Books were viewed as playing an important role in the reform, as they were designed to provide considerable support to teachers. It was assumed that many would not be used to the new pedagogical ideas included in Series Eight. As I noted:

> The new methodology needed to be explained. Variations in students' needs and abilities, and the availability of resources had to be considered. Many teachers would require language support, help with grammatical explanations

and background information on the cultural elements in the series. Our response to these needs evolved as the writing proceeded: unfortunately we did not have the prescience to address them all from the outset. (Adamson, 1995: 21)

A variety of methods were designed in order to handle these issues:

> The question of methodology was tackled by including an introductory chapter in Chinese on the theoretical basis and practical applications underpinning the course. Detailed, step-by-step lesson plans were written and interleaved with the relevant pages from the Student's Book. Occasionally, a brief explanation was given as to the purpose of an activity. Suggestions were offered on how to simplify or extend activities to suit individual needs and interests. I assumed that minimal resources were available, by describing ways of carrying out, for example, a listening exercise if the teacher had no tape recorder. Verbatim classroom language was included for the teachers to use, such as "Say to your students: *Please look at the picture. What can you see?*", and notes on grammar and cultural issues were incorporated. Liu Daoyi provided very useful insights into the teachers' needs as far as grammar and cultural notes were concerned, as I tended to assume too much as common knowledge. (Adamson, 1995: 21–22)

Liu Daoyi's contribution is once again a reflection of her perception that the interests of teachers had to be safeguarded and that too great a leap forward in pedagogy would be unwise. The techniques adopted in writing the Teacher's Books were rooted in my previous experience of teacher education in China:

> My task was to draft the books, with Liu Daoyi acting as editorial supervisor. My approach was to think back to lesson planning conferences that I used to have with a junior secondary school teacher in Taiyuan, Shanxi Province, where I worked in a Teachers' College. Miss Zhao had basic training in ELT [English Language teaching], taught in an ordinary school with large classes and poor resources, and always raised very practical objections to my suggestions for her teaching. I wrote the Teacher's Books with her in mind. (Adamson, 1995: 21)

Overall, the development process of the 1993 curriculum was more complex than its predecessors. The consultative relationship between outside agencies and the PEP was formalized with the establishment of the research-oriented CTMRI. More autonomy was granted to regional authorities to produce textbook series, although they had to be approved by ministry officials in the NECPSST. The PEP (and Liu Daoyi in particular) had strong views as to the kind of textbook series that would be suitable for the new curriculum: communicative in orientation, but with a structured progression, and containing moral messages. Despite the involvement of a foreign publisher, it was not direct transfer of Western pedagogy. There was a process of synthesis, with the project director, Liu Daoyi, having the final say with regard to the end product. The collaboration with outside agencies and teachers was enhanced: Series Eight, which emerged from the PEP project, was the result of extensive consultation with teachers and teacher researchers (local officials in charge of supporting curriculum development). Another new feature was the PEP's continuing support once implementation had begun. For previous series, the PEP had provided all textbook resources in advance. For Series Eight, new materials were added after the series had been published.

Assessment, which previously had not been a major issue in curriculum development, was more significant in the 1993 curriculum, as the importance of examinations for access to higher education grew. The new pedagogy led to a tension with prevailing assessment practices, particularly with the increased attention to developing oral and listening ability — skills which had rarely been assessed before. In the classroom, this placed teachers in a dilemma: whether they should teach specifically for the examinations or follow the recommended syllabus. Liu Daoyi was determined that the new curriculum should force changes in the examinations, rather than allowing the examinations to circumscribe the pedagogy in the textbook series (Liu, 1995). In the event, however, it is clear that Book 3 and Book 4 in Series Eight have a stronger orientation towards reading and writing skills than the earlier books.

Two major innovations in Series Eight in terms of the nature of the resources are the increased size of the textbooks and the wide range of resources accompanying the series, which are more comprehensive than for any previous series. The page-size of the Students' Book is double that of previous textbooks, measuring 26 cm x 18.5 cm ($10\frac{1}{4}$ inches x $7\frac{1}{4}$ inches; see Figure A.12, p. 214). This provides room for the inclusion of more material (thus aiding integration of the four skills) and allows a more generous spacing in the layout of contents. There are more illustrations throughout including several pages containing reproductions of colour photographs, and the cover is made of thick paper (glossy in most editions) with bright coloured designs. The resources include four Students' Books (Book 4 was intended for those areas of China which operate a four-year junior secondary school system) and Teacher's Books; Workbooks for written exercises; readers; cassette tapes; videos, CD-ROMs and wallcharts. In some versions of the series, the four Student's Books were sub-divided into eight books to lighten the physical burden for students.

These innovations helped to address two goals. Teacher support was identified by Liu Daoyi and Neville Grant as crucial to the success of the new curriculum. The larger page size allowed for all the prescribed material for an individual lesson to be consolidated on a single page: thus effectively delineating the expected contents of each lesson. The detailed notes in the Teacher's Book were designed to provide support for teachers unfamiliar with the new approaches. The use of multi-media permitted a greater variety in the learning experiences than previously available, reflecting the belief underlying the Functional/Notional Approach that language is embedded in a socio-cultural context — the videos, pictures, CD-ROMs and other media allowed realistic, contextualized English to be present in the language classroom.

The organization of Series Eight has some similarities and differences from previous series. One innovation is the arrangement of the content into material for an individual class period, rather than for approximately one week's work, as was the previous practice. The material is divided into lessons and units. The textbooks have 30 units in Book 1, 28 in Book 2, 24 in Books 3 and 4. Each lesson occupies one page and there is a corresponding set of exercises in the Workbook, intended for classwork and/or homework. Four lessons constitute a unit devoted to a particular theme, in terms either of topic or linguistic function. There are recurring characters: Chinese and Western children who attend a school in Beijing, and their family and teachers. Some topics focus on the children's daily life as they interact in school or engage in more culturally-specific activities at home. The characters do not appear in every lesson: sometimes the reading passages or dialogues are stories based in Western countries or they focus on a topic of general interest. The latter trend is particularly evident in Books 3 and 4, towards the end of the course. The use of Western children is not new, but their placement in a specific school context is. Liu Daoyi recalls that this decision arose from an idea by Neville Grant in response to the instructions he had received from the PEP:

> We just told Neville the materials and the contents of the materials should be close to the students' life, so actually the texts are relevant to the students' daily life — the children's interests and needs … [and] we chose to include different nationalities, different characters from Australia, the States, China: in that way we can include foreign culture.[6]

Each book in the series contains a contents page, a few pages with full colour illustrations or photographs (to which references are made in the main body of the book), and various appendices. In all the books, the appendices include notes on the phonic relationship between letters and sounds; a summary of grammar points introduced in the book; a list of words and expressions arranged according to the units in which they are presented for the first time, and an alphabetical vocabulary list. Books 2, 3 and 4 also have an appendix that provides notes in Chinese glossing difficult vocabulary and structures that appear in the reading passages. Books 3 and 4 have a further section presenting the forms of irregular verbs. The use of colour pictures is not an innovation, nor are the various appendices, but Series Eight is more comprehensive in providing such material than previous series.

Pedagogy

As noted above, each unit is divided into four lessons. In Books 1 and 2, there is no clear pattern in the arrangement of the lessons in a unit, other than in that the first lesson usually contains a functional dialogue and the fourth lesson a 'Checkpoint' which lists the principal grammar items and expressions that were introduced in the unit. Most of Book 1 focuses on oral development, with short dialogues or structure-based spoken drills. This is supported by games, songs and a range of listening exercises. Some written practice, such as copying and simple compositions, is also found. Reading passages start to appear towards the end of Book 1, with the passage in Lesson 92, a description of the students in Miss Gao's class, being the first instance of a strongly realistic written text. As the length of reading passages increases, a pattern emerges in the organization of lessons in Book 2. The first two lessons in a unit usually include a functional dialogue and related speech work. The third lesson incorporates a reading passage, and the fourth lesson usually comprises word study, discrete structure or function practice, a listening exercise and/or a short written composition task and a checkpoint. In Book 3, the length of reading passages has grown to the extent that the whole of the second lesson in each unit and often much of the third are devoted to the reading passage, a pattern which continues in Book 4.

These organizational patterns reflect the traditional orientation of previous series, with the initial emphasis being placed on oral development, and the later stages concentrating more on reading skills. The grammar items, too, are arranged according to the sequence established in earlier series, reflecting the Structural Approach, but this is now integrated with the Functional/ Notional Approach — which some teachers found problematic, according to Liu Daoyi:

> To a certain extent I have to admit we have been following the traditional construction because our teachers are quite used to the traditional grammar, and besides, we know the features and characteristics in the students' learning, especially their cognitive competence ... so the sequence of introducing grammatical structures is about the same as the old book, but the structures are mixed up with functional items. So in the new book, the skeleton doesn't look so distinct as before. That's why the teachers think it's *tai luan* (too chaotic). But actually that's not true.[7]

As with some previous series, most notably Series One, the lessons in a unit in Series Eight are linked thematically. The theme may be a topic, such as the weather, or a function, such as taking messages in different contexts. The links are tenuous at times. For instance, in Book 4 Lesson 15, the themes of different lessons are related to building a rabbit hutch and the story of Benjamin Franklin as a child. The link is actually 'making things'. The grammar and vocabulary items are either related to, or derived from, the reading passage: in the example quoted above, the grammar points are clauses of purpose (which are then used in the reading passage to explain the purpose of different inventions) and, after the reading passage, structures using *had never seen/heard* (etc.) *such ... before* and *neither ... nor*. The inclusion of the latter two structures may be contrived, as the guiding principle is covering the prescribed lists of structures, functions and vocabulary in the syllabus.

These lists created difficulties for the textbook writer, whose contributions were modified or rejected by the editorial team, in a further example of how the process of synthesis operated. Liu Daoyi acknowledges the problem:

> Really it was ... difficult for Neville [Grant] because the vocabulary (list) is actually the smallest in the world, but our demand is so high, because we wanted an interesting book ... Every time we received his drafts, we gave him our comments or suggestions. Sometimes we wrote texts or dialogues to replace his versions.[8]

Series Eight is oriented towards strongly realistic discourse from an early stage, reflecting the communicative aims of the curriculum. The discourse may be divided into the following principal genres: everyday interactions; anecdotes and short stories; scientific and other educational topics; moral education and cultural information. This is similar to the genres in previous series. The positive portrayal of foreign countries, and Western countries in particular, in Series Eight is not entirely new, but is much more evident than before. Everyday interactions form the largest and broadest category, and comprise mainly functional dialogues. Examples are found in every unit of the series. Stories and anecdotes are also common, with the latter being found in Book 2, where their shorter length is deemed more appropriate for the students to handle. Stories are a feature of Books 3 and 4 in particular, and a number of them appeared in previous series, as these were identified as successful by teachers in the survey carried out during the process of planning Series Eight.

Scientific and other academically-oriented passages are found particularly in the later books in the series, probably because of the higher vocabulary demands they make upon the students. Examples include 'A Great Inventor' (about Thomas Edison) in Book 3 Lesson 42 and 'The Great Green Wall' (about afforestation) in Book 3 Lesson 74. In accordance with the stated aim of developing the students' moral character, there is also a focus on ethical behaviour. Cultural information about other countries is presented in the form of descriptions of food (e.g., 'Take-away food' in Book 2 Lesson 78), festivals (e.g., 'Christmas Day' in Book 3 Lesson 54, and 'Mother's Day' in Book 4 Lesson 38), places of interest (e.g., Ayers Rock in Book 3 Lesson 94), sport (e.g., American football in Book 2 Lesson 27) and language (e.g., 'The English Language' in Book 3 Lesson 62, and 'American English and British English' in Book 4 Lesson 77).

Table 7.3   Antecedents of some passages in Series Eight

Passage	Location	Source (with adaptations)
'Thomas Edison'	Book 3 Lessons 42 and 43	Series Seven Book 5 Lesson 9
'Standing Room Only'	Book 3 Lesson 78	Series Seven Book 4 supplementary reading passage 1
'The Seagulls of Salt Lake City'	Book 4 Lessons 14 and 15	Series Seven Book 5 Lesson 5
'The Pyramids'	Book 4 Lesson 34	Series Seven Book 5 Lesson 7
'The King and the Artist' (listening passage)	Book 4 Lesson 56	Series Seven Book 3 Lesson 5
'Florence Nightingale'	Book 4 Lesson 62	Series Seven Book 5 supplementary reading passage 5
'Good Manners'	Book 4 Lesson 86	Series Seven Book 6 Lesson 8

The thematic arrangement of Series Eight means that the topic of an individual unit serves as the cohesive agent for the linguistic components. Thus, in Book 1 Unit 19, where the topic is food and drink, the new functional items, grammatical components and vocabulary are all related, or made to relate, to the theme. The functional items, offering and accepting offers of food and drink, overlap with some of the grammatical structures: *Would you like ...? What would you like? I would like (I'd like) a cup of tea/some milk.* Other new grammatical structures include *How many ... can you see?* and *It's time to ...* . These structures are linked to the topic by being presented in the context of discussing food and drink. The new vocabulary in the unit is connected either directly to the topic (*a bottle of milk, rice, meat, bread,* etc.) or to the new grammatical structures that are presented within the context of the topic (*It's time to ...*). Although there is a complex interrelationship among the various elements, the development of each element is controlled as Series Eight develops. Functional items start in Book 1 with a focus on oneself and friends, family and others. The scope then widens in Book 2 and Book 3 to general social interactions in a variety of settings. Book 4 revises and expands these interactions. The development of the grammar syllabus follows the pattern observed in previous series, commencing with the verb *to be* and then other verbs in the present indefinite tense. In Book 2 the present continuous, past indefinite and future indefinite tenses are presented, followed in Book 3 by the past continuous, present perfect and past perfect tenses. Other grammar structures are progressively introduced in a similar order to previous practice.

The intended pedagogy, 'The Five Steps', is outlined in the Teacher's Books. These five steps are not the same as those associated with Kairov's pedagogy that was influential in the 1950s. The steps are concerned with the learning of new language items, divided into three categories: vocabulary, structures and functions (the language of social interaction) and are associated with the PPP (presentation-practice-production) model of teaching that was prevalent in Western English Language teaching in the 1980s (e.g., Hubbard et al., 1983). The first step is revision, which involves recycling relevant known language in order to link it to new material. The course follows a cyclical rather than linear approach to syllabus-realization, so revision represents an important element in enabling the learner to establish conceptual frameworks of language. The second step is the presentation of the new language items. New vocabulary is introduced by appropriate means: realia, picture, mime, definition or translation. Structures and functions are presented by means of a teacher-centred demonstration or a listening exercise. Form-orientated practice then follows in the form of drills, contextualized and communicative where possible. A variety of drilling techniques are explained in the Teacher's Book, including transformation drills, cued drills, backchaining, repetition and question-and-answer drills. The next step consists of learner-centred message-orientated activities, moving from controlled to guided and, finally, free practice whereby the students are given the opportunity to use the new language items independently. Teachers are encouraged to arrange group- and pair-work as appropriate. The fifth step comprises further activities designed to consolidate the new language and to give extra practice in grammatical points. Many of the exercises in the Workbooks are devoted to form-orientated practice to cater for teachers and students who wish to spend more time on developing grammatical competence.

Not all the lessons in the coursebook contain new language items. Some are given over to the practice of listening, reading, and communicative writing skills. The methodology suggested for the learning of receptive skills consists of providing practice in comprehending gist and specific information through pre- and post-reading or listening exercises. In the early stages, communicative writing skills exercises are carefully controlled, offering models for imitation or picture-stimuli for guided writing. From the third year onwards, exercises become freer, with advice on aspects such as logical ordering and paragraphing being offered. The fourth (i.e., final) lesson in each unit concentrates on speech work and revision. Learners imitate the pronunciation, stress and intonation of words and phrases presented by a native speaker on the course cassette tapes. The teacher is advised to allocate several minutes to grammatical explanation of items covered in the course of the unit and to give a short test in the form of a dictation or other written work.

The pedagogical approach implicit in the contents of the new course materials and explicit in the Teacher's Books corresponds to what Tang Lixing (1983) classifies as an eclectic approach in that: there is a general focus on communication; the four skills of listening, speaking, reading and writing all receive attention; the use of the mother tongue is permitted; there are elements of the Structural Approach in the graded linguistic syllabus, and of Audiolingualism, which the 'Five Steps' extends by including free practice; and the teacher is free to select suitable strategies. Unlike the former textbook series, which switch from the Structural Approach and Audiolingualism to the Grammar-Translation Method, the approach of the Series Eight remains consistently eclectic throughout. The series therefore extends the parameters of the intended pedagogy to focus more on holistic, communication-oriented constituents. The Teacher's Book notes state that teachers are free to choose their own pedagogy to suit the individual needs of classes and students, but stress should be placed upon the cultivation of language competence and performance in English rather than upon knowledge of the language. Most notably meaningful oral communication is viewed as the prime aim. The eclectic approach allows for a blend of new and familiar pedagogy: the Structural Approach and Audiolingualism are retained, but the approach to reading passages, for instance, is more in keeping with Liu Zhaoyi's 'Global Teaching' method, with its emphasis on reading for meaning, rather than with the Grammar-Translation Method of analysing the linguistic composition of the passage.

Linguistic components

In Series Eight, the Teacher's Books offer a comprehensive breakdown of the linguistic components. Two elements are listed: functional items and grammatical structures. A list of vocabulary is provided at the back of the Student's Books. The interrelationship among these three linguistic components is complex. A functional item, such as telling the time, is realized through grammatical structures (e.g., *What's the time? It's ...*) and vocabulary (e.g., *o'clock, past, to*). Sometimes, a new functional item will be presented in the series involving new structures and new vocabulary; at other times the structure or the vocabulary may be familiar. At other times, the lines of definition between the three elements become very fuzzy: *Excuse me!* might, for example, be regarded as a functional item (i.e., politely negotiating one's way through a crowd), or as a grammatical structure (i.e., an imperative) or as a single vocabulary item (as a formulaic expression). Series Eight acknowledges this problem by labelling all the new linguistic components in individual lessons as 'New language items'. The arrangement indicates a holistic conception of language, in which the various linguistic components interact to produce contextualized communication, rather than a narrower grammar-based conception that tends to ignore the sociolinguistic factors that influence language choices. As noted earlier, there was a conscious decision by the textbook writing team to blend the grammatical structures with the functional/notional components.

The number of new vocabulary items, which served in the past as an indicator of the level of difficulty of a series, is also regulated in Series Eight, but with a new conception: categorizing the new language items (including vocabulary, expressions and sentence patterns) into four skills. 'One skill' words or expressions are for the students to recognize by listening only; 'two skills' involves recognition by listening and reading; 'three skills' is listening, reading and saying the words or expressions; and 'four skills' is listening, reading, saying and writing the words or expressions. The purpose of these classifications is to reduce the learning load on students, although the move was criticized by teachers and some university scholars as too complicated, according to Liu Daoyi.[9] It does, however, represent a more sophisticated system of regulating difficulty than the former method of simple word counts.

Content

As Table 7.4 indicates, the number of passages with political themes are particularly sparse. Moral messages are present, but a large majority of the discourse examples have no obvious political or moral connotation. This reflects the statements in the syllabus that political messages should be restricted to patriotism and socialism, but that foreign culture should be included for the sake of international understanding.

Table 7.4   Political and moral messages in Series Eight

Discourse total	Messages total	Nil	Moral	Political	Political (attitude)	Political (information)	Political (role model)
570	572	434 (75.87%)	113 (19.76%)	25 (4.37%)	22	0	3

The PEP decided that political messages should be avoided in the light of previous experience. Interestingly, Liu Daoyi had to turn down a suggestion by Neville Grant for a passage with political content:

> For instance, once Neville suggested writing a story about Zhou Enlai. I said "What about Mao Zedong? Lenin? Stalin? Or Liu Shaoqi? Or other leaders?" So no political leaders. It was good lesson: in the history of developing textbooks after 1949, especially for Chinese Language, they used to use a lot of political essays, written by the famous leaders, for instance Hua Guofeng. Then Hua Guofeng left his position. Oh goodness! The book can't be used, although he didn't make a mistake, we just couldn't use that book .... . I don't want to keep rewriting books. Very difficult.[10]

Lesson 18

 Read

Read the passage below as quickly as you can and find out: "Does Xue Tingfang like being an only child?" Put your hand up when you have found out. Then read the passage again, and answer the questions on page 18 of your workbook.

HAPPY FAMILIES

Today, many parents in China have only one child. What do people think of this? I asked Song Haiyun. She is going to have a baby next March.

"I live in Shuang Feng Village," she said. "It's only a 20 minute bicycle ride from Hangzhou. I'm a cook in a hotel there. My husband is a farmer. We have waited for five years to have our baby."

"Some people say that they don't mind if they only have one child — as long as it's a boy. What do you think?"

"Even if it is a girl, I don't want another child," Song Haiyun answered. "I prefer girls, because they're easier to bring up, and more hard-working. They're also less trouble. My husband thinks the same."

"Do you think an only child will feel lonely?"

"We live near my husband's brother and sister-in-law. They also have a child, so the children will not feel lonely. I know a little about the population problem. I hear that the China's population is more than a billion and it's still growing. I think that slowing it down is very important."

What is it like to be an only child? I asked a girl called Xue Tingfang what she thought. Xue Tingfang is one of Shanghai's 1,500,000 only children. She is eleven years old. Like many children of her age, Tingfang is a Young Pioneer. She wears the bright red pioneer scarf round her neck. Her father works in a factory. Her mother is also a cook like Song Haiyun, in a hotel. How does Tingfang like being an only child?

"I sometimes think I would like to have a brother or sister, because I feel rather lonely at home at times. But I have many friends at school, and we play together on the sports ground.

"Sometimes I do feel a bit lonely at home. But then I think it is good I am an only child, because I can eat good food and wear nice clothes. When I feel lonely, that's what I tell myself!"

18

Figure 7.1   Reading passage from Book 4

The passage considers the topical issue of the one-child policy.

Instead, the PEP decided that the focus would be on moral education. The notion that reading passages could be selected or written for their inherent interest was rejected by Liu Daoyi: they should contain some educative message. For example, at one stage, Grant's suggestion that a reading passage could be a science fiction story about aliens landing on earth from the moon was not accepted by Liu Daoyi on the grounds that such materials 'were not so educational'.[11] Instead, some of the passages from earlier series were used, because they were perceived to be interesting stories with a moral message. As Liu Daoyi also comments:

> We cannot make things so serious. We can't teach the students by lecturing them, but we must give the students some moral education in the reading passages, while the students do not really feel "Oh, that is a moral lesson!" ... We cannot insert political ideas, political slogans, as we did during the Cultural Revolution, but actually we are educating our students. We are trying to influence their moral character.[12]

The moral messages are mainly concerned with social behaviour. In Book 4 Unit 22, for instance, an article on 'Good Manners' includes politeness to others and orderly behaviour, such as queuing for a bus. Another section points out cultural differences:

> Ideas of what are good manners are not always the same in different countries. For example, in Britain or America it is not polite to ask people how much money they get in their jobs. People don't like talking about the cost of things around the home, though in America they don't mind so much. But in both Britain and America it is not polite to ask people how old they are.
>
> There are other interesting differences between China and foreign countries. In China, if someone says something good about you, it is polite to answer "No, not at all!" In Britain or America, a person answers "Thank you!" with a big smile. This may be bad manners in China, but good manners in Britain or America. (Series Eight, Book 4: 87)

The political passages are very mild, being mainly related to positive portrayals of China. One political role model is provided by the characters in the book who go to help on a farm (Book 2 Lesson 17), which echoes a past theme of students combining academic study with manual labour. There is no mention of CCP leaders, and no passages casting foreign countries in a poor light. Indeed, some passages promote international friendship with Western nations, which is associated with open-door policies rather than hard-line ideology. Thus in the description of Miss Gao's class (Book 1 Lesson 92), mention is made of English, Chinese and American children, and concludes:

> "American — English — Chinese! There's no difference!" says Wei Hua. "We are all friends!" (Series Eight, Book 1: 92)

1 Practise   Practise this dialogue. Use the words in this unit.

A: Which do you like better, beef or pork?
B: I like pork better than beef.
A: Which do you like best, tomatoes, cabbage or peas?
B: I like tomatoes best of all.

2 🔊 Read

Take-away food

In England, the most popular food is fish and chips. Sometimes people cook this food at home, but usually they go to a fish and chip shop. They put the food in paper bags, and take it home, or to their work place. Sometimes they eat it in the park or on the road. This "take-away" food is very popular.

Chinese take-away food is also popular. There are many "Chinese take-aways" in England and in the U.S.A. – and in Australia, too. They also have fish and chip shops in Australia, but there are not so many in the U.S.A. What is the most popular food in the U.S.A.? I think it is fried chicken.

		Right		Wrong	
1	The most popular food in England is Chinese take-away food.	/	/	/	/
2	They usually cook fish and chips at home.	/	/	/	/
3	People eat fish and chips on the road.	/	/	/	/
4	Chinese take-away food is also popular.	/	/	/	/
5	Fish and chip shops are very popular in the U.S.A.	/	/	/	/

3 Ask and answer

What kind of meat is more popular in China, pork or beef?
Which is the most popular, rice, bread or noodles?

78

Figure 7.2   Reading passage from Series Eight Book 2 Lesson 78

The passage contains cultural information about English-speaking countries. The pre-reading exercise allows the students to create their own dialogues about food (Series Eight Book 2: 78).

The analysis of vocabulary reveals that the percentage of non-Thorndike words is low (23.41%, or 492 words out of 2,102) and very few have explicit political connotations: *Young Pioneer, comrade* (in the context of a story about neighbours in Moscow), *PLA, Party member* and *League member* being rare examples. Many of the non-Thorndike words are foreign names of people or places, reflecting the cultural content of the series.

Summary

The 1993 curriculum, with its pluralistic processes of curriculum development and the sophistication of Series Eight, is the most complex in terms of process and product of all the curricula since 1949. This curriculum also saw the formal break in the symbiotic relationship between the syllabus and the PEP textbook resources. The CTMRI syllabus is applicable to all regional textbook producers, except for those in Shanghai and Zhejiang. In these regards, the 1993 curriculum represents the start of a new era in English Language curriculum development in China. The contribution made by non-Chinese bodies (namely Longman International and UNDP) is noteworthy as unprecedented in the history of English Language teaching in China. However, the nature of their contribution is entirely in keeping with the historical maxim of *zhongxue weiti xixue weiyong* in that the PEP sought to tailor foreign ideas to the Chinese experience, so that the curriculum would suit teachers and students alike. The role of the outside agencies remained the same as for the previous curriculum innovations of 1978 and 1982, although the relationship with the PEP was strengthened and the scope for writing materials was increased by the policy of decentralization. The role of the teachers (the classroom teachers) in the pre-writing period was greatly enlarged with their involvement in the research stage and an extensive piloting exercise. The support of foreign funding and the increasing economic prosperity of the nation enabled the PEP to produce a more lavish set of textbooks than previously. In sum, the 1993 curriculum reflects both change and continuity. In many respects, it marks a new departure in curriculum development in China, but the innovations are also strongly linked to their antecedents.

The 1993 curriculum was revised in draft form in 2000, in preparation for a thorough review in 2005. The 2000 draft set higher standards in terms of the learning targets (for example, expecting students to learn an extra 200 vocabulary items at each level), and incorporating task-based learning in the intended pedagogy. The decentralization of textbook publication and collaborations with foreign publishers brought new market forces into play. The PEP, having revised *Junior English for China* (Series Eight) to take account of teacher feedback and to provide for the different needs of various regions of China, began work on an alternative set of textbooks, which involved revising a series that was designed for the international English language teaching market. The PEP employed foreign writers as part of the team carrying out these revisions which included the introduction of table-based learning. Other collaborations included a venture with Ohana Foundation in the USA to produce DVDs and web-based material to support Series Eight. In carrying out these initiatives, the PEP has striven to maintain its channels of feedback from teachers and consultants, but competition in the market has put pressure on the PEP's timelines. A new phase of curriculum development is emerging, in which the writing of the syllabus and of the PEP textbooks is no longer symbiotic, and the economic imperatives of commercialization and competition are producing new dynamics and tensions in the processes of textbook publishing.

8 *China's English*

The official English Language curriculum for junior secondary schools in China is a product of navigation, mainly by the PEP, through political, socio-economic and educational currents. Over time, the English Language curriculum has reflected the vagaries of the socio-political climate in China. The curriculum has served as a mechanism for the state to appropriate English to serve its different aspirations, be they revolutionary or economic in orientation. The (often sudden) shifts in state priorities have required curriculum developers to be nimble-footed in ensuring the political correctness of the resources, but within the constraints, they have maintained the principle of selective appropriation of pedagogy and have evolved a system that allows stakeholders a considerable role in helping to make sure that the finished product is teachable at the chalkface in China. Navigation has been particularly hazardous at times because of the controversy surrounding the role and status of English in China: an alien language with negative historical connotations, but viewed by the state as necessary for future prosperity. At times of politicization, the status of English was extremely low, and because of the grave political risks that it involved, English Language teaching was either abandoned or taught with a high degree of circumspection. At other times, the study of English has been enthusiastically embraced by the state and the populace.

At present, the role and status of English in China is higher than ever in history as evidenced by its position as a key subject in the curriculum, with its growing use as a medium of instruction as many schools adopt a bilingual approach to education; and as a crucial determinant for university entrance and procuring well-paid jobs in the commercial sector. CCP leaders value the contribution that English can make to the nation's modernization programme, particularly with China's entry into the World Trade Organization, and, indeed, many politicians at the highest levels are competent in the language. The success of bids for prestigious international sporting events, such as the Olympic Games, has been dependent to some extent upon China's ability to cater for the linguistic needs of the foreign mass media and tourists. Despite the occasional and generally ineffective campaigns to control the diffusion of Western thought, *mores* and cultural artefacts such as pop music, films and websites that are deemed unsuitable, English — once spoken only by the despised social outcasts of Chinese society — is now the main second language of the nation's political, academic, industrial and commercial communities.

Because China has the capacity for producing its own school textbooks — unlike many other developing nations — the state has a degree of control over the curriculum (Altbach, 1991). As a result, both the curriculum development processes and the products — the syllabus, textbooks and other resources — reflect the contemporary tensions, and the shifts in the curriculum over time are like a weathervane indicating the changes in the state's priorities. Figure 8.1 (see p. 197) provides an overview of the changing characteristics of the English Language curriculum since 1949. It distinguishes two dimensions, namely the degree to which the curriculum stressed political or economic goals (both in terms of the policy that initiated curriculum change, and the product), and, secondly, the degree of openness of the system of curriculum development (which is linked to the pluralism evident in the process).

Five distinct phases are evident, as summarized in Table 8.1 (see p. 198). During the first phase, English was largely neglected, due to the political ascendancy of the USSR, which was aiding China's economic development, and to the associated antipathy towards the USA. After 1955, however, English Language was restored to the school curriculum to some extent, as there was:

> a gradual awareness that the complete rejection of English and other foreign languages was a short-sighted view, and that to communicate in other languages ... was absolutely necessary for the progress of the country. (Tang Lixing, 1983: 41)

The curriculum was heavily influenced by Russian approaches to pedagogy and the textbooks had a significant proportion of political texts, especially at times of movements such as the Anti-Rightist Campaign and the Great Leap Forward that took place at the end of the 1950s. In the second phase, during the early 1960s, when the politicization died down, and attention was turned to international affairs and economic progress, there was engagement with pedagogical approaches emerging from the West, such as Audiolingualism. Foreign teachers were invited to serve as curriculum consultants alongside Chinese specialists, and the textbooks contained fewer political references. This period was short-lived. The political turmoil of the Great Proletarian Cultural Revolution started in 1966, with schools being closed down so that students could take the lead in revolutionary activities, which were often violent and

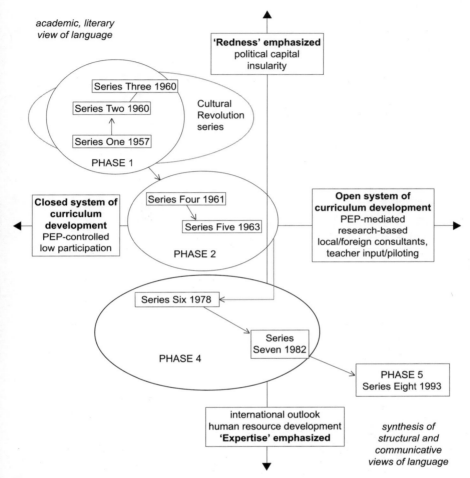

*academic, literary
view of language*

'Redness' emphasized
political capital
insularity

Series Three 1960

Series Two 1960

Cultural
Revolution
series

Series One 1957

PHASE 1

**Closed system of
curriculum
development**
PEP-controlled
low participation

Series Four 1961

Series Five 1963

PHASE 2

**Open system of
curriculum development**
PEP-mediated
research-based
local/foreign consultants,
teacher input/piloting

Series Six 1978

Series
Seven 1982

PHASE 4

PHASE 5
Series Eight 1993

international outlook
human resource development
'Expertise' emphasized

*synthesis of
structural and
communicative
views of language*

Notes:
1. The dotted arrow denotes the disruption to the curriculum development process caused by the Cultural Revolution.
2. For simplification, the various Cultural Revolution series (Phase 3) are not shown individually, but would be located in the top left-hand sector.

Figure 8.1   English Language curriculum development in China since 1949

targeted at those with any affiliation with the West — so English Language teachers were particularly vulnerable. The country lurched into a state of near anarchy before a semblance of normality was restored. Following the visit to China by the US President Richard Nixon in 1972, English Language curricula started to appear in some regions. During this phase, the locally-produced textbooks were heavily politicized, although the series published in Beijing

Table 8.1   Features of the English Language curriculum in China since 1949

	Phase 1: The End of Soviet Influence	Phase 2: Towards Quality in Education	Phase 3: The Cultural Revolution	Phase 4: Modernization under Deng Xiaoping	Phase 5: Integrating with Globalization
Macro National Priorities	National socialist construction	Quality in education to support development	Social revolution	Economic modernization	Economic modernization and compulsory schooling
Role of English	Access to scientific and technical information	Developing cultural and scientific knowledge	Vehicle for political propaganda	Developing trade; cultural and scientific knowledge	Developing trade; cultural and scientific knowledge
Curriculum Innovations	1957, 1960	1961, 1963	1966–1976	1978, 1983	1993, 2000
Sets of Official Textbooks	'English' Series 1–3	'English' Series 4–5	No national series, but some produced regionally	'English' Series 6–7	'Junior English for China' (Series 8) and competing series by commercial publishers
Content of Textbooks	Anecdotes, stories, scientific and politicized texts	Anecdotes, stories, scientific texts; some politicized texts	Highly politicized texts	Anecdotes, stories, scientific texts; some politicized texts	Anecdotes, stories; scientific and cultural information
Intended Pedagogy	Structural and Grammar-Translation, Kairov's Five Steps	Structural and Grammar-Translation; some Audiolingualism	Structural, Grammar-Translation and Audiolingualism	Audiolingualism, Structural and Grammar-Translation	Eclectic: functional/ notional-structural, plus task-based learning (since 2000)

and Shanghai were more moderate in this respect. At the end of the Cultural Revolution, the fourth phase was one of recovery, before the Four Modernizations drive for economic development and the Open Door Policy instituted by the new paramount leader, Deng Xiaoping, made English highly desirable for trade, careers, study and overseas travel, which formed the backdrop to the fifth phase of curriculum development. The modernization drive was cranked up a gear in the mid-1980s, and educational reform set goals for nationwide provision of compulsory schooling and decentralization of educational policy-making (including the preparation of curriculum materials, such as textbooks). The pedagogy underpinning the fifth phase was an amalgam of communicative and structural approaches. Political texts were no longer evident.

In terms of the nature of China's English, the overall pattern is one in which the nature of the curriculum has shifted from a structural, literary orientation in the first phase (Series One to Three) to a synthesis of such an orientation with more holistic, communicative emphases. The pattern was not oscillatory, as many portrayals of the history of education policy in China suggest (e.g., Chen, 1981); rather, it was evolutionary, although it was disrupted during the Cultural Revolution until the evolution resumed with the restoration of the PEP in the late 1970s. Although state goals might arguably be seen to oscillate between political and academic/economic priorities, these forces often acted simply as the trigger for curriculum change. Although the oscillation theory provides a broad picture of the shifts in education policy in general and English Language curriculum innovation in particular, it does not indicate the amplitude or duration of each 'oscillation', nor does it fully encapsulate the range of influences at a given time, the specific details and degrees of those influences, the complexities of the processes that handled the influences, nor the accumulated momentum of chronological developments. For instance, the actual impetus for innovation was more complex than just the launching of a particular new economic policy or changing political agenda — Series Four and Five were produced in response to a call for improved pedagogical qualities by state leaders. In Series Seven, as well as reducing the political content, the PEP was responding to complaints about the pedagogical quality from teachers and supporting the policy to establish key schools. Moreover, despite many overt similarities, the actual nature, degrees and complexities of the influences on, and processes of education policy and English Language curriculum innovation in the 'academic' phase of the early 1960s were very different from those in the 'academic' phase in the late 1970s — there had been radical political changes, including the death of Mao; shifts in the international political climate (e.g., *détente* between China and the USA); changes in pedagogical ideas in China and abroad; different personnel at the PEP, and so on.

In the process of curriculum development, there are other forces at work other than general shifts in the orientation of state policy. The power of stakeholders within the education system concerned with academic and pedagogical aspects increased, especially during phases when state policy stressed economic-oriented goals. Curriculum change in English Language has been increasingly influenced by interaction between the PEP, outside agencies and teachers, while pressure for curriculum change has been exerted sporadically and decreasingly by external interest groups (if the definition is extended to radical factions of the CCP, whose criticisms of Series One, for instance, led to its replacement with the more politicized Series Two). Also, the key role of individuals in the curriculum process (despite its pluralistic nature) meant that people such as Liu Daoyi and Tang Jun have been highly influential in shaping the curriculum. This applies to earlier curricula to some extent (e.g., for Series One, the leaders of the textbook writing team, Ying Manrong and Fan Ying, were very important in determining the curriculum content; likewise Tang Jun and others in the 1960s and 1970s).

The process of curriculum development evolved into a complex, pluralistic system, albeit one still dominated by the PEP. In each of the phases except the Cultural Revolution, the PEP reflected macro policy decisions made by the national government, but was also significantly influenced by contributions by outside agencies and, increasingly, by teachers in developing the curriculum. Outside agencies supplied expertise through their knowledge of second language acquisition theories and pedagogical models, and through syllabus design and textbook writing in the first phase of curriculum development. They also, from the early 1960s, provided an important source of staff recruitment for the PEP. The most recent phase of curriculum reforms, which started in 1993, saw a broadening of the range of outside agencies with the involvement of foreign publishers working in partnership with the PEP.

The contribution of the grassroots teachers started as *post hoc* feedback on an existing curriculum — which often resulted in significant innovations. For instance, the editorial team producing Series Seven took into account teachers' complaints about the workload demands of Series Six. Small groups of teachers also contributed to the process by piloting draft versions of textbook series, and their comments were respected: for example, Series Three was abandoned largely because of negative feedback from the teachers who piloted the course. Later the teachers became more involved as consultants and critics in the design and development of a new curriculum (as in Series Five), or even as pioneers through their pedagogical experiments (as in Series Eight). This pattern of involvement of the PEP, outside agencies and teachers indicates a growing pluralism: the evolution of a clear procedure that facilitates negotiation between the various agencies. While the process remained centrally-dominated — the PEP presided over the process of curriculum design, ensuring that the end product was in line with the prevailing political requirements — the mechanism that evolved was more sensitive and responsive to the views of experts in linguistics and language pedagogy, and to those of teachers responsible for the actual implementation of the curriculum, carrying out experiments or piloting new series.

Overall, the processes of curriculum development evolved through a pattern of pragmatism–consultation–co-option/partnership–partnership, with partnership being strengthened in the last phase of the study (Table 8.2, see p. 202). Within this pattern, however, there was a single break — during the Cultural Revolution — which caused abrupt decentralization, returning to partnership after a transition period in the late 1970s.

As to Elmore and Sykes' (1992) concept of rationality or irrationality of curriculum change, there are indications of both. To account for this paradox, a distinction needs to be drawn between the trigger for curriculum change and the forces that shape the actual product. The trigger is related to state policy, which may be oriented towards specific economic, political or educational goals. The goals and the policy are rationally congruent: for example, when economic modernization has been perceived as a priority and a goal that is dependent upon a skilled workforce, the curriculum has changed to focus on relevant skills. Apparently less rational is the interplay of forces in the process of curriculum development. The constraints of available resources, human and otherwise, have forced the process into pragmatism at times; the resolution of socio-political and educational tensions has sometimes been the result of horse-trading or, in more than one case, of teachers casting a veto on a proposed solution; at times, too, the dominant position of the Chief Editor in the PEP (for, despite the development of a pluralistic system, the ultimate decision-making power has rested with one person) has resulted in an individual choice of pedagogy or textbook content. In a sense, though, this negotiation of the curriculum has its own rationale. Decisions and choices are explainable, not illogical. The process is 'irrational' only in the relative incoherence of the curriculum product.

The awareness of the curriculum developers that the final product needed to be accepted by frontline teachers served as a brake on experimentation. Some innovative pedagogical features were introduced when conditions allowed — the shift in the curriculum towards communicative goals is broadly associated with two major movements: the relative depoliticization in the socio-political context and a more pluralistic process of curriculum development. The increasing focus on communicative competence was a product of greater interaction with Westerners arising from open door policies in the 1960s and from the late 1970s onwards. The more liberal socio-political climate allowed more opportunities for experimentation in current Western ideas to graft on to indigenous methods and other established pedagogies. During periods of politicization, the curriculum tends to be centred more on written texts, with transmissive pedagogy — appropriate means of disseminating propaganda. The foreign pedagogies (Table 8.3, see p. 203) that influenced the curriculum

Table 8.2   Decision-making mechanisms in English Language curriculum development

Phase	Series	Role of Agencies	Notes
1. The Soviet influence 1949–60	Series One (1957)	PEP: commissioning, publishing textbooks Consultants: writing syllabus and textbooks Teachers: nil	Pragmatism: PEP's lack of expertise and choice; outside agency chosen as only agency offering vaguely relevant courses
	Series Two (1960)	PEP: commissioning, publishing textbooks Consultants: writing syllabus and resources Teachers: nil	Pragmatism: two different outside agencies chosen because of PEP's lack of expertise and severe time constraints
	Series Three (1960)	PEP: commissioning, publishing textbooks Consultants: advice, writing syllabus and resources Teachers: piloting and feedback	Consultation: outside agency chosen due to contribution to consultation process and PEP's lack of expertise; teachers pilot series
2. Towards quality in education 1961–66	Series Four (1961)	PEP: writing syllabus and resources; publishing resources Consultants: writing syllabus and resources Teachers: piloting and feedback	Co-option/Partnership: writing and editorial teams from PEP and outside agencies; input from teachers
	Series Five (1963)	PEP: production of syllabus and resources Consultants: advice and feedback Teachers: feedback on Series Four and on piloted resources	Partnership: PEP/outside research; outside agencies on editorial committee; more teachers input
3. The Cultural Revolution 1966–76	Cultural Revolution series	PEP: inoperative Consultants: inoperative Teachers: producers of resources	Forced decentralization: teachers produced own resources
4. Modernization under Deng Xiaoping 1978–1993	Series Six (1978)	PEP: commissioning, publishing syllabus and resources Consultants: writing syllabus and resources Teachers: some input to syllabus and resources	Pragmatism/Transition: outside (and a few teachers) agencies chosen — PEP lacked staff; no piloting (lack of time)
	Series Seven (1982)	PEP: writing, publishing syllabus and resources Consultants: advice and feedback Teachers: consultants, piloting and feedback	Partnership: wide consultation; outside agencies on editorial committee; teachers piloting
5. Integrating with globalization 1993 onwards	Series Eight (1993)	PEP: writing, publishing syllabus and resources Consultants: advice and feedback, writing syllabus and resources Teachers: consultants, piloting and feedback	Partnership: wide consultation; joint venture with overseas outside agencies; major input from teachers

Table 8.3   Pedagogical influences on the English Language curriculum

Phase	Pedagogical influences	Pedagogical features
1. The Soviet influence 1949–60	Kairov's pedagogy from the USSR and traditional Chinese/Western ELT methods (Grammar-Translation/ Structural approach)	teacher-centred; focus on accuracy and written language; memorization; Kairov's 'Five Steps' (review old materials, orient new materials, explain new materials, consolidate newly-learned materials, give assignments)
2. Towards quality in education 1961–66	traditional Chinese/Western ELT methods (Grammar-Translation/Structural Approach) and some modern Western influence (Audiolingualism)	reading aloud, oral practice, memorization, sentence writing, students' independent learning
3. The Cultural Revolution 1966–76	variable: traditional Chinese/Western ELT methods (Grammar-Translation/Structural Approach) and modern Western influence (Audiolingualism)	various: mainly teacher-centred; focus on accuracy and written language; memorization; some reading aloud and oral practice
4. Modernization under Deng Xiaoping 1978–1993	traditional Chinese/Western ELT methods (Grammar-Translation/Structural Approach) and modern Western influence (Audiolingualism and Functional/Notional Approach)	oral practice in contextualized situations, memorization, sentence writing, students' independent learning, accuracy and written language
5. Integrating with globalization 1993 onwards	traditional Chinese/Western ELT methods (Structural Approach) and modern Western influence (Audiolingualism, Functional/Notional Approach and Task-based Learning)	oral and written practice in contextualized situations, memorization, sentence writing, students' independent learning, accuracy and written language

are generally linked to the socio-political climate: thus, for example, Kairov's ideas were influential during the Sino-Soviet co-operation, but were rejected after the schism. During the later periods of depoliticization, Western pedagogies were actively researched by curriculum developers, PEP staff travelled to Western countries to study applied linguistics, and Westerners were engaged as consultants (and then as co-writers). But even when a foreign publisher had the major responsibility for writing materials (i.e., Series Eight), the PEP was concerned that the series should be appropriate to the Chinese context, with the result that an eclectic approach was adopted. The process of grafting new ideas onto traditional ones can create challenges for the textbook writers. For Grammar-Translation, the assimilation was relatively smooth as this pedagogy shared much in common with Chinese mother tongue teaching and learning. Other pedagogies, such as the Functional/ Notional Approach were introduced through the use of a thematic arrangement of content, whereby a common theme or topic linked the disparate components of a lesson or unit. Neville Grant's struggles in writing Series Eight (see Chapter 7) to keep within the prescribed vocabulary limits when attempting to produce realistic discourse is indicative of the kind of problems that the grafting process entailed.

The process of synthesis, by which traditional Chinese approaches blend with ideas from overseas, accords with the time-honoured Self-Strengthening principle of *zhongxue weiti xixue weiyong* (Chinese essence, Western practice). It also corresponds to the notion of *mosuo* (or 'feeling one's way') described by Paine (1992), in which experimental teaching serves as a pioneer before being adopted as officially sanctioned nation-wide practice. Experiments by Chinese teachers were influential throughout the study — many were based on ideas from abroad, and the experiments endowed pedagogies such as Audiolingualism and the Functional/Notional Approach with Chinese characteristics.

The traditional pedagogies remained in the curriculum in the use of the extent of vocabulary learning as a measure of student progress, and the central position accorded to the reading passages (often with a moral content). Both these characteristics have links to mother tongue learning. As part of a mass literacy campaign in the 1950s, the Chinese government prescribed the number of characters that could be used in mass media publications. Newspapers were limited to a vocabulary of 3,000 characters. A similar principle has been adopted for the English Language curriculum, with the syllabus defining the number of vocabulary items to be mastered and even, at times, the percentage of correct retention expected. For instance, the 1993 curriculum sets out the following targets for vocabulary:

- an active oral and written command of around 600–700 frequently used words plus 200 common expressions;
- a passive command of around 400–500 other words;

- the ability to use the rules of reading to remember the spelling of words;
- the ability to identify the meaning and parts of speech of derivatives and compounds;
- the ability to identify the meaning and parts of speech of polysemants in context. (1993 syllabus)

The vocabulary in the various curricula was initially based on the word-lists drawn up in the West in the first half of the twentieth century. Conscious of China's specific needs, curriculum developers amended the lists to include relevant cultural, political or economic items. In 1983, Tang Jun, the leader of the curriculum development at the time, drew up the list with Liu Jinfang based on a needs analysis they conducted.[1]

Reading passages predominate in part because of the status of literary texts in the Chinese language. Texts perform an educative role: for instance, the works of Confucius are studied for their philosophical and moral content rather than for their historical or rhetorical interest. The reification of the written word was reinforced during times of isolation, when China's contact with English was mainly through books and scientific journals. Reading passages are also less threatening to a teacher, as time can be spent preparing the presentation and exploitation of a passage, whereas an oral lesson can be less predictable. The educative value of reading passages has continued to be recognized, in the form of moral and/or political messages. Both kinds of message have waxed and waned in the English Language curriculum over time. As one might expect, the presence of political messages is strongest during periods of politicization, and weakest at times of depoliticization (most notably in the 1993 curriculum). In terms of political messages, as Table 8.4 (see p. 206) shows, two types predominate: those promoting an ideological goal or attitude (such as loyalty to the CCP and its policies) and those providing a role model for emulation. Moral messages, which are more evident during times of depoliticization, mainly promote a 'healthy' lifestyle, such as early rising and studying diligently, or participation in outdoor activities — often inculcating civic responsibility. The moral messages are conveyed through traditional fables (from China or Aesop's Fables), modern stories or everyday anecdotes and dialogues.

The influences of socio-political and pedagogical forces on the English Language curriculum are both competing and complementary. Attention to political education often occurs at the cost of pedagogical quality, which is associated with clearly structured learning activities and controlled sequencing of linguistic components. Thus, in the first phase, which encompasses a period of pedagogical innovation through Soviet influence as well as periods of politicization, the textbook resources decline in pedagogical quality as the political content increases. This also occurs during the Cultural Revolution: the more politically charged materials show less attention to pedagogical

Table 8.4   Presence of political and moral messages in the English Language curriculum 1949–94

Phase		Total no. of discourse	Total messages	Nil	Moral	Political	Political (attitude)	Political (information)	Political (role model)
1. The Soviet influence 1949–60	Series One	88	94	38 (40.43%)	30 (31.91%)	26 (27.66%)	16	2	8
	Series Two	90	102	12 (11.76%)	21 (20.59%)	79 (67.65%)	28	12	29
	Series Three	119	125	3 (2.40%)	1 (0.80%)	121 (96.80%)	43	29	49
2. Towards quality in education 1961–66	Series Four	81	82	19 (23.17%)	18 (21.95%)	45 (54.87%)	26	8	11
	Series Five	175	177	85 (48.02%)	26 (14.69%)	66 (37.29%)	30	3	23
3. The Cultural Revolution 1966–76	Shanghai Series	39	39	4 (10.26%)	4 (10.26%)	31 (79.48%)	11	1	19
	Shaanxi Series	15	15	1 (6.67%)	0 (0%)	14 (93.33%)	8	0	6
	Tianjin Series	19	20	1 (5.00%)	4 (20.00%)	15 (75.00%)	4	3	8
	Beijing Series	62	63	25 (39.68%)	3 (4.76%)	35 (55.56%)	17	10	8
4. Modernization under Deng Xiaoping 1978–1993	Series Six	159	163	86 (52.76%)	46 (28.22%)	31 (19.02%)	18	3	10
	Series Seven	168	169	108 (63.91%)	47 (27.81%)	14 (8.28%)	6	1	7
5. Integrating with globalization 1993 onwards	Series Eight	570	572	434 (75.87%)	113 (19.76%)	25 (4.37%)	22	0	3

concerns. Intermediate cases are the Beijing and Shanghai series published towards the end of the Cultural Revolution and Series Six, published immediately afterwards. In all these cases, the political climate was unclear, with first the *rapprochement* with the USA after the mass political mobilization, and then, after Mao's death, the struggle between his nominated successor, Hua Guofeng, and the popular Deng Xiaoping. The Cultural Revolution series are strongly politicized, but do pay attention to pedagogical concerns. For Series Six, there were indications of moves to improve the economy and restore the central education system, but the tension of the times is evident in the tentative and defensive message in the syllabus, stressing both economic and political goals. There was also a restoration of some of the pedagogically innovative approaches of the early 1960s, but, as shown in Chapter 6, the quality proved deficient. There are several reasons for this inversely proportional relationship. First, political movements occurred quickly, and proponents demanded rapid responses in the curriculum to ensure that education was politicized appropriately. This meant that the process of curriculum development was brutish and short, leaving little opportunity for research into, and piloting of pedagogical approaches. Second, under the circumstances where anything that might be construed as politically heterodox may have negative consequences, the textbook writers reverted to a style which had features of traditional Chinese English Language teaching, stressing memorization of literary texts, and which was congruent with the goal of transmitting ideology through political tracts. Third, the writers were inexperienced (either because textbook writing was in its infancy in China or because those with experience had been rusticated), although the writers of the Cultural Revolution series did make some use of previous materials.

Summary

Emerging from this study, it is evident that, since the resolution of the civil war in 1949, English as a school subject in China has had an essentially oxymoronic status, in that it has been perceived officially as something akin to a 'desirable evil' with the relative emphasis on desirability and evilness shifting according to the socio-political climate. In this regard, the fluctuating official status of English in China is in keeping with earlier historical trends, dating back to the Qing dynasty. The state has appropriated English to promote economic and political goals at various times. This recurring tension between the forces of politicization and economic modernization resulted in shifts in both the processes and products of curriculum development. Periods of politicization placed constraints upon curriculum developers, whereas relative depoliticization allowed for the evolution of a centrally-dominated but pluralistic process which was able to absorb historical, pedagogical and socio-political forces. The final phase, when economic-oriented reforms have been intensified with little disruption from 'red' forces, has witnessed the evolution of a highly complex process of curriculum development.

Whilst there is clearly a link between the nation's shifting priorities in terms of the open-door versus anti-capitalist debate, the general strategy of curriculum development in junior secondary school English Language and the specific nature of curriculum content, curriculum change in English Language in China is best explained by a combination of macro- and meso-/micro-level factors, both external and internal. These factors have varied in nature and degree of influence according to the prevailing socio-political climate and the evolutionary stage of the pluralistic process of curriculum development. Thus, for example, teachers' influence on the development of the 1993 curriculum was greater than on the 1982 curriculum not just because of the relatively liberal socio-political context and the higher economic returns associated with competence in English, but also because the evolutionary processes facilitated greater interaction between the PEP and the teachers, and past experience had shown the benefits of such interaction.

In many respects, this history of the English Language curriculum in China is a history of China itself. The evolutionary process has moved from state-determined towards client-determined; from centralization towards decentralization; from closed systems towards pluralism. The building of self-reliant, pluralistic systems; the ambiguous portrayals of the outside world; the periods of turmoil; international collaboration and commercialization — all these reflect the experience of the Chinese nation since 1949. The principles of curriculum development are those of the Self-Strengtheners in response to the Western gunboats: take foreign learning and make it serve China through synthesis. English Language teaching with Chinese characteristics is viewed (as is Western learning in general) as a tool that can promote the economic and cultural well-being of the citizens of China, and can enable the country to enjoy international status as a strong, independent nation, rather than one subjugated by foreign powers.

Information transfer in general and the English language in particular are double-edged swords. Self-strengthening has had a cultural cost in China: the imperial system, which in its heyday was a cohesive political, religious and social force, was an early victim. The erosive qualities of the English language have already been identified in other cultures and, to date, English Language curriculum developers in China have shown a good deal of circumspection in this regard, with the pluralistic system serving as a filtering mechanism. It is filtering mechanisms such as the one described in this book that form a crucial aspect of China's relationship with modernized countries. English has been a particularly prickly subject for China to grasp, to the extent that people who have been associated with promoting English Language teaching have lost their lives, but now it is sustained in the school curriculum by a complex network of tension resolutions that attempt to satisfy most parties. In future, as China's English enters a new phase in the education system — one in which the commercialization of the curriculum resources becomes significant — the English Language curriculum will continue to reflect China's domestic socio-political affairs and international relations. On those grounds alone, the English Language curriculum commends itself as a fascinating topic for study.

Appendix

The covers from the various series show the development of production quality, especially after the Cultural Revolution.

Figure A.1   Series One (1957)

Figure A.2   Series Two (1960)

Figure A.3   Series Three (1960)

Figure A.4   Series Four (1961)

Figure A.5   Series Five (1963)

Figure A.6   Beijing Series

Figure A.7   Shaanxi Series

Figure A.8   Shanghai Series (Tianjin edition)

Figure A.9   Tianjin Series

Figure A.10   Series Six (1978)

Figure A.11   Series Seven (1983)

Figure A.12   Series Eight (1993)

Notes

CHAPTER 1

1. To distinguish between the language and the school subject, this book uses 'English language' for the former and 'English Language' for the latter.
2. Details of the data collection are as follows. Liu Daoyi: 10–13 June 1994 (informal discussions); 16 August 1994 (discussions and tour of PEP archives); 15 December 1995 (semi-structured interview); 16 December 1995 (informal discussion); 18–22 May 1996 (discussions); 22 May 1996 (semi-structured interview); 6 November 1996 (discussion); 3 April 1997, 22 July 1997, 25 November 1997 (letters responding to queries); 15 May 1998 (discussion); 21 May 1998 (discussion). Most of our interactions were in English. Liu Daoyi also read and commented on my PhD thesis that forms the basis for this book. Tang Jun: 12 July 1995 (22-page memoir and a letter, both in Chinese, responding to queries); 22 March 1998 (letter in English responding to queries). In both instances, Tang Jun also liaised with Ying Manrong and Fan Ying, clarifying issues concerning the 1957 curriculum. Liu Jinfang: 17 December 1997 (discussion); 15 May 1998 (semi-structured interview). Interactions were conducted in English and Chinese (for reiteration and clarification). Neville Grant: 18–30 June 1998 (email correspondence). During our periodical meetings over more than ten years, Grant took an interest in my study and offered useful insights and lines of investigation. My own reflections on the development of the 1993 curriculum were written up as a journal article (i.e., Adamson, 1995).

CHAPTER 3

1. Tang Jun, memoir, 12 July 1995.
2. In a discussion with Tang Jun, reported in Tang Jun, letter, 22 March 1998.
3. Tang Jun, memoir, 12 July 1995.
4. In a discussion with Tang Jun, reported in Tang Jun, letter, 22 March 1998.
5. In a discussion with Tang Jun, reported in Tang Jun, letter, 12 July 1995.
6. Bibliographical details of textbooks are found in a separate section of the References at the end of this book.

7. In a discussion with Tang Jun, reported in Tang Jun, letter, 12 July 1995.
8. Interview, 15 December 1995.
9. Memoir, 12 July 1995.
10. Letter, 12 July 1995.
11. Interview, 15 May 1998.
12. Memoir, 12 July 1995.
13. Memoir, 12 July 1995.
14. Series Three, Book 7 Introduction, p. 2 (in translation).
15. Tang Jun, letter, 12 July 1995.
16. Tang Jun, letter, 12 July 1995.

CHAPTER 4

1. The evidence for this chapter is mainly derived from analysis of the textbook resources and the syllabus produced during the phase, and from the reminiscences of Tang Jun, who joined the PEP from Beijing Foreign Languages Institute in 1960.
2. Confirmed by Tang Jun (letter, 15 May 1998) and Liu Daoyi (informal discussion, 21 May 1998).
3. Memoir, 12 July 1995.
4. Memoir, 12 July 1995.
5. Informal discussion, 21 May 1998.
6. Memoir, 12 July 1995.
7. Letter, 22 March 1998.
8. Letter, 22 March 1998.
9. Liu Daoyi, informal discussion, 15 May 1998.
10. Liu Jinfang, interview, 15 May 1998.
11. Interview, 22 May 1996.
12. Memoir, 12 July 1995.
13. Letter, 21 July 1995.

CHAPTER 5

1. Interview, 15 May 1998.

CHAPTER 6

1. Liu Jinfang, interview, 15 May 1998.
2. Liu Jinfang, interview, 15 May 1998.
3. Liu Daoyi, interview, 15 December 1995.
4. Liu Daoyi, interview, 15 December 1995.
5. Liu Jinfang, interview, 15 May 1998.
6. Liu Jinfang, interview, 15 May 1998.
7. Tang Jun, letter, 22 March 1998.
8. Extracted and translated from PEP, 1978: 23–7.
9. Tang Jun, letter, 22 March 1998.

10. Liu Jinfang, interview, 15 May 1998.
11. Liu Jinfang, interview, 15 May 1998.
12. Liu Jinfang, interview, 15 May 1998.
13. Liu Daoyi, interview, 15 December 1995; Tang Jun, memoir, 12 July 1995.
14. Liu Jinfang, interview 15 May 1998.
15. Liu Daoyi, interview, 15 December 1995.
16. Liu Daoyi, interview, 15 May 1998.
17. Liu Jinfang, interview, 15 May 1998.

CHAPTER 7

1. Grant, email, 25 June 1998.
2. Liu Daoyi, interview, 22 May 1996.
3. Grant, email, 25 June 1998.
4. Liu Daoyi, interview, 22 May 1996.
5. Liu Daoyi, interview, 22 May 1996.
6. Liu Daoyi, interview, 22 May 1996.
7. Liu Daoyi, interview, 22 May 1996.
8. Liu Daoyi, interview, 22 May 1996.
9. Liu Daoyi, interview, 22 May 1996.
10. Liu Daoyi, interview, 22 May 1996.
11. Liu Daoyi, interview, 22 May 1996.
12. Liu Daoyi, interview, 22 May 1996.

CHAPTER 8

1. Liu Jinfang, interview, 15 May 1998.

References

Textbooks references

The following textbooks, organized according to series, were consulted for this book. Each series published by the People's Education Press is numbered chronologically (Series One to Eight) to avoid confusion arising from the similar titles given to the textbooks. The Cultural Revolution textbooks are organized according to the place in which they were written (although they may have been used in various places) — except for the 'Tianjin' series, which was an adaptation of a series originally written in Beijing.

Series One

People's Education Press (1957) *English Book 1*. Beijing: People's Education Press.
People's Education Press (1959) *English Book 2*. Beijing: People's Education Press. (First published 1958.)

Series Two

People's Education Press (1962) *English Book 1*. Beijing: People's Education Press. (First published 1960.)
People's Education Press (1962) *English Book 2*. Beijing: People's Education Press. (First published 1960.)
People's Education Press (1961) *English Book 3*. Beijing: People's Education Press. (First published 1960.)

Series Three

People's Education Press (1960) *English Book 7*. Beijing: People's Education Press.
People's Education Press (1960) *English Book 8*. Beijing: People's Education Press.
People's Education Press (1960) *English Book 9*. Beijing: People's Education Press.

People's Education Press (1960) *English Book 10*. Beijing: People's Education Press.
People's Education Press (1960) *English Book 11*. Beijing: People's Education Press.
People's Education Press (1960) *English Book 12*. Beijing: People's Education Press.

Series Four

People's Education Press (1961) *English Book 1*. Beijing: People's Education Press.
People's Education Press (1961) *English Book 2*. Beijing: People's Education Press.
People's Education Press (1964) *English Book 3*. Beijing: People's Education Press. (First published 1962.)

Series Five

People's Education Press (1965) *English Book 1*. Beijing: People's Education Press. (First published 1963.)
People's Education Press (1965) *English Book 2*. Beijing: People's Education Press. (First published 1963.)
People's Education Press (1966) *English Book 3*. Beijing: People's Education Press. (First published 1964.)
People's Education Press (1965) *English Book 4*. Beijing: People's Education Press. (First published 1964.)
People's Education Press (1966) *English Book 5*. Beijing: People's Education Press. (First published 1965.)
People's Education Press (1965) *English Book 6*. Beijing: People's Education Press.

Shanghai Series

Tianjin People's Education Press (1975) *English Book 7*. Tianjin: Tianjin People's Education Press (First published 1973 by Shanghai People's Education Press.)
Tianjin People's Education Press (1974) *English Book 8*. Tianjin: Tianjin People's Education Press (First published 1973 by Shanghai People's Education Press.)
Tianjin People's Education Press (1974) *English Book 9*. Tianjin: Tianjin People's Education Press (First published 1973 by Shanghai People's Education Press.)

Beijing Series

Tianjin People's Education Press (1978) *English Book 2*. Tianjin: Tianjin People's Education Press (First published 1974 by Beijing People's Education Press.)
Tianjin People's Education Press (1978) *English Book 5*. Tianjin: Tianjin People's Education Press (First published 1975 by Beijing People's Education Press.)
Beijing People's Education Press (1978) *English Book 6*. Beijing: Beijing People's Education Press (First published 1975.)

Tianjin Series

Tianjin People's Education Press (1974) *English Book 4*. Tianjin: Tianjin People's Education Press. (This book was based on a textbook published in 1973 by Beijing People's Education Press, with adaptations based on *English Book 3*, published by Tianjin People's Education Press in 1972.)

Shaanxi Series

Shaanxi People's Education Press (1978) *English Book 1*. Xi'an: Shaanxi People's Education Press (First published 1973.)

Series Six

People's Education Press (1980) *English Book 1*. Beijing: People's Education Press. (First published 1978.)
People's Education Press (1980) *English Book 2*. Beijing: People's Education Press. (First published 1978.)
People's Education Press (1980) *English Book 3*. Beijing: People's Education Press. (First published 1979.)
People's Education Press (1980) *English Book 4*. Beijing: People's Education Press. (First published 1979.)
People's Education Press (1980) *English Book 5*. Beijing: People's Education Press. (First published 1979.)
People's Education Press (1980) *English Book 6*. Beijing: People's Education Press.

Series Seven

People's Education Press (1983) *English Book 1*. Beijing: People's Education Press. (First published 1982.)
People's Education Press (1984) *English Book 2*. Beijing: People's Education Press. (First published 1982.)
People's Education Press (1983) *English Book 3*. Beijing: People's Education Press. (First published 1982.)
People's Education Press (1983) *English Book 4*. Beijing: People's Education Press.
People's Education Press (1984) *English Book 5*. Beijing: People's Education Press. (First published 1983.)
People's Education Press (1984) *English Book 6*. Beijing: People's Education Press.

Series Eight

People's Education Press (1990) *Junior English for China Book 1*. Beijing: People's Education Press.

People's Education Press (1991) *Junior English for China Book 2*. Beijing: People's Education Press.
People's Education Press (1992) *Junior English for China Book 3*. Beijing: People's Education Press.
People's Education Press (1993) *Junior English for China Book 4*. Beijing: People's Education Press.

Other references

Abe, Hiroshi (1987) Borrowing from Japan: China's first modern educational system. In *China's Education and the Industrialized World: Studies in Cultural Transfer*, 1987. Edited by Ruth Hayhoe and Marianne Bastid. Armonk: M.E. Sharpe, pp. 57–80.
Adamson, Bob (1995) Writing the Teacher's Books for "Junior English for China". *Teacher Education Study Unit Forum*, **2** (1) 19–22.
Altbach, Philip G. (1991) Textbooks: the international dimension. In *The Politics of the Textbook*. Edited by Michael Apple and Linda K. Christian-Smith. London: Routledge, pp. 242–58.
Apple, Michael and Christian-Smith, Linda K. (1991) The politics of the textbook. In *The Politics of the Textbook*. Edited by Michael Apple and Linda K. Christian-Smith. London: Routledge, pp. 1–21.
Ayers, William (1971) *Chang Chih-tung and Educational Reform in China*. Cambridge, MA: Harvard University Press.
Bastid, Marianne (1987) Servitude or liberation? The introduction of foreign educational practices and systems to China from 1840 to the present. In *China's Education and the Industrialized World: Studies in Cultural Transfer*. Edited by Ruth Hayhoe and Marianne Bastid. Armonk: M.E. Sharpe, pp. 3–20.
Biggerstaff, E. Knight (1961) *The Earliest Modern Government Schools in China*. Ithaca: Cornell University Press.
Bolton, Kingsley (2002) Chinese Englishes: From Canton jargon to global English. *World Englishes* **21**, (2) 181–99.
Bolton, Kingsley (2003) *Chinese Englishes: A Sociolinguistic History*. Cambridge: Cambridge University Press.
Borthwick, Sally (1982) *Education and Social Change in China: The Beginnings of the Modern Era*. Stanford: Hoover Press.
Brandt, Conrad, Schwartz, Benjamin and Fairbank, John K. (1952) *A Documentary History of Chinese Communism*. London: George Allen and Unwin.
Carter, Ronald (1993) *Introducing Applied Linguistics*. London: Penguin.
Chang, Jung (1991) *Wild Swans*. New York: Simon and Schuster.
Chen, Hsi-en T. (1981) *Chinese Education since 1949: Academic and Revolutionary Models*. New York: Pergamon.
Chen, Li Fu (1986) *The Confucian Way*. London: KPI.
Cherryholmes, Cleo H. (1988) *Power and Criticism: Poststructural Investigations in Education*. New York: Teachers College Press.
Clark, John L. (1987) *Curriculum Renewal in School Foreign Language Learning*. Oxford: Oxford University Press.
Cleverley, John (1991) *The Schooling of China*. Second edition. Sydney: Allen and Unwin.

Dzau Y. Francis (1990) Historical background. In *English in China.* Edited by Francis Y. Dzau. Hong Kong: API Press, pp. 11–40.

Elmore, Richard and Sykes, Gary (1992) Curriculum policy. In *Handbook of Research on Curriculum.* Edited by Philip W. Jackson. New York: Macmillan, pp. 185–215.

Gillin, Donald G. (1967) *Warlord Yen His-shan in Shansi Province, 1911–1949.* Princeton: Princeton University Press.

Gu, Yueguo (1996) Steering a middle course: educational dilemmas in managing tertiary foreign language education in China. In *Issues in Language in Education.* Edited by Peter Storey, Vivien Berry, David Bunton and Philip Hoare. Hong Kong: Hong Kong Institute of Education, pp. 145–51.

Hayhoe, Ruth (1984) The evolution of modern Chinese educational institutions. In *Contemporary Chinese Education.* Edited by Ruth Hayhoe. London: Croom Helm, pp. 26–46.

Hsü, Immanuel C.Y. (1990) *The Rise of Modern China.* Oxford: Oxford University Press.

Hubbard, Peter, Jones, Hywel, Thornton, Barbara and Wheeler, Rod (1983) *A Training Course for TEFL.* Oxford: Oxford University Press.

Hymes, Del (1972) On communicative competence. In *Sociolinguistics.* Edited by John B. Pride and Janet Holmes. Harmondsworth: Penguin, pp. 263–93.

Johnson, R. Keith (1989) A decision-making framework for the coherent language curriculum. In *The Second Language Curriculum.* Edited by R. Keith Johnson. Cambridge: Cambridge University Press, pp. 1–23.

Keenan, Barry (1977) *The Dewey Experiment in China: Educational Reform and Political Power in the Early Republic.* Cambridge, Mass.: Harvard University Press.

Kwong, Julia (1985) Changing political culture and changing curriculum. *Comparative Education,* **21**(2), 197–207.

Lai, Winnie Y.W. Auyeung (1994) The Chinese language curriculum in the People's Republic of China from 1978–1986: Curriculum change, diversity and complexity. Unpublished PhD dissertation, Faculty of Education, The University of Hong Kong.

Larsen-Freeman, Diane (1986) *Techniques and Principles in Language Teaching.* Oxford: Oxford University Press.

Leung, Y.M. Julian (1989) A study of curriculum innovation in post-1976 China, with special reference to the design and implementation of the senior middle school geography curriculum. Unpublished PhD dissertation, Faculty of Education, University of Sussex.

Leung, Y.M. Julian (1991) Curriculum development in the People's Republic of China. In *Curriculum Development in East Asia.* Edited by Colin Marsh and Paul Morris. London: Falmer, pp. 61–81.

Li, Kwok-sing (1995) *A Glossary of Political Terms of the People's Republic of China.* Hong Kong: The Chinese University Press.

Liao, Kuang-sheng (1990) *Antiforeignism and Modernization in China.* Hong Kong: The Chinese University Press.

Littlewood, William (1993) Cognitive principles underlying task-centred L2 learning. In *Language and Content.* Edited by Norman Bird, John Harris and Michael Ingham. Hong Kong: Institute of Language in Education, pp. 39–55.

Liu, Daoyi (1995) English language teaching in schools in China. Paper presented at the International Language in Education Conference, The University of Hong Kong, 13–15 December.

Löfstedt, Jan-Ingvar (1980) *Chinese Educational Policy: Changes and Contradictions 1949–79*. Stockholm: Amqvist and Wiksell International.

Mackerras, Colin (1991) *Western Images of China*. Oxford: Oxford University Press.

McDonough, Jo and Shaw, Christopher (1993) *Materials and Methods in ELT*. Oxford: Blackwell.

Ministry of Education (1950a) *Gaodeng Waiyu Jiaoxue Jihua (Cao'an)* (Draft foreign language teaching plan for tertiary institutions). Beijing: Ministry of Education.

Ministry of Education (1950b) *Zhongxue Zanxing Jiaoxue Jihua (Cao'an)* (Draft temporary secondary school teaching plan). Beijing: Ministry of Education.

Ministry of Education (1984) *Achievement of Education in China: Statistics 1949–1983*. Beijing: People's Education Press.

Paine, Lynn (1992) The educational policy process: A case study of bureaucratic action in China. In *Bureaucracy, Politics and Decision-making in Post-Mao China*. Edited by Kenneth Lieberthal and David Lampton. Berkeley: University of California Press, pp. 181–215.

Paine, Lynn (1997) Chinese teachers as mirrors of reform possibilities. In *The Challenge of Eastern Asian Education*. Edited by William K. Cummings, and Philip G. Altbach. Albany: State University of New York Press, pp. 65–83.

Penner, Janice (1991) Opening the door with the English key — foreign involvement in EFL teacher education in China: An annotated bibliography. Vancouver: University of British Columbia (mimeograph).

People's Education Press (1963) *Yingyu Jiaoxue Dagang* (English syllabus). Beijing: People's Education Press.

People's Education Press (1978) *Zhong Xiao Xue Yingyu Jiaoxue Dagang* (English syllabus for primary and secondary schools). Beijing: People's Education Press.

People's Education Press (1986) *Yingyu Jiaoxue Dagang (English Syllabus)*. Beijing: People's Education Press.

People's Education Press (1989) Program for the compilation of the English teaching materials for Nine-Year Compulsory Education in the full-time secondary schools. Beijing: People's Education Press (mimeograph).

People's Education Press (1990) *Millions of Books with Deep Love for People's Education*. Beijing: People's Education Press.

People's Education Press (1993) *Yingyu Jiaoxue Dagang* (English syllabus). Beijing: People's Education Press.

Pepper, Suzanne (1996) *Radicalism and Education Reform in 20th-Century China*. Cambridge: Cambridge University Press.

Price, Ronald F. (1979) *Education in Modern China*. London: Routledge and Kegan Paul.

Price, Ronald F. (1992) Moral-political education and modernization. In *Education and Modernization: The Chinese Experience*. Edited by Ruth Hayhoe. Oxford: Pergamon, pp. 211–38.

Pu-Yi, Aisin-Guoro (1964) *From Emperor to Citizen*. Beijing: Foreign Languages Press.

Qun Yi and Li Qingting (1991) *Waiyu Jiaoyu Fazhen Zhanlüe Yanjiu* (Research into foreign language education development strategies). Sichuan: Sichuan Education Press.

Richards, Jack C. and Rodgers, Theodore S. (1986) *Approaches and Methods in Language Teaching: A Description and Analysis*. Cambridge: Cambridge University Press.

Ridley, Charles P., Godwin, Paul H.B., and Doolin, Dennis J. (1971) *The Making of a Model Citizen in Communist China*. Stanford: The Hoover Institution Press.

Ross, Heidi (1992) Foreign language education as a barometer of modernization. In *Education and Modernization: The Chinese Experience.* Edited by Ruth Hayhoe. Oxford: Pergamon, pp. 239–54.

Ross, Heidi A. (1993) *China Learns English: Language Teaching and Social Change in the People's Republic.* New Haven: Yale University Press.

Short, Philip (1982) *The Dragon and the Bear: Inside China and Russia Today.* London: Abacus.

Spence, Jonathan (1980) *To Change China: Western Advisers in China 1620–1960.* London: Penguin.

State Education Commission (1995) *Zhongguo Jiaoyu Nianjian* (China Education Yearbook). Beijing: People's Education Press.

Tang Jun (1986) *Sanshier nian laide zhongxue yingyu jiaocai* (Thirty-two years of secondary school English teaching materials). In *Zhongxue Waiyu Jiaocai He Jiaofa* (Foreign language materials and methodology for secondary schools). Edited by Curriculum, Materials and Methodology Association. Beijing: People's Education Press, pp. 49–60.

Tang Lixing (1983) *TEFL in China: Methods and Techniques.* Shanghai: Shanghai Foreign Languages Press.

Teng Ssu-yü and Fairbank, John K. (1979) *China's Response to the West: A Documentary Survey, 1839–1923.* Cambridge, MA: Harvard University Press.

The Chinese Repository (1834) Editorial. *The Chinese Repository,* (2) 1–5.

Thorndike, Edward L. and Lorge, Irving (1944) *The Teacher's Word Book of 30,000 Words.* New York: Teachers College, Columbia University.

Tsang Chiu Sam (1967) *Nationalism in School Education in China.* Hong Kong: Progressive Education Publishers.

Unger, Jonathan (1982) *Education under Mao: Class and Competition in Canton Schools 1960–1980.* New York: Columbia University Press.

Van Ek, Jan A. (1980) *The Threshold Level in a European Unit/Credit System for Modern Language Learning by Adults.* Systems Development in Adult Language Learning. Strasbourg: Council of Europe.

Venezky, Richard L. (1992) Textbooks in school and society. In *Handbook of Research on Curriculum.* Edited by Philip W. Jackson. New York: Macmillan, pp. 436–61.

Wang, James C.F. (1995) *Contemporary Chinese Politics: An Introduction.* Englewood Cliffs: Prentice Hall.

White, Ronald V. (1988) *The ELT Curriculum.* Oxford: Blackwell.

Wilson, Dick (1984) *Chou: The Story of Zhou Enlai 1898–1976.* London: Hutchinson.

Yang Huizhong (2001) Towards improving marker reliability. Seminar paper presented at the University of Hong Kong, 24 May 2001.

Yu Chen-chung (1984) Cultural principles underlying English teaching in China. *Language Learning and Communication* 3 (1) pp. 29–40.

Zhou Liuxi (Editor) (1995) *Zhongguo Zhongxue Yingyu Jiaoyu Baikequanshu* (An encyclopaedia of English education in middle schools of China). Shenyang: Northeastern University Press.

Zhou Liuxi and Weng Yanxing (1995) *Waiyuxueke jiaoxuelun* (Foreign language pedagogy). In *Zhongguo Zhongxue Yingyu Jiaoyu Baikequanshu* (An encyclopaedia of English education in middle schools of China). Edited by Zhou Liuxi. Shenyang: Northeastern University Press, pp. 114–208.

Index